Immigrants as outsiders in the two Irelands

MANCHESTER
1824

Manchester University Press

Immigrants as outsiders in the two Irelands

Edited by
Bryan Fanning and Lucy Michael

Manchester University Press

Published by Manchester University Press
Altrincham Street, Manchester M1 7JA
www.manchesteruniversitypress.co.uk

British Library Cataloguing-in-Publication Data is available

ISBN 978 1 5261 4559 8 paperback
ISBN 978 1 5261 4089 0 hardback

First published 2019

Typeset by Toppan Best-set Premedia Limited

Contents

List of figures and tables

Figures

Tables

Notes on contributors

Patricia Brazil is the Averil Deverell Lecturer in Law at Trinity College Dublin where she teaches refugee and immigration law, family law and child law. She has also practised as a barrister since 2004, specialising in asylum and immigration, and family and child law, and regularly publishes in these areas.

Teresa Buczkowska is the Integration Team Coordinator at the Immigrant Council of Ireland, where she works to promote cultural, social, economic and political integration of people of migrant background living in Ireland. Delivering diverse anti-racism projects is a cornerstone of her work. She has researched and published on Polish migrants' integration and patterns of racism in Ireland.

Catherine Cosgrave is the Legal Services Manager with the Immigrant Council of Ireland. She spent thirteen years in legal practice specialising in human rights and migration law. She was also appointed as the founding Director of the Law Centre for Children and Young People (Ireland) in 2013.

Siobhan Curran is the Advocacy and Policy Advisor on Human Rights and Democratic Space with Trócaire. She previously coordinated the Roma project in Pavee Point Traveller and Roma Centre and led the development of the participatory research project *Roma in Ireland: A National Needs Assessment*. She has worked in the areas of human rights and community development, with a focus on gender and ethnicity, for the past fifteen years. She has a Master's in Human Rights Law and Transitional Justice and a Master's in Social Policy, and has published articles focusing on the themes of human rights, discrimination and racism, gender, and health rights.

Merike Darmody is a Research Officer at the Economic and Social Research Institute, Dublin and an Adjunct Assistant Professor of Sociology at the Department of Sociology, Trinity College Dublin. Her key area of interest lies in ethnic, cultural, linguistic and religious diversity in contemporary societies and education systems.

Bryan Fanning is a Professor of Migration and Social Policy at University College Dublin. He is the author of *New Guests of the Irish Nation* (2009), *Immigration and Social Cohesion in the Republic of Ireland* (2011), *Racism and Social Change in the Republic of Ireland* (second edition, 2012) and *Migration and the Making of Ireland* (2018), as well as several other books on the modernisation of Irish society.

Ronnie Fay is a founder member and Co-Director of Pavee Point Traveller and Roma Centre which seeks to promote Traveller and Roma human rights both within Ireland and in international arenas, through research, local action, national resourcing and policy advocacy. She was responsible for establishing the first Primary Health Care for Travellers Project in Ireland which has been replicated nationally. Ronnie has worked to ensure an evidence base is used to inform policy development and services in addressing health inequalities. She has represented Traveller organisations nationally in overseeing the groundbreaking national research *Our Geels: All Ireland Traveller Health Study* (2010) and supported implementation of *Roma in Ireland: A National Needs Assessment* (2018). Ronnie has represented the community and Traveller/Roma sectors of national social partnership arrangements and policy settings.

Marta Kempny holds a PhD in Social Anthropology from Queen's University Belfast, where she has subsequently worked as a teaching assistant. Her expertise lies in the field of migration and diaspora studies, narrative approaches to identity and qualitative methodologies. She has undertaken extensive fieldwork among Polish migrants in Northern Ireland.

Orla McGarry is a Postdoctoral Researcher at University College Cork. She has conducted extensive research in the areas of youth migration, intercultural engagement, and religious and cultural adaptation. She also has a specific interest in, and expertise on, the development of culturally responsive and age-appropriate participatory research methodologies. She has published widely on the themes of youth migration, intercultural engagement, research methods, researcher positionalities and social theory. She was awarded a PhD by the School of Political Science and Sociology, National University of Ireland Galway in 2012.

Frances McGinnity is an Associate Research Professor at the Economic and Social Research Institute and an Adjunct Professor of Sociology at Trinity College Dublin. Her research focuses on labour market inequality, work–life balance, childcare, discrimination and migrant integration in Ireland from a comparative perspective.

Katie Mannion is a practising solicitor with the Immigrant Council of Ireland and is the author of *Child Migration Matters – Children and Young People's Experiences of Migration*, published in 2016. She is also a Board member of the Children's Rights Alliance, Dublin.

Lucy Michael is a Lecturer in Sociology at Ulster University and President of the Sociological Association of Ireland. Dr Michael completed her PhD from Keele University on civic leadership in Muslim communities under surveillance, and holds an MA in Criminology and Research Methods from Keele University, and a Bachelor Degree in Civil Law from University College Dublin. Her current research addresses racist violence, employment discrimination and racist incident reporting in Ireland and Northern Ireland. She is author of the iReport.ie racist incident reporting system with the European Network Against Racism Ireland and works closely with civil society organisations and public bodies to improve reporting and recording of racist incidents. She regularly publishes analyses from the data for policymaker and NGO use in Ireland and Europe, utilised by the OSCE Office for Democratic Institutions and Human Rights, and the European Commission against Racism and Intolerance, as well as by a wide range of Irish governmental and non-governmental organisations.

Fiona Murphy is a Research Fellow and Anthropologist based at the Institute for the Study of Conflict Transformation and Social Justice at Queen's University Belfast. Her research interests include migration, indigenous rights and sustainability. She is the co-author of *Integration in Ireland: The Everyday Lives of African Migrants* (2012).

Bríd Ni Chonaill is a Senior Lecturer at the Institute of Technology Blanchardstown, currently delivering modules in the Department of Humanities on cultural diversity and intercultural competency and combating racism. She has researched and published on linguistic and cultural diversity in France, language policy and more recently on issues concerning immigration in the Irish context.

Philip J. O'Connell is Director of the Geary Institute and a Professor in the School of Social Policy, Social Work and Social Justice at University College Dublin. Prior to that, he was Research Professor and Head of Social Research at the Economic and Social Research Institute Irelandand Adjunct Professor of Sociology at Trinity College Dublin. He received his doctorate from Indiana University, Bloomington and taught at the University of North Carolina, Chapel Hill. He has served as a consultant to the European Commission and the OECD. He is a government-appointed member of the Irish national Labour Market Council.

Bashir Otukoya is a Lecturer in Law at Griffith College Dublin and a PhD student in the UCD Sutherland School of Law and in the School of Politics & International Relations. He has a Bachelor of Arts in Law, a Bachelor of Law in Laws, and a Master of Laws in Public Law. His current research focuses on citizenship, in particular exploring the politico-legal process of becoming an Irish citizen, and its influence on the sociological idea of *being*

Irish. Bashir is a member of the Irish Refugee Council and is experienced in advising migrants in politico-socio-economic integration matters.

Pablo Rojas Coppari is Migration and Freedom of Movement Advisor at the OSCE Office for Democratic Institutions and Human Rights, Warsaw. Previously, he held the posts of Policy & Research Officer and Strategic Advocacy Officer of the Migrant Rights Centre Ireland, focusing on irregular migration and trafficking for forced labour. He was awarded an Irish Research Council scholarship to conduct doctoral research in the areas of labour market policy and economic integration of migrants in the Department of Sociology, Maynooth University. He also previously held positions on the Board of Directors of Cairde – a national health advocacy organisation for ethnic minorities in Ireland, and in the Advisory Panel to the Director of the European Union's Fundamental Rights Agency, and chaired the Working Group on Labour Rights for the Platform for International Cooperation on Undocumented Migrants, Brussels. He is currently completing his doctoral research at Maynooth University.

Ulrike M. Vieten is a Lecturer in Sociology in the School of Social Sciences, Education and Social Work at Queen's University Belfast. Before coming to Queen's she worked at the University of Luxembourg, University of Sheffield and VU University Amsterdam. She is the author of *Gender and Cosmopolitanism in Europe: A Feminist Perspective* (2012). Her research has focused on the far-right in Europe and on asylum seekers.

Bethany Waterhouse-Bradley is a Lecturer in Health and Social Care Policy at Ulster University, Northern Ireland. She completed her PhD in Social Policy in 2012 at Ulster on the representation of marginalised groups in policy decisions. Bethany previously worked in the area of migration policy in Northern Ireland supporting policy transposition from Westminster, and as Research Associate in the Psychology Research Institute at Ulster University researching veteran health and wellbeing. She has a strong interest in interdisciplinary examination of social justice issues, and her research explores social movements, political engagement and representation of traditionally excluded groups. She has worked as a researcher and support practitioner in both the US and Northern Ireland across a range of services, including homelessness, migration and asylum, ageing and dementia.

Bryan Fanning and Lucy Michael

Introduction: immigrants and other outsiders

Immigrants as outsiders in the two Irelands examines how a wide range of immigrant groups who settled in the Republic of Ireland and in Northern Ireland since the 1990s are faring today. Most of these are first-generation immigrants, although many have formed families and growing numbers have Irish-born children. The body of academic literature on immigration in both Irish cases has focused on issues such as racism in the labour market and on racialised responses to groups such as asylum seekers. Much of this literature draws on research that is now more than a decade old. The aim of this volume is to take stock of the experiences of a range of immigrants during the second decade of the twenty-first century. The intellectual project of this book is to contribute to the knowledge and understanding of barriers encountered by some immigrant communities that urgently need to be addressed.

The island of Ireland was partitioned in 1922, and six northern counties remained within the UK. Partition, and the resulting differences in legal and policy contexts, have inevitably affected the experiences of immigrants and responses to immigrants. Yet there are significant commonalities which warrant the comparative and all-island approach of *Immigrants as Outsiders in the Two Irelands*. Northern Ireland and the Republic of Ireland have experienced similar waves of immigration. During the nineteenth century Litvak Jews settled in Belfast as well as Dublin, Limerick and Cork. More recently Chinese, Polish, Roma and other migrants have settled in both Irelands. The first wave of Chinese immigration to both occurred during the 1960s, when migrants from Hong Kong relocated to Northern Ireland and to the Republic from the British mainland as restauranteurs. Commonwealth citizenship entitled them to settle in Britain, and a reciprocal common travel area agreement facilitated residency in the Republic without work permits.

The peace process in Northern Ireland, and the economic prosperity that followed in both jurisdictions, prompted new attention to citizenship and immigration issues across the island. Economic prosperity during the 'Celtic Tiger' years triggered large- scale immigration to the Republic, a phenomenon paralleled on a lesser scale in Northern Ireland. The Belfast 'Good Friday' Agreement of 1998 (hereafter 'the Good Friday Agreement') extended Irish citizenship rights to children born in Northern Ireland, upheld in a European Court ruling preventing the UK from deporting Chinese citizen Man Levette Chen, whose baby was born in Belfast and as such had the usual right of an Irish citizen to reside there. The case was one of a number of prompts for the 2004 Referendum in the Republic removing the *jus soli* right of Irish-born children of immigrants to become Irish citizens, significantly reordering Ireland's immigration regime.

Responses to asylum seekers in the Republic of Ireland and in Northern Ireland as part of the UK emerged not so much in the context of the 1998 agreement but of longstanding common travel area agreements between the UK and the Republic. In 1999 the Irish government introduced a punitive Direct Provision system in response to fears that the UK's new dispersal and voucher scheme under the 1999 Immigration and Asylum Act would drive more asylum seekers to Ireland.

Both jurisdictions experienced similar waves of post-EU Enlargement immigration and both also have attracted immigrants from non-EU countries into areas of employment such as healthcare. By 2011 there were 81,318 migrants in Northern Ireland not from elsewhere in the UK or the Republic.[1] Just under a quarter (19,658) were Polish. Lithuanians (7,241) comprised the next largest group. In the Republic Poles became the largest immigrant community, followed by Lithuanians. The 2006 Republic of Ireland Census identified 419,733 non-Irish citizens resident, increasing to 544,357 by 2011.[2]

Twenty years on from the first significant immigration rise in the Republic of Ireland and the Good Friday Agreement, it is evident that immigration has diversified both jurisdictions, and racism and xenophobia are established matters of public debate. Integration policy has however barely featured on the political agenda of either the Republic of Ireland or Northern Ireland. A bold statement in the former on integration in 2008, 'Migration Nation', was severely undermined by austerity, while attempts in Northern Ireland to adhere migrant integration to wider questions of community relations have resulted in its becoming invisible and under-resourced.[3] Ireland's policies have been described as 'fragmented, cost-effective, de facto assimilationist and laissez-faire'.[4] A new migrant strategy, launched in 2017, fails to acknowledge the decade of institutional silence on racism and the systematic undermining of key agencies and partnerships between the state and non-governmental organisations (NGOs) to support integration. Academics working on immigration and the experiences of immigrants and their children in a range of different institutional contexts have frequently commented on the lack of discernible policy direction. Yet this should not distract from the lengthy history of forced assimilation of Travellers, and the failure of the police and other statutory bodies to capture and address the racist crime and discrimination which underpin and emerge from the political failure to take seriously the question of integration policy. Our starting point is, given these approaches to integration in both jurisdictions, what are the experiences of immigrants? How does a laissez-faire approach to integration impact on community relations, racism, opportunities and formation of immigrant communities?

The chapters that follow address some of the following questions:

- How and to what extent are immigrants who have settled in Ireland 'outsiders' within Irish society?
- Are there particular areas or domains where exclusions are prevalent, and to what extent?
- Are some groups particularly marginalised?
- What are the specific consequences of institutional barriers, of racism and of discrimination?
- How do groups respond to experiences of exclusion such as racism or institutional barriers?
- How and to what extent (if at all) do some groups choose to remain outsiders?

When proposing the terms of reference for this book the editors simply asked contributors to use these questions to consider how and to what extent (if at all) immigrants are outsiders in the Republic of Ireland and in Northern Ireland. Various chapters examine concrete experiences of exclusion and inclusion in many different domains. A focus on immigrants as outsiders – barely represented, for example, in the media, politics and the public sectors of both Irelands – might situate specific experiences of exclusion (and the extent of such exclusion) within a detailed overall picture of the range of ways in which a particular group has succeeded economically, politically, religiously or otherwise in building viable lives in Ireland. Also addressed are the experiences of a range of different groups whose experiences in both Irelands have been influenced, in part, by host society responses and the ways in which these have variously experienced stratifications of rights and entitlements that distinguish between citizens and non-citizens, asylum seekers, migrants from other EU member states and from non-EU countries.

We utilise the term 'integration' to mean a two-way process of adaptation between migrants and host society, and the ease with which migrants can access and be included in the existing social structures of the host country. The term has been employed internationally with a wide range of imagined relations between migrants and host society, giving it a vagueness that can often deplete its usefulness. The implicit assertion is that there is a single national culture into which immigrants can integrate, and general silence on adaptations that might result from or induce greater interaction and intimacies with migrants. A tendency to focus on norms and values, rather than social practices, leaves integration debates lacking in explanatory power. With this in mind, the approach taken in this book is to explore the social practices of migrants as they reveal adaptations across a range of social institutions and spaces, and highlight the barriers migrants face in Ireland to full participation.

Ireland has been heavily influenced by European approaches to integration, and specifically EU protocols. This is revealed in the focus in the early 2000s on temporary economic migration from the EU, the neoliberal approach to neo-EU immigrant selection and the economy as the central concern of migration policies. The EU's Common Basic Principles on integration have emphasised that it is a 'dynamic, two-way process of mutual accommodation by all immigrants and residents of Member States'.[5] In Irish policy, the term 'integration' has also been used to understand a two-way process, but since 2005 specifically as a relationship between migrants and the state, rather than the members of the communities in which they live. The citizenship referendum of 2004 ensured that integration has been defined in terms of law and order, and the dominant narrative of social cohesion is as a security concern.[6] The main policy debates on integration before this focused on work. There have however been no significant debates on values as there have been in, for example, the UK or France, and to date fewer distinctive ethno-cultural rules of belonging pertain in the Irish case than in most European countries. Without the lengthy histories of immigration of other EU states, the emphasis is on avoiding mistakes made elsewhere. The Migrant Integration Strategy launched in 2017, for example, explicitly names among its aims the 'avoidance of urban ghettoes' and solutions to address African underemployment.[7]

There is no one Ireland (or two Irelands) into which migrants might be integrated. Northern Ireland (see Chapters 2, 3 and 7) cannot be understood as a homogeneous society just as the migrants who have settled there are not ethnically homogeneous. Both Northern Ireland and the Republic of Ireland are stratified on the basis of social class and socio-economic status and migrants have arrived with different kinds and levels of social and human capital. A Muslim doctor who lives with her family in either Dublin or Belfast might have very different experiences than an undocumented immigrant from the same country of origin or the same religion who works in a restaurant in either city. The Ireland that an immigrant software engineer or university lecturer slots into might be a very different one from the Ireland seen by immigrants from the same places who, because they can't speak English or have lesser skills, cannot move on from low-wage jobs and must live in deprived areas with fewer resources to aid their assimilation.

Immigrants, of course, are not the only outsiders in the Republic of Ireland or in Northern Ireland. Nor are the kinds of marginalisation experienced by some immigrants – in education, access to public services, employment or political representation – unique within Irish society. Debates about integration often focus on processes of cultural adaptation but it is also the case that integration in practical terms relates to many issues that also affect other potentially marginalised groups in society. In seeking to contextualise the kinds of barrier potentially faced by some immigrants, this book includes (in Chapter 1) a focus on Travellers, an Irish ethnic minority who have experienced intergenerational racism and discrimination. The experiences of Travellers and the failure of the Irish state to address their experiences as outsiders offer a salutary lesson for Irish society in a context where some first-generation immigrants undergo various kinds of marginalisation, racism and exclusion, and have come to perceive themselves as outsiders.

While both jurisdictions have immigrant populations from the same countries of origin and there have been many commonalities between the experiences of those who settled in each jurisdiction, there is also a need to take account of differences between Northern Ireland and the Republic of Ireland. Academic critiques of racism in Northern Ireland have tended to focus on state racisms and particularly racism among Protestant loyalists.[8] Those focused on the Republic have again emphasised state racisms but also legacies of mono-ethnic Catholic nationalism.[9]

The relationship between state racisms and the integration of immigrants and ethnic minorities is best understood through both action by the state and its agents, and the ability of those targeted by discriminatory processes to thrive in spite of them. State racisms set the tone for how members of the dominant cultural groups receive and interact with migrants and ethnic minorities, as well as being shaped by them. It is necessary therefore, to better understand the levels of exclusion experienced by racialised 'outsiders', to employ a framework which allows us to map the full range of factors which determine their marginalisation.

In the following section, we explore the ways in which discriminatory processes are embedded in the range of rules which have emerged to delineate different rights for these racialised groups, and the ways in which their rights (and indeed right to claim 'rights') have been limited. This provides a backdrop against which state racisms against each of the groups described in this book can be understood. As we then explore in each chapter the ways in which these groups have adapted to interact with wider society economically, socially and politically, it becomes evident that each has developed pathways to integration which are shaped by this administrative exclusion, the openness of dominant cultural groups to interaction, and the shared particular aspirations and histories of the migrant group as it emerges in Irish society.

Racism, rules and rights

This book is a sequel to an earlier edited volume, *Immigration and Social Change in the Republic of Ireland*, that took stock of institutional responses to migrants and the experiences of some groups at that time. Here we retain the conceptual focus of that volume on the ways in which racism and systems of rules and rights can stratify immigrants on arrival.[10] Efforts to challenge racism in the politics and social policies of many Western states have been bounded by presumptions about citizenship. Forms of discrimination sanctioned by legislation, such as the lesser benefits entitlements of asylum seekers or non-citizen immigrants, are all too easily excluded from debates about racism and inequality. Nation states in the current era of global migration still explicitly discriminate between citizens and non-citizens, notwithstanding some reciprocal entitlements to domicile, employment or welfare services resulting from agreements between nation states or international conventions emphasising universal human rights. In the Irish case this discrimination is a particularly pressing issue because a large proportion of immigrants (who now amount to a significant proportion of Irish society) are recent ones. As the proportion of non-citizens living in Irish society has increased, so too the rules that distinguish their rights and entitlements of those from citizens have become more pronounced. This can be seen especially in the case of asylum seekers who have been placed deliberately on the fringes of the societies in which they reside by systems of rules and lesser rights than apply to other people. Concerns about future reductions in the rights to free movement, social security, education and healthcare of migrants from the EU countries living in the United Kingdom of Great Britain and Northern Ireland have been central to post-2016 Brexit negotiations.

For Hannah Arendt the big practical problem with the concept of human rights was the absence of a 'right to rights'.[11] The rights of migrants who are not citizens have depended considerably upon what host states (and their citizens) do about these. Nation states including the Republic of Ireland and the UK have ratified the UN Convention on the Rights of Refugees (1956) and are required to admit persons seeking asylum. Both Ireland and the UK have operated a common travel area that allows respective citizens of one state living in the other the right to vote as well as the right to work and rights to social security benefits and public services. European Union member states have extended most of these rights (except the right to vote) to each other's citizens on a reciprocal basis. Migrants from EU countries benefited from a lack of restrictions on movement between both jurisdictions that are now at risk following the decision of the UK in 2016 to leave the European Union.

The legal systems of the nation state distinguish between citizens and non-citizens and furthermore sift non-citizens into groups with different levels of rights and entitlements. Migrants from EU countries enjoy rights to free movement, social security, education and healthcare that are not enjoyed by some migrants from non-EU countries, who also have a variety of different levels of rights. Administrative categories determine the entitlements of people to welfare, education and healthcare. Ideas about race and ethnicity continue to circumscribe the lives of human beings bring written implicitly into these hierarchies. Further, in recent years the category of asylum seeker has become a vilified one in many Western countries. Laws have been passed in various countries that have removed various rights from people so administratively categorised. Borders have been tightened to prevent refugees claiming rights to asylum already embedded in law. As a result it has recently become natural that asylum seekers have lesser welfare and education rights or that they be excluded from the remit of policies aimed at addressing poverty and disadvantage. Within the administrative logic of such systems human beings become defined by the categories in which they find themselves placed.

Max Weber argued that human objects of bureaucratic tasks cease to be subjects of moral demands.[12] Moral considerations and social solidarity become subordinated to organisational goals and legal rules. Such bureaucratic rationality is evident within the administrative and decision-making processes of Western societies where these affect groups such as immigrant workers, refugees and citizen welfare recipients as well as persecuted minorities. The way in which refugees or immigrants are administratively classified determines the extent to which they are regarded as members of the society within which they live. Gradations of rights between citizens and non-citizens, immigrant 'guest' workers, undocumented workers, refugees and asylum seekers have emerged in a number of Western countries that as recently as a century ago operated few restrictions on immigration. In effect, these are the result of placing human beings in different administrative boxes. Under the logic of citizenship it becomes 'natural' that the non-citizen should not have social and economic rights. Citizenship grants privileges to those who belong at the very same time as it denies them to the non-citizen.

However, nation states can also cooperate to extend reciprocal rights to the citizens of one another. Free movement, the right to work, access to social protection and other rights have been extended across the European Union. It perhaps made little concrete difference to some migrants from EU countries whether they settled in Dublin or in Belfast but it may matter more in the future should the UK cease to extend equivalent rights to such people.

A large body of research in a wide range of societies has illustrated how racism interacts with other social and political processes to produce distinct forms of 'racialised' inequality.[13] The concept of racialisation describes the ways in which racist ideologies and beliefs function as a mechanism for demarcating defined groups, such as ethnic minorities, in ways that legitimise their marginalisation or social exclusion.[14] Racism, then, is an imprecise term often loosely used to describe a collection of inter-related prejudices, beliefs and ideologies which assume the biological or cultural inferiority of distinct groups. Racism can be broadly defined as referring to any beliefs or practices which attribute negative characteristics to any group of persons, either intentionally or unintentionally, on the basis of supposed 'race' or ethnicity within the context of differential relations of power.[15] The term 'racism' can also be used to describe a tendency to portray the cultures and ways of life of minority ethnic groups as inferior or as threatening to those of majority groups in society.[16] It is used to describe negative attitudes and practices towards persons because of their membership of groups perceived to differ in physical or cultural characteristics from the perceiver. The ethnicity paradigm, which developed from the 1970s, extended accounts of racialised discrimination to include groups who experienced this on the basis of cultural difference.[17]

Racism, as such, describes a number of interlocking ways of thinking which emerged in turn, were superimposed upon each other, and which can be seen to persist within ideological and everyday understandings of social difference. For example, the UNESCO Declaration on Race and Racial Prejudice emphasised the role of structural and institutional barriers in producing racist barriers in society. It defined racism to include racist ideologies, prejudiced attitudes, discriminatory behaviour, structural arrangements and institutional practices 'resulting in racial inequality'. It notes that racism 'is reflected in discriminatory provisions in legislation or regulations and discriminatory practices as well as in anti-social beliefs and acts'.[18] Racism finds expression in the rules and structures of organisations, social norms and legislation. The Apartheid system in South Africa institutionalised overt legal discrimination against non-whites from 1948. Hitler institutionalised discrimination against the Jews through the Nuremberg Laws. In both these cases 'racial' categories became legal ones and became vehicles of overt discrimination. Such overt racist discrimination has been challenged in the West in the decades since the Holocaust. Examples include international conventions on human rights, de-segregation legislation in the United States and, crucially, shifts in social norms where overt expressions of racist beliefs have become less and less acceptable. Migrants who become citizens or refugees often continue to experience exclusion because of this policy context and the particular attitude that supports and emanates from it.

Non-citizens with lesser rights and entitlements encounter structural barriers to participation in society that may compound institutional barriers resulting from racism. First, they may be categorised by the state as outside the remit of a range of policies and programmes aimed at tackling disadvantage. Secondly, they may be excluded from official equality discourse, that is, excluded from how inequalities in society are conceptualised and discussed in official research, reports and within the remit of policies. This can be seen as a form of ideological exclusion whereby asylum seekers and other non-citizen groups are deemed not to be part of the host society.

The tensions between rules and rights evident within such examples of structural discrimination have deepened in recent decades. Present day constitutional, legislative and administrative norms affecting the treatment of non-citizens have developed over time. Commitments to extending rights and entitlements of non-citizens resulted from the ratification of international conventions. Yet the main thrust of legislation since the 1990s shaped by international norms and national political responses to immigration has often been to circumscribe rights and entitlements. Political responses to refugees in Ireland have often mirrored those in other parts of 'Fortress Europe'. Social policy systems of entitlement for non-citizen immigrants have become subordinated to the control imperatives of border policies.[19] New forms of institutional and structural discrimination have emerged. Older ones, to a considerable extent, have persisted.

Debates about poverty, social exclusion and even the integration of minority groups remain anchored in the paradigm of citizenship. Goals of promoting equal opportunity within citizenship coexist with the its use as a mechanism of exclusion. Institutional racisms within citizenship persist but they are augmented by structural racisms fostered by stratified rights and entitlements on the basis of citizenship entitlement. Legal and administrative distinctions between citizens and non-citizens have become a site of racism and ethnic discrimination. However, beliefs about 'race' or 'ethnicity' are no longer the sole basis of discrimination. Status itself has become racialised. Asylum seekers in Ireland (persons from dozens of countries and ethnic groups) have been demonised as a category. That said, links to older manifestations of racism remain evident.

Immigrant outsiders and segmented assimilation

Identity politics within both host societies – in the Republic of Ireland and in Northern Ireland as part of the UK – clearly influence responses to immigrants but this influence is often indirect. From the perspective of immigrants there is more to being an outsider than not feeling Irish or being accepted as 'Irish'. The opening chapters of the book address legacies of sectarianism and of anti-Traveller racism where religious, cultural and ethnic differences within Ireland's host populations play out. There is, to be clear, no monolithic Irish host society into which migrants might or might not be integrated. The two Irelands we examine are further divided on the basis of class and gender. So, to introduce one of the examples discussed in the book (Chapter 7), Poles variously settle in Catholic, Protestant and multi-ethnic areas of Belfast and perceive the immediate host society to differ in each case, while Poles who settle in Dublin might have very dissimilar experiences from those who move to rural areas. Immigrants who settle in middle-class areas may have very different experiences of racism, harassment and anti-social behaviour from those who settle in deprived localities or in social housing (see Chapter 8).

Theories of integration (perhaps best described as variations on 'classic assimilation theory') see migrant groups as becoming more similar to the majority population over time in norms, values, behaviours and characteristics. These mostly presume that it is easy to agree what the 'mainstream' entails. Length of residence of migrants might predict greater similarities to develop, modified primarily perhaps by levels of exposure between migrant groups and wider society. But an acknowledgement that the 'mainstream' is itself a subject of contention, particularly in a society demonstrating rapid social change, requires a more nuanced approach to understanding available pathways to assimilation or integration. Even those integration theories that acknowledge that the incorporation of immigrant groups also involves change and acceptance by the mainstream population do not adequately address the extent to which 'mainstream' society is itself not homogeneous.[20]

Theories of integration which focus on state approaches (multiculturalism, etc.) are useful for understanding many of the structural factors which may facilitate or impede integration, and even how migrants can be encouraged to orientate themselves to the state, but they are less useful for measuring the progress of different groups. Tools such as the Migrant Integration Policy Index similarly are useful for mapping the policies facilitating or impeding migrants in the host country but offer no understanding of how groups experience these and exercise agency in relation to them.[21] The Republic of Ireland, for example, ranked 19 out of 38 countries in the 2015 Migrant Integration Policy Index, but migrants living here are more likely to be cut off from family members, with family reunification the lowest in Europe.[22]

The canonical theory of assimilation as it developed in the case of the United States presumes a progression across three generations: a first generation that may not speak English experiences poverty and discrimination; a second generation advances economically but retains some distinct 'ethnic' cultural and linguistic traits; a third generation becomes fully assimilated, and disconnected from the place of origin of their grandparents. Across these three generations, education levels rise and the second and third generations climb the ladder of social class. Most of the groups this theory referred to were white emigrants from Europe: Italians, Poles and Irish. By comparison, some European countries that became emigrant destinations after the Second World War admitted migrants from their own former empires. Migrants from colonies and ex-colonies experienced overt racism and discrimination that contributed to the marginalisation of subsequent generations.

Integration, envisaged as a two-way process, is presumed to require some change in the host society as well as adaptations to its rules and norms by immigrant newcomers.[23] Many chapters in this book contest the inference of much policy and political discourse that it is a one-way process for which migrants or ethnic minorities are responsible. The societies into which immigrants to the island of Ireland have settled have been changed by their presence. However, these have been changing economically, politically and culturally on an ongoing basis for other reasons. Migrants seeking to find a place to live and flourish in either of the twenty-first-century Irelands are not the only ones facing challenges. A comprehensive mapping of the changes to Irish society is beyond the scope of this book. We focus therefore on the factors which can be explored through the experiences of migrant groups and their engagement with those 'core' institutions of structural integration: the economy and labour market, housing system, welfare state institutions and political citizenship.[24] Although it is true that Ireland is experiencing rapid social change in some respects (decreasing religiosity, liberal social attitudes), nonetheless there are strong characteristics/elements of Irish society which remain relatively stable (family formation, class mobility).

We might therefore more usefully in this collection talk about assimilation rather than integration. In making sense of the range of immigrant experiences of belonging and marginalisation described in this book, we are drawn to conceptual debates about segmented assimilation that acknowledge the varieties of ways in which migrants who come from different places on different terms must navigate the complexities of host societies.[25] This theory, as it has been developed in both the United States and Europe, facilitates the mapping of multiple pathways to assimilation which are navigated by immigrant groups depending on their national origins, socioeconomic status, contexts of reception in the host society, and family resources, both social and financial. Research in the UK on migrant perceptions of factors affecting integration has highlighted some common themes, namely labour market experiences, experiences related to social opportunities and social interactions, as well as the placing of responsibility on migrants for social integration.[26] Ager and Strang suggest that the key integration domains are housing, employment, education and health, with citizenship and rights underpinning both access to and achievement within these, as well as mediating the processes of social connections and how they relate to access and outcomes.[27]

Our consideration of the theory of segmented assimilation at this juncture is not therefore a rejection of the concept or possibility of two-way integration in Irish society, but a recognition that, in this project, we are best able to measure the extents to which migrant and minority groups have assimilated (by choice or necessity) into mainstream institutions, and explore the various pathways that various groups have taken. We do not propose a normative idea of assimilation but recognise the ways in which structural and cultural assimilation occurs over time, and how it is equally resisted for a range of reasons.

Segmented assimilation focuses on identifying the contextual, structural and cultural factors that separate successful assimilation from unsuccessful, or even 'negative', assimilation. While the proximate causal mechanisms of assimilation relate to individual and group relationships and characteristics, distal sources are embedded within the larger structures of institutions, the state and market.[28] As well as accounting for both the impact of government policies and the influence of existing ethnic communities in the host society, the theory accommodates factors including societal values and biases of the host society, residential location and the presence or absence of opportunities for mobility as contextual factors. Immigrant group characteristics are explored through their history (human capital possessed by the first generation and the context of the host society at time of arrival), acculturation, economic and cultural barriers, and access to family or community resources. Adding the theory of spatial assimilation further allows us to explore the phenomenon of immigrant groups moving into or away from ethnic enclaves or multi-ethnic neighbourhoods (as we see in Chapter 7), and which can affect *exposure* between majority and minority groups and *centralisation* of a group's activities around key resources.[29]

The theory also allows us to explore a much-debated point, which is what exactly immigrants are assimilating into. We might ask what is a 'host' community,[30] how disadvantage in labour or housing markets affects exposure to and interaction with specific segments of wider society, and how class and other stratifications shape assimilation pathways. It rejects the ethnocentric deficit model of assimilation, which posts distinctive ethnic-origin traits of new immigrant groups (e.g. cultural customs or native language) as shortcomings which need to be discarded to successfully assimilate.[31] Immigrants and their children do not have to shed their 'cultural distinctiveness' in order to succeed, and the tossing of the deficit model permits us to examine the persistence of inequality and conflict among and between different population groups as being the result of other factors.[32] Assimilation is conceived of as an incremental process which occurs across generations in different ways for different groups.[33] Segmented assimilation provides the foundation for a longitudinal approach which seeks to understand the range of experiences and choices made by migrants and post-migrant cohorts.

There are key differences, of course, between Ireland and the United States or Europe, where this theory has been applied. The absence of 'urban ghettoes' or even distinct ethnic enclaves in Ireland, and the absence of a comparative group similar to African-Americans or, in Europe, immigrants from the historical dominions, make simple application impossible. We are also cautious about the application of the original theory's concept of 'downward assimilation', which identified assimilation into these historically excluded groups as negative. However, the findings of this book in relation to the second generation, citizenship rights, education and inclusion suggest strongly to us that there are good reasons to be concerned about the long-term impacts of the structural barriers to and failures of anti-discrimination. Employing a model that emphasises assimilation is not to assume that the endpoint is complete acculturation to the point that ethnicity is mainly symbolic or expressive. Economic and spatial assimilation are important stages which determine the life chances of migrants and their children.

Acculturation of the migrant group is not necessarily unidirectional. Migrants (like the Poles in Belfast discussed in Chapter 7) may choose to adapt into a particular culture, depending on their experiences of discrimination and prejudice, or their orientation to a particular type of assimilation (e.g. spatial). Newly arrived immigrant groups might even choose to adapt into an existing minority ethnic culture if it provides valuable knowledge and resources for success in the host society. Such a case is not easily imagined in Ireland since 2000, as extant minority groups have been small and often highly dispersed or significantly marginalised. Indeed in the case of Travellers we see such high levels of exclusion that there may even be prejudice against them in newly arrived immigrant groups. Thus we do not posit the goal of complete assimilation, and we hold that it is possible for migrants and minorities to move beyond simple participation to develop a 'sense of belonging' vis-à-vis the core institutions in society (identificational integration)[34] without losing their own cultural identities, as suggested (if not taken seriously) in most Irish integration policy.[35]

Most commonly used to map the progress of groups across generations, it might be counter-argued that it is too early in Ireland to use such a theoretical tool to understand integration here. True there are longstanding, if small, migrant groups which preceded the 1997 peak moment of inward migration. But most of the groups discussed in this book, excepting the Travellers, are migrants to Ireland mainly post-1997, and thus we are only starting to see the emergence of the next significant adult generation. We also acknowledge that the inductive nature of the exercise behind this book is not entirely suited for testing the application of the theory in either Ireland or Northern Ireland. This is not however to remove the usefulness of the concepts it employs for better describing and examining the processes underpinning and mobilising integration in such a context. An understanding of how racism operates in Ireland to block the pathways of children of immigrants or ethnic groups, particularly as a consequence of racialisation, is important for a long-term view.

Future generations

The historic context of migrants' entry into the host society is an important factor determining the multiplicity and effectiveness of pathways to integration that follow. Policies on inclusion and equality offer an insight into the wider policy context and its impact on migrant mobility and access to rights and opportunities as well as subjection to rules and regulations. Anti-Traveller and sectarian legacies that preceded the large-scale immigration of the late 1990s and early 2000s demonstrate this context well. We start this book, then, with an insight into how the most marginalised of Irish groups, Travellers, have been impacted by and sought to change the policy context in which they are blamed for their own economic, political and social exclusion. This starting point allows us not just to understand the relative success of migrant groups in integration, but also how shared resources among outsider groups (including Travellers) – oriented towards anti-racism and anti-discrimination – have shifted host society biases and the cultural barriers to integration that racism so easily establishes.

Although not an immigrant group, as a small indigenous minority group experiencing decades of exclusion, Travellers' experiences of state attempts to force assimilation demonstrate keenly the importance for some ethnic groups to interact with wider society without losing their cultural distinctiveness. This orientation has been distinctly at odds with both governmental and public attitudes, such that Fay (in Chapter 1) notes that nearly a fifth of the population of Ireland in a 2010 survey would deny Irish citizenship to Travellers. Significant health inequalities, including rates of suicide among Traveller men seven times higher than the national rate, are the outcome of decades of exclusion as Travellers have sought to cope with the health consequences of discrimination and structural poverty without engaging at length with discriminatory health providers. Fay maps the shift in government position which seeks to move (if only slightly) away from treating Traveller culture as one of poverty, a position which reflected the deficit model of assimilation, and the limited subsequent impact of this on the rights available to Travellers. In doing so, she illustrates how economic, social and political integration of Travellers is blocked by the continuing assimilationist orientation of policy and service provision. This is amply demonstrated by the 2017 state recognition of Traveller ethnicity, which has not been supported in law to facilitate the claims of rights on the grounds of ethnicity by Travellers, and the failure of the state to address the disproportionate suicide rates of the group. The work she describes demonstrates how models of service provision which incorporate collective resolution, from the point of view of the minority group, support the importance of facilitating multiple pathways to integration and how activism by one ethnic minority group can impact on the mobility of others.

The tenuous access of minority groups to policymakers in the Republic of Ireland is mirrored in Waterhouse-Bradley's investigation of Northern Ireland's policy context (Chapter 2). Despite the promise held of greater immigration displacing the dominance of the two-community model of community relations, the legislative and policy frameworks promoting equality appear in fact to mitigate against the inclusion of 'outsiders'. Increased migration into the region after the Good Friday Agreement and again after the 2004 ('A8') Enlargement of the EU attracted greater policy interest and resources to the community sector which initially benefited longstanding minority ethnic communities and supported mobilisation for political inclusion and access to rights and justice. However, the marginalisation of ethnic minorities and migrants continued, and the disinterest of policymakers in incorporating migrants into equality considerations (demonstrated by the refusal even to collect data on these groups) highlights the intractability of the two-community model. Like Fay, Waterhouse-Bradley explores the policy goal of 'mainstreaming', which seeks to integrate the specialist support of minority groups into existing institutions and services. Ideally, mainstreaming is the systematic integration of an equality perspective which tackles structures, behaviours and attitudes that contribute to or sustain inequality and discrimination. It requires an understanding that inequalities exist, an acknowledgement that discrimination is occurring, and a willingness to take action to prevent and reduce the occurrence and redress the consequences of discrimination.

State failures to consistently develop and monitor equality and integration frameworks are also examined in Chapter 3's examination of anti-racism in both jurisdictions. Both Chapter 2 and Chapter 3 emphasise the importance of accountability to communities affected by racism at a local level, and in contexts where groups are affected by racism at a national level, the importance of states being held to account by international rights-monitoring bodies. Failures to adequately identify and develop strategies to respond to racism speak both to the biases of the host society and the structural barriers which migrants face in both jurisdictions. Chapter 3 identifies political indifference to racism on both sides of the border which has led, if anything, to worsening institutional responses since 2008 and an over-reliance on NGO efforts to highlight experiences of racism and discrimination that are being ignored by governments.

Access to basic safety for migrants at home and in their neighbourhoods has significant impact on equal access to health, education and employment, and on migrant orientations to integration, a point taken up by several authors in their explorations of residential mobility and spatial assimilation in Belfast and Dublin. Murphy and Vieten (Chapter 4) suggest that the ambivalence of African refugees in both jurisdictions to 'place' is not only connected to their changing immigration status but also intimately tied up with their vulnerability to violence, which makes them fearful of relations with neighbours, and their keen awareness of the constraints on access to key institutions of integration posed by spatial segregation.

The responses of African refugees are distinct from those of Poles who, in Kempny's analysis, find that their whiteness affords them much greater access to the city, even facilitating cross-community mobility in Belfast which evades Irish Catholics. This contribution to our exploration of segmented assimilation keenly illustrates how migrants' knowledge on arrival and reliance on shared community resources change over a decade, offering a surprising diversion of integration pathways within the Polish group which is informed by their knowledge not only of spheres of 'safety', but also of what there is to become integrated into culturally. Spatial assimilation is highly evident in this exploration of Polish pathways to integration in Northern Ireland, as migrants develop independent knowledge of the host society over a decade and select the neighbourhoods, and neighbourhood cultures, of their preference. Even in the context of post-conflict Belfast, with its loyalist–nationalist– Protestant–Catholic lines of segregation which constrain spatial mobility, Polish migrants demonstrate varying orientations towards and away from 'diverse' migrant areas, and a multiplicity of pathways to integration into the dominant host cultures become evident. In this we see that despite the racialisation of Catholicism which hallmarked sectarian divisions in the region, Poles have been able and motivated to thrive in loyalist areas, partaking in loyalist traditions and positive reciprocal relations with their neighbours, and community groups working against racism towards Poles in those areas have been able to find sufficient common ground between host society and migrants to provide the basis for mutual interest to develop.

The enduring problem of racism, and poor supports to address it, are key factors in constraining spatial assimilation. While migrant groups are distributed across owner-occupier, private rental and public sector social housing sectors, it is the latter that apparently have the most protection. Migrants in social housing are already among the most economically marginalised of migrants, and additionally among the most vilified of migrants at the height of a national housing crisis, but they are the named responsibility of public sector authorities. Yet, as Buczkowska and Ní Chonaill (Chapter 8) describe in their exploration of experiences of migrants in Dublin's social housing sector, the protections which appear to be in place have no substance in practice, leaving victims of racism exposed and, in some cases, homeless. Ireland's legislative framework, which fails to adequately address hate crimes, and poorly effected statutory duty on local authorities to consider equality issues combine to ensure that migrants' housing allocations and transfers are made without proper considerations of the impact of racism on neighbourhood integration. They highlight the effectiveness of all-community approaches to producing positive relations and high-visibility protection of victims to avoid ghettoisation of migrants in the social housing sector. These contrast with the much-criticised voluntary repatriation of Roma from Belfast's social housing sector in 2009 discussed in Chapter 3 as well as the more normalised residential transfer of victims in social housing in the Republic.

Employment provides opportunities not only for economic integration, but also for social integration, and as such plays a key role in determining pathways to integration. Regardless of the human capital that migrants bring, there is little that they can do to alter the labour market in the host society, and the conditions that circumscribe their entry and success in it. In this collection, we see the impacts of the labour market on migrants and their economic success, but also on their orientations to integration. In Chapter 6 Coppari examines the marginalisation of Filipino-Irish care workers. While some Filipinos, like several of Coppari's interviewees, have become Irish citizens, many remain economically marginalised in precarious work. Filipino isolation from Irish society is particularly gendered, so it is no surprise to see residential co-location among Filipinos not only to reduce economic pressures but also to meet basic needs like childcare and provide a buffer against isolation and 'hyper-precarity'.

O'Connell in Chapter 5 investigates the experiences of Africans in the Irish labour market and seeks to explain how a relatively well-educated group of prime working age demonstrates low labour market participation. Understanding routes into the labour market through a longer lens of immigration and settlement offers some better clues to accounting for this pattern of disadvantage. Here, too, an investigation of gender effects raises questions about the relative impacts of cultural behaviours of the migrant group(s) versus the discrimination which they experience, which is both gendered and racialised. This point about the cumulative and intersecting effects of discrimination is particularly addressed by Curran (Chapter 9) in her exploration of Roma women's economic (in)activity, which she connects to the extraordinary levels of explicit and open discrimination experienced by few other migrant groups. Together, these contributions constitute an extended examination of the impact of societal biases on access to employment, and shift the focus from that of migrant deficits to structural barriers in the Irish labour market.

Biases against these 'outsider' groups are most explicitly exposed in contemporary popular discourses about Roma, Travellers and asylum seekers as well as other migrant groups, which we address through an examination of Irish media. Michael (Chapter 10) addresses the question of societal values and the biases of the host society sharply in a review of the treatment of ethnic minorities and migrants by Irish media. It is, sadly, unremarkable in Europe in 2019 to say that there is extensive evidence of racism in digital, print and social media against migrant groups, and in particular asylum seekers. It is possible however to see an increasingly normalised range of racist discourses employed in the presentation of news and opinion in Ireland, such that the overlaps with extremist discourses can be identified. The regulatory frameworks which govern Irish print, digital and broadcast media appear to offer some protection to minority groups, but in practice have failed to stem the gross stereotyping of highly disadvantaged groups (including Travellers and Roma) and of asylum seekers and migrants more generally, and these stereotypes are increasingly touted in media discourses as being beyond regulation.

The latter part of this collection is more future-orientated – in addressing the experiences particularly of young people and the uncertainties thrown up by Brexit, we set the stage for questions to be asked about future integration of migrants across the island. The activation by the UK of Article 50, initiating their departure from the European Union, has drawn our attention once again to the impact of the different range of rights and opportunities which attract migrants to different countries. Previous responses by Ireland to shifting regimes of rights in other countries have been largely punitive towards migrants, to deter further immigration occurring through displacement or preference. A prime example of this is the urgent establishment of the extra-legal system of Direct Provision in response to the UK's dispersal of asylum seekers. Similar responses might be expected as it becomes clear how migrant rights are affected by Brexit in the UK as a whole, or in Northern Ireland and Ireland, and how migrants interpret the opportunities available to them in that context. In any case, migrant choices about residential location, applications for naturalisation or visas, political engagement and investment in their neighbourhoods and communities may signal changing commitments to the host societies of Ireland and Northern Ireland post-Brexit, and shifting biases towards or against certain groups in host societies will shift the context into which they can and do assimilate.

Children including those of immigrants must navigate an education system that in the Republic of Ireland (the case examined in Chapter 12) works to reproduce intergenerational inequalities on the basis of social class and socio-economic status. Some immigrant-origin children face disproportionate challenges because they do not have the kinds of residency status (see Chapter 11) that grant them the same degree of access to education as Irish citizens. Chapter 12 notes immigrant-origin children are disproportionately shunted towards schools in disadvantaged areas. Within education, language proficiency and engagement in sport and cultural activities are some key determinants of 'insiderness'. Some immigrant-origin children, like the Muslim teenagers discussed in Chapter 13, appear to have successfully navigated their school environments. In both Irelands, as elsewhere, schools can do much to support children from culturally diverse backgrounds but structural issues which reproduce class inequalities for the population have proven difficult to address. As noted in the Conclusion, this is because societal inequalities owe much to the concentration of social capital in economically advantaged areas. Immigrant-origin and other children who live in better off and more deprived neighbourhoods are, in effect, expected to integrate in society under different terms and conditions.

The segmented assimilation model suggests that the Irish-born children of foreign-born immigrants will experience integration differently from children who are themselves first-generation immigrants.[36] This is found to be the case in Chapter 12, which compares the experiences of Muslim teenagers who are variously newly arrived children of asylum seekers (who must contend with a range of structural barriers not experienced by others) and the Irish-born children of well-established immigrants. The former appear to consider themselves as outsiders to a greater extent than the latter. In Chapter 15 Otukoya examines how immigrants who have become Irish citizens can feel as outsiders. He examines the impact of efforts by young immigrant-origin people to become 'insiders' on their relationships with others from the same ethnic and cultural groups. The difficulties of mapping the boundaries of what it means to be an 'outsider inside' are well demonstrated in the existing literature on migration,[37] and Otukoya's investigation of the subtleties of statutory discretion (particularly around 'loyalty' to the nation) goes some way to demonstrating the precarity of 'insiderness' in Ireland and addressing this wider lacuna in the literature.

In summary

Immigrants as outsiders in the two Irelands offers contributions which speak to the full range of factors shaping new and available pathways to integration, from the context into which immigrants arrive, the characteristics of immigrant groups affecting their emigration and immigration, the biases and structural barriers they encounter in the host society, and the multiple ways in which they seek to adapt to and change the institutions which facilitate integration. Using the concepts associated with the theory of segmented assimilation to frame these contributions, we establish a framework through which we invite our readers to view the successes and adaptations of the migrants represented here as well as the structural powerlessness with which many of them, but not all, are faced. We note the limited choices that attend 'outsider' status, and the impact of these economically, politically and culturally, and the ways in which combinations of 'insider' and 'outsider' positions affect integration, the ability of migrants (and children of migrants) to thrive, and their future orientations to the opportunities available on the island of Ireland.

The rights and stratifications which attend migrant identities on the island, of which racism is one, vary by national and ethnic identity, but in practice the ability to claim rights is further delimited by class and gender. While we might note the cultural preferences of some groups which appear to constrain the choices and opportunities of their members, including those of women, it serves us well to consider how these fit easily into the discriminatory frameworks (on the basis of gender, class and age) which already exist in the host society and which poorly serve inclusion across the wider population.

It is evident that the biases and racism experienced by migrants in the key institutions of integration – employment, housing and education at least – are mirrored in and reflect state policy, and are not inevitable. Rather, we observe a consistent picture of political refusal to seriously address racism and xenophobia, and to provide even the most basic of supports for efforts towards integration. A laissez-faire policy towards integration may be less harmful than a poorly designed or overly ideological one, but the assurance of basic access to human rights must be recognised as essential to the ability of migrants to meet their own needs, as well as their ability to contribute to Irish society (as they are so often asked to prove that they do).

Notes

1 Anna Krausova and Carlos Vargas-Silva, *Northern Ireland Census Profile* (2011), www.nirsa.gov.uk.
2 Republic of Ireland's Central Statistic Office, www.cso.ie, accessed 30 January 2019.
3 Office of Minister of State for Integration Policy, *Migration Nation: Statement on Integration Strategy and Diversity Management* (Dublin: Stationery Office, 2008); R. McVeigh and B. Rolston, 'From Good Friday to good relations: sectarianism, racism and the Northern Ireland state', *Race and Class*, 48:4 (2007), 1–23.
4 G. Boucher, 'Ireland's lack of a coherent integration policy', *Translocations*, 3:1 (2008), 5–28, p. 19.
5 Cited in Office of Minister of State for Integration Policy, *Migration Nation*, p. 32.
6 Boucher, 'Ireland's lack of a coherent integration policy', p. 19.
7 Department of Justice and Equality, *Migrant Integration Strategy – A Blueprint for the Future* (Dublin: DJE, 2017).
8 McVeigh and Rolston, 'From Good Friday to good relations'.
9 B. Fanning, *Racism and Social Change in the Republic of Ireland* (Manchester: Manchester University Press, 2012), pp. 42–46.
10 B. Fanning (ed.), *Immigration and Social Change in the Republic of Ireland* (Manchester: Manchester University Press, 2007).
11 H. Arendt, *The Origins of Totalitarianism* (London: George Allen and Unwin, 1961), p. 294.
12 M. Weber, *The Protestant Ethic and the Spirit of Capitalism* (New York: Scribner's Press, 1958), p. 182.
13 J. Solomos and L. Back, *Racism and Society* (London: Macmillan, 1996), p. 65.

14 R. Miles, 'Racialisation', *Dictionary of Race and Ethnic Studies* (London: Routledge, 1996), p. 307.
15 S. Hall, 'Racism and reaction', in Commission for Racial Equality (ed.), *Five Views of Multi-Racial Britain* (London: Commission for Racial Equality, 1978).
16 M. Barker, *The New Racism* (London: Junction Books, 1981).
17 S. Cornell and P. Hartmann, *Ethnicity and Race – Making Identities in a Changing World* (Thousand Oaks, CA: Pine Forge Press, 1998), p. 17.
18 United Nations Educational Scientific and Cultural Organisation (UNESCO), General Conference, 27 November 1978. Declaration on Race and Racial Prejudice, Article 2.
19 T. Kostakopoulou, *Citizenship, Identity and Immigration in the European Union* (Manchester: Manchester University Press, 2001), pp. 148–149.
20 R. D. Alba and V. Nee, *Remaking the American Mainstream: Assimilation and the New Immigration* (Cambridge, MA: Harvard University Press, 2003).
21 Migrant Integration Policy Index, mipex.eu, accessed 3 January 2019.
22 T. Huddleston, O. Bilgili, A. L. Joki and Z. Vankova, *Migrant Integration Policy Index 2015* (Barcelona and Brussels: CIDOB and MPG, 2015).
23 W. Bosswick and F. Heckmann, *Integration of Migrants: Contribution of Local and Regional Authorities* (Dublin: European Foundation for the Improvement of Living and Working Conditions, 2006), pp. 3–10.
24 Ibid., p. 10.
25 A. Portes and M. Zhou, 'The new second generation: segmented assimilation and its variants among post-1965 immigrant youth', *Annals of the American Academy of Political and Social Science*, 530 (1993), 74–98.
26 J. Rutter, L. Cooley and N. Jones, *Moving Up Together* (London: IPPR, 2008), p. 8; A. Bloch, 'Refugee settlement in Britain: the impact of policy on participation', *Journal of Ethnic and Migration Studies*, 26:1 (2000), 75–88, p. 86.
27 A. Ager and A. Strang, 'Understanding integration: a conceptual framework', *Journal of Refugee Studies*, 21:2 (2008), 166–191, p. 166.
28 Alba and Nee, *Remaking the American Mainstream*.
29 D. Massey and N. Denton, *American Apartheid: Segregation and the Making of the Underclass* (Cambridge, MA: Harvard University Press, 1993).
30 T. Threadgold and G. Court, *Refugee Inclusion: A Literature Review* (Cardiff: Cardiff School of Journalism, Media and Cultural Studies, 2005), p. 5.
31 M. Zhou, 'Coming of age: the current situation of Asian American children', *Amerasia Journal*, 25:1 (1999), 1–27.
32 B. S. Heisler, 'The sociology of immigration: from assimilation to segmented integration, from the American experience to the global arena', in C. B. Brettell and J. F. Hollifield (eds), *Migration theory: Talking across Disciplines* (New York: Routledge, 2000), pp. 77–96.
33 Alba and Nee, *Remaking the American Mainstream*.
34 Bosswick and Heckman, *Integration of Migrants*, p. 11.
35 Following Bernard (1973), cited in T. Kuhlman, 'The economic integration of refugees in developing countries: a research model', *Journal of Refugee Studies*, 4:1 (1991), 1–20, p. 4.
36 Zhou, 'Coming of age'.
37 See for example B. Walter, *Outsiders Inside: Whiteness, Place and Irish Women* (London: Routledge, 2001).

1 Ronnie Fay

Traveller health inequalities as legacies of exclusion

Irish Travellers (often referred to as the Travelling Community) are a small indigenous minority ethnic group in Ireland; a distinct community but with cultural parallels with Gypsy (also called 'Traveller') communities in Britain and Roma communities in other parts of Europe. Travellers' language, customs and values have been profoundly shaped by their traditions, history of nomadism and a long history of being an important part of community life in Ireland while also experiencing marginalisation, racism and exclusion. Travellers are not an immigrant community although many Travellers have migrated from and to Ireland, with some emigrating back and forth to countries such as Britain and the United States where there are Irish Traveller communities that can trace their roots back to the nineteenth century. The 2016 Census identified some 30,987 Travellers in the Republic of Ireland, or approximately 0.7 per cent of the total population. According to Traveller organisations this figure most likely underestimates the total number by several thousand.[1] As a racialised and long discriminated against minority ethnic group failed by generations of policymakers, their experiences, and the struggles of Traveller organisations to secure access to healthcare examined here, are instructive when considering how other groups, including some immigrants, may also come to be marginalised. In particular, common issues and concerns have been identified in respect of Roma in Ireland, whose experiences as outsiders in Ireland are addressed in Chapter 9.

The Equal Status Act 2000 defined Travellers as 'The community of people who are commonly called Travellers and who are identified (both by themselves and others) as people with a shared history, culture and traditions, including an affinity to a nomadic way of life on the island of Ireland' (Part 1, Section 2). However, Traveller ethnicity was only formally acknowledged by the state in March 2017 when, in a statement to the Dáil, An Taoiseach (Prime Minister) Enda Kenny declared that 'Our Traveller Community is an integral part of our society for over a millennium, with their own distinct identity – a people within our people.'[2]

While an aspiration of nomadism remains a fundamental part of Traveller culture, many Travellers are no longer nomadic de facto, either by choice or due to the lack of support for and the incremental criminalisation of, nomadism by the Irish state which gained pace following the 1963 publication of the *Report of the Commission on Itinerancy*, the first national report on Travellers.[3]

I am the Director of the Pavee Point Traveller and Roma Centre, the longest established Traveller human rights organisation in Ireland. In 2015 we celebrated thirty years of direct engagement with Travellers[4] and fifteen years with the Roma community living in Ireland.[5] We recognised the need for solidarity between Roma and Irish Travellers based on shared experiences of racism and discrimination, and common cultural traditions including nomadism. We have worked directly with Roma living in Ireland since 1998 and we officially changed our name from Pavee Point to the Pavee Point Traveller and Roma Centre in 2012.

The Centre has made significant contributions to the development of both local and national Traveller organisations in Ireland, as well as to Traveller policy developments. These organisations include the Irish Traveller Movement, Mincéirs Whiden, the National Traveller Women's Forum, and the Parish of the Travelling People. Alongside a number of these we are members of the European Network against Racism Ireland. Our work is based on two essential premises: (1) Travellers must be involved in the most important decisions that affect their lives, and (2) racism and exclusionary policies of inclusion have been at the root of Traveller inequalities. Pavee Point was the first organisation to recognise the importance of, and campaign for, state acknowledgement of Traveller ethnicity. Community development, with its principles of social justice, solidarity, equality and human rights, and an approach that involves participation, empowerment and collective action, has been fundamental in informing our work with Travellers and Roma.

A central tenet in our approach is the belief that delivering services based on equality does not mean treating people the same but rather comprises designing policies and implementing programmes that are inclusive, culturally appropriate and appropriate to the needs of groups in society. This can lead to better outcomes for disadvantaged groups, including Travellers and Roma. Fundamentally, we believe that Travellers and Roma should be afforded rights to their cultural identity without experiencing marginalisation and discrimination. There is a need for an urgent response and positive action measures to address current and historic processes of discrimination and to address the social determinants that lead to unacceptable health inequalities.

Traveller health inequalities

In 2010 the *All Ireland Traveller Health Study* (*AITHS*), based on research undertaken in the Republic of Ireland and in Northern Ireland in 2008, found that at all ages and for all causes of death Travellers experience a higher mortality than the general population. It concluded:

> The problem is endemic and complex and will not be solved in the short term without considering the wider contextual issues. The fact that an identifiable disadvantaged group in our society is living with the mortality experience of previous generations 50–70 years ago cannot be ignored. The fact that the gap between Traveller mortality and that in the general population has widened in the past 20 years shows that comprehensive approaches to address this situation are required and are indeed vital.[6]

Eight years since the publication of the *AITHS*, Traveller health inequalities remain the same, and in some instances, due to improvements in the national population, health disparities have even widened. The *AITHS* documented:

- Life expectancy for Traveller men is 15.1 years and for Traveller women 11.5 years less than men/women in the general population.
- Traveller men have four times the mortality rate and Traveller women three times the mortality rate of the general population.
- Traveller infant mortality rate is 3.6 times higher than the national rate.
- Suicide rates are six times the national average, accounting for 11 per cent of all Traveller deaths.

The *AITHS* confirmed that health services available to Travellers were perceived as inadequate and substandard, resulting in Travellers' low engagement and poor health outcomes. Findings from the study indicate various institutional, cultural, social and structural barriers that restrict Travellers from accessing and engaging with health services. These include discrimination and racism (at both individual and institutional levels); lack of trust in healthcare providers and inappropriate service provision; and lack of engagement from service providers with Travellers and Traveller organisations.[7]

Unfortunately, a lack of understanding of diversity among senior policy-makers and political leaders has resulted in Travellers being frequently blamed for their own marginalisation, echoing wider society biases against Travellers. Developing a more inclusive and intercultural society is about inclusion by design, not as an add-on or afterthought. Too often a so-called 'mainstreaming approach' has been claimed which in reality fails to meet the health needs of Travellers to the same extent as other groups in society. This, de facto, results in negative outcomes for Travellers and other marginalised groups as their needs are not taken account of and it is assumed that a common/universal approach benefits everyone equally.

Discrimination and racism

Travellers' marginalisation and discrimination have been observed both nationally and internationally by human rights organisations and monitoring bodies. In an urgent site visit to Ireland in 2016, Nils Muižnieks, Council of Europe Commissioner for Human Rights, was 'deeply concerned at the persisting social exclusion and discrimination Travellers are confronted with in Ireland' and recommended that targeted policy measures and more effective involvement of Travellers is required to address the 'serious inequalities that continue to affect the members of this [Traveller] community in accommodation, health, education and, in fact, all fields of life'.[8] Muižnieks reiterated previous Commissioners' calls for targeted measures to redress social exclusion and marginalisation of Travellers. Academic research has contributed to this policy area by consistently reporting the extent to which anti-Traveller racism and discrimination exist in Ireland. In 2010, a national survey of attitudes and prejudices towards Travellers reported:

- 40 per cent of respondents were unwilling to employ a Traveller;
- 79.6 per cent were reluctant to purchase a house next to a Traveller; and
- 18.2 per cent would deny Irish citizenship to Travellers.[9]

A more recent 2017 analysis on discrimination found that Travellers are almost ten times more likely than their settled peers to experience discrimination in seeking work. It also found that Travellers are twenty-two times more likely to experience discrimination in accessing private services such as restaurants and banks.[10] The 2016 Census recorded Traveller unemployment at 80.2 per cent. All these findings recall those of research across Europe into the kinds and levels of discrimination experienced by Roma.

Travellers' poor health outcomes cannot be decoupled from the historical, social and political context in which they live. As Krieger and others have established, health inequalities do not simply exist in a vacuum; there is a clear link between health inequalities and self-reported experiences of racism and discrimination.[11] This is reflected in Travellers' overall vital demographics and in the alarming rates of suicide among young Traveller men, which are currently seven times higher than the national rate.

There is a strong recognition that Irish health services are not equitable and/or operating in a culturally competent manner, making it more difficult for Travellers to access the services they require. Racism and discrimination underpin Travellers' lack of engagement and access to mainstream health services and supports.[12] This was highlighted in the *AITHS*, which reported:

- 53 per cent of Travellers were 'worried about experiencing unfair treatment' from health providers;
- over 40 per cent of Travellers had a concern that they were not always treated with respect and dignity;
- over 50 per cent of Travellers had concerns about the quality of care they received when they engaged with services.

In a 2004 survey of access to hospital facilities, some 66.7 per cent of participating health service providers agreed that discrimination against

Travellers occurs sometimes in their use of health services, and that anti-Traveller discrimination and racism resulted in substandard treatment of Traveller service users. Such barriers have discouraged Travellers from engaging effectively with mainstream health services and supports, particularly with respect to preventative healthcare, as Travellers anticipate inadequate care and discrimination. Mainstream services are often only accessed as a last resort and there has been a tendency to use Accident and Emergency departments as an initial point of contact.[13]

Traveller identity and public policy

To understand the context of Traveller health inequalities, it is useful to consider Irish Travellers' relationship with the Irish state. This relationship, notwithstanding some inclusionary rhetoric, has largely been defined by a state project of assimilation of Travellers, by a lack of respect for cultural identity and by an unwillingness to acknowledge the racist nature of discrimination against Travellers.

The first phase of official concern with the situation of Travellers began with the creation of the Government Commission on Itinerancy in 1960. The Commission excluded Traveller representatives and explicitly focused on assimilation.[14] A subsequent Review Body was established in 1981 tasked with revaluating Traveller-specific policy. This committee had limited Traveller participation. Its key objective was to review 'policies and services for the travelling people and to make recommendations to improve the current situation'; it also sought to address the needs of Travellers 'who wish to continue a nomadic way of life'.[15] A slight shift from the previous explicit assimilationist approach was reflected in the language used by the Review Body, with 'Traveller' replacing the Commission's pejorative use of the term 'itinerant'.[16] In response the state published a key implementation plan leading to a policy of 'sharing out the problem [i.e. Travellers]' whereby each local authority was tasked with building Traveller accommodation within their geographic boundary. Some years later, in 1993, following pressure from Traveller organisations using national social partnership structures, the state established the Task Force on the Travelling Community. Representatives from independent national Traveller organisations actively participated in, and shaped, the committee's inquiry and subsequent policy recommendations for the first time.

The 1995 Report of the Task Force represented a positive shift in the state's conceptualisation and assessment of equality and diversity. It also envisaged a shift in the new relationship between Traveller organisations and the state – from a charity-based welfare approach to a more rights-based approach inspired by a partnership process – in seeking to improve the living circumstances and general welfare of Travellers. It acknowledged the change in nature of the discourse relating to Travellers and, while not formally acknowledging the ethnic distinctiveness of Travellers, stated that culture, ethnicity, racism and discrimination had entered the debate about the situation of Travellers. This represented a degree of movement towards acknowledgement of Traveller cultural distinctiveness and away from racist stereotypes that denigrated Traveller identity as a culture of poverty.[17]

This paradigm shift can be attributed largely to the work of Pavee Point and our sister Traveller representative organisations. A key legacy of the Task Force, which has stood the test of time, is the recognition of the need for mainstreaming, targeting and participation. While successful in achieving a change in rhetoric, this was not however translated into practice by many public services and policymakers, nor into positive outcomes for Travellers on the ground.

A more recent policy impetus has been the European Framework for National Roma Integration Strategies announced by the European Commission in May 2011, which includes Travellers in its remit alongside Sinti, Kalé, Gens du Voyage and other groups listed under the umbrella term 'Roma'.[18] The EU Framework has set targets for the Irish state in relation to education (ensuring that all children complete primary schooling at a minimum), employment (reducing the gap between Travellers/Roma and other citizens), housing (ensuring access to accommodation and basic services such as water and electricity) and health (reducing the gap in health status between Travellers/Roma and the rest of the population).

The strategy drawn up by the Department of Justice and Equality in 2012 in response to the EU Framework was flawed in many respects. First, there had been no consultation of Traveller and Roma organisations when this was drawn up. Secondly, it contained no clear goals, targets, indicators or related timeframes, or monitoring and evaluation mechanisms. The European Commission's assessments of the strategy in 2013 and 2014 were highly critical of Ireland. It was not until 2015–2016 that a comprehensive national consultation process was undertaken involving Travellers and Roma. This also included all government departments and a range of statutory agencies. In 2017, a revised *National Traveller and Roma Inclusion Strategy* was published and submitted to the EU. In the foreword, the Minister of State acknowledged the marginalisation of Travellers and Roma, stating that

> during the years of the financial crisis from which Ireland is emerging, those at the margins of our society frequently– and regrettably – suffered disproportionately from the effects of financial adjustments. Now that Ireland's economy is back on a firmer footing, it is a moral and societal imperative that we work together to address the real needs of these communities.[19]

However, the Minister's comments on some other positive rhetoric have not been backed up by concrete support. The Republic of Ireland's 2017 budget allocated no additional resources to implementation of the *National Traveller and Roma Inclusion Strategy* or to Traveller health development, despite the need to reverse disproportionate cuts to Traveller services imposed during the austerity period.[20] Traveller organisations remain concerned that yet another policy with the potential to effect positive change may merely prove to be lip service.

Pavee Point and Traveller health

The community development ethos of Pavee Point has advocated a multi-faceted approach to addressing Travellers' human rights. This approach means that gender equality and other needs of Travellers must be addressed if equality for all Travellers is to be realised. As part of addressing Traveller gender equality concerns, specific programmes were established for Traveller women and run in 1988–1991. Through the work of these programmes Traveller women articulated the need to address their and their families' health requirements. In response to this, Pavee Point identified the model of Primary Health Care (PHC) as being particularly suitable in tackling Traveller health inequalities.

PHC ensures that Travellers are involved at all stages of the development and delivery of the project. It facilitates the involvement of both literate and pre-literate participants and can therefore be inclusive of those most marginalised in the community. It addresses the causes (social determinants) of ill health rather than the consequences (health inequalities). It reflects a community-based response to health issues rather than a medical response and supports community groups collectively in resolving problems they identify. It is a model endorsed by the World Health Organisation[21] and therefore had currency with the health boards from which funding was sought to progress this work.

Traveller health inequalities have been documented since the publication of the 1988 *Travellers' Health Status Study* and of a further report the following year.[22] These reports highlighted an infant mortality rate more than three times the national average and documented that Traveller men and women died much earlier than their settled counterparts, reaching only the life expectancy that Irish people had attained in the 1940s. However, these revelations were met with little action by the state, health professionals or service providers, or attention from academics. It was largely left to Pavee Point to show leadership in tackling Traveller health inequalities. Prior to the establishment of Traveller Primary Health Care Projects, Traveller women's access to health screening services was severely limited. Through the work of Pavee Point and peer-led Traveller Community Health Workers rates of breast and cervical screening among Traveller women reached almost twice the level for women in the general population, a necessary intervention given low historic rates of engagement.

The work of Pavee Point in addressing health inequalities through a PHC model has significantly influenced government policy since 1994 when the approach was first piloted. It has proven to be an effective way of delivering healthcare to a community that was difficult for the Health Service Executive (HSE) to reach and it has increased the appropriate use of health services by Travellers, thus representing value for money. Pavee Point's health work strongly influenced the approach to health adopted in the 1995 *Task Force Report*, with discrimination acknowledged as a key influence on the poor health status of Travellers. It also acknowledged the link between lack of accommodation and poor health status and the need to facilitate the participation of Travellers in the planning of health services.[23]

Pavee Point drove the development of the 2002 National Traveller Health Strategy.[24] Following consultation with Travellers and Traveller organisations, the Strategy recommended an all-island health study that later became known as the *AITHS*. Some four hundred Travellers, mostly women, acted as peer researchers, and the study achieved an 80 per cent participation rate among a so-called 'hard to reach' group. Pavee Point also campaigned for better data in order to recognise and combat discrimination. Since 1993 it has successfully lobbied for an ethnic question in the national Census as well as the collection, monitoring and use of ethnic status in all routine administrative data collection systems.[25] Work was undertaken to raise Travellers' awareness of the need and role of ethnic data as a tool for attaining human rights as well as addressing data protection concerns. Pilot projects were also undertaken in a range of health settings and the learning documented.[26] This involved working in solidarity with a range of other minority ethnic groups, including migrant representative organisations, recognising that disaggregated ethnic data benefits everyone, not just Travellers.

Many hospitals and primary care health settings now collect and use ethnic data to inform service provision. Nevertheless, in the absence of a comprehensive national approach to ethnic data collection, it has been difficult to monitor access, participation and outcomes for Travellers, Roma and other minority ethnic groups.

Conclusion

The *All Ireland Traveller Health Study* has provided robust evidence of persisting Traveller health inequalities in Ireland despite the valuable work that has been undertaken in developing primary healthcare. Travellers were recognised as an ethnic group in 2017, yet echoes of the deeply flawed assimilationist approach of the 1960s persist. One benefit of Pavee Point's longstanding community development approach has been the emergence of strong Traveller leaders who continue to advocate for policy and service improvements, including those related to health policy. A major problem is that the recommendations of the *AITHS* were never implemented. State funding for all Traveller health and other initiatives was disproportionately cut back during the post-2008 financial crisis compared with other areas of government policy. 'Mainstreaming' policies were adopted by government as a rationale for reducing such funding, but few resources were dedicated to making mainstream approaches effective and no accountability mechanisms were put in place. Demands from Traveller groups to improve funding have been ignored by successive governments despite ongoing criticism of Ireland in international UN human rights reports and from EU bodies.[27] However, following a period of sustained advocacy, there is commitment to develop a National Action Plan for Traveller Health. While this is welcome it follows a period of eight years of cutbacks in the health services and Traveller-specific services and many missed opportunities.

A coherent National Action Plan for Traveller Health might seek to build upon a range of initiatives in which Pavee Point has played a leading role. These include:

• Programmes addressing the specific health needs of men, women and children have been undertaken. Initiatives to address high suicide rates and poor mental health of Travellers have been piloted and rolled out nationally.
• Piloting and implementation of ethnic equality monitoring in a range of healthcare settings, including hospitals, maternity and drugs services.[28] Traveller Proofing[29] and health and health equality impact assessment tools have been developed and training provided for health professionals and Traveller organisations.
• The model of PHC embedded in a community development approach involving the active participation and empowerment of Travellers working collectively to address health inequalities has proven an effective model in our work with Travellers and has been replicated with other marginalised communities in Ireland.

There has been significant progress in the acknowledgement of Traveller health inequalities in Ireland and improved understanding of how to address these issues, even if monitoring, funding and policy implementation are not yet adequate. Section 42 of the Irish Human Rights and Equality Act (2014) requires all public bodies 'to promote equality, prevent discrimination and protect the human rights of their employees, customers, service users and everyone affected by their policies and plans'[30] This legislation requires that measures are taken to address health inequalities experienced by Travellers and other groups. The advocacy and health policy development work of Pavee Point offers a model to also support other marginal groups. For example, visual health education materials developed by Traveller organisations have been adapted by mainstream providers for use with other disadvantaged groups who may also face literacy and/or language constraints. Pavee Point's work in addressing Traveller health inequalities has contributed to greater understanding of the dynamics of exclusion and inclusion in Ireland, and can inform the development of inclusive policies and intercultural service provision within Ireland which benefits all of society, not just Travellers, Roma and other minority ethnic groups and immigrants.

Notes

1 Pavee Point, 'Traveller numbers "up by 32%" in new census', 29 March 2012, www.paveepoint.ie/traveller-numbers-up-by-32-in-new-census/, accessed 4 February 2019.

2 Dail Eireann debate, Wednesday 1 March 2017, Traveller Ethnicity: Statements, oireachtas.ie/en/debates/debate/dail/2017-03-01/37/, accessed 4 February 2019.

3 Commission on Itinerancy, *Report of the Commission on Itinerancy* (Dublin: The Stationery Office, 1963).

4 R. Fay and C. McCabe, *30 Years of Pavee Point* (Dublin: Pavee Point, 2015).

5 Roma Support Group and Pavee Point, *Roma in Ireland: An Initial Needs Analysis* (Dublin: Pavee Point, 2001).

6 UCD Study Team, *Our Geels: All Ireland Traveller Health Study* (Dublin: Department of Health, 2010), p. 13.

7 Pavee Point, *Evidence and Recommendations on Mental Health, Suicide and Travellers* (Dublin: Pavee Point, 2015).

8 Statement by Nils Muižnieks,25 November 2016, www.coe.int/en/web/commissioner/-/ireland-advance-equality-of-travellers-and-women, accessed 4 February 2019.

9 M. Mac Gréil, *Emancipation of the Travelling People: A Report on the Attitudes and Prejudices of the Irish People towards the Travellers Based on a National Social Survey 2007–2008* (Maynooth: NUI Maynooth Publications, 2010).

10 F. McGinnity, R. Grotti, O. Kenny and H. Russell, *Who Experiences Discrimination in Ireland? Evidence from the QNHS Equality Modules* (Dublin: ERSI, 2017).

11 N. Krieger, 'Embodying inequality: a review of concepts, measures, and methods for studying health consequences of discrimination', *International Journal of Health Services*, 29:2 (1999), 295–352.

12 Pavee Point Traveller and Roma Centre, *Submission to the Joint Oireachtas Committee on the Future of Mental Health Care* (Dublin: Pavee Point Traveller and Roma Centre, 2017).

13 Traveller Health Unit Eastern Region, *Use of Hospital Facilities by the Traveller Community – Summary Report* (Dublin: Traveller Health Unit Eastern Region, 2004).

14 Commission on Itinerancy, *Report of the Commission on Itinerancy* (Dublin: The Stationery Office, 1963), p. 11.

15 Travelling People Review Body, *Report of the Travelling People Review Body* (Dublin: The Stationery Office, 1983), pp. 1, 3.

16 J. O'Connell, 'Travellers in Ireland: an examination of discrimination and racism', in R. Lentin and R. McVeigh (eds), *Racism and Anti-Racism in Ireland* (Belfast: Beyond the Pale Publications Ltd., 2002), p. 49.

17 Department of Justice, Equality and Law Reform, *Report of the Task Force on the Travelling Community* (Dublin: The Stationery Office, 1995), pp. 62–63.

18 European Commission, 'An EU Framework for National Roma Integration Strategies up to 2020', COM(2011) 173/4.

19 Department of Justice and Equality, *National Traveller and Roma Inclusion Strategy 2017–2021* (Dublin: DJE, 2017), p. 3.

20 B. Harvey, *Travelling With Austerity* (Dublin: Pavee Point, 2013).

21 World Health Organisation, *Declaration of Alma Ata*, International Conference on Primary Health Care, Alma-Ata, USSR, 6–12 September 1978, who.int/publications/almaata_declaration_en.pdf, accessed 4 February 2019.

22 J. Barry and L. Daly, *The Travellers' Health Status Study: Census of Travelling People* (Dublin: The Health Research Board, 1988); J. Barry, B. Herity and J. Solan, *The Travellers' Health Status Study: Vital Statistics of Travelling People* (Dublin: The Health Research Board, 1989).

23 Department of Justice, Equality and Law Reform, *Report of the Task Force on the Travelling Community*.

24 Department of Health and Children, *Traveller Health: A National Strategy 2002–2005* (Dublin: Department of Health and Children, 2002).

25 Pavee Point Submission to the Central Statistics Office, 'Towards an ethnic equality question in Census 2021', paveepoint.ie/wp-content/uploads/2015/04/Census2021Submission.pdf. accessed 16 January 2019.

26 Pavee Point, *Policy and Practice in Ethnic Data Collection and Monitoring: Counting Us In – Human Rights Count!* (Dublin: Pavee Point, 2016).

27 Examples include Pavee Point, *Submission for the Universal Periodic Review Ireland* (Dublin: Pavee Point, 2015); Pavee Point, *Irish Travellers and Roma: Shadow Report: A Response to Ireland's Third and Fourth Report on the International Convention on the Elimination of All Forms of Racial Discrimination (CERD)* (Dublin: Pavee Point, 2011); Pavee Point Travellers Centre, *Shadow Report: Ireland's First and Second Report on CERD* (Dublin: Pavee Point, 2005); Pavee Point, *Irish Traveller and Roma: Shadow Report: A Response to Ireland's Consolidated Third and Fourth Report to the UN Committee on the Rights of the Child* (Dublin: Pavee Point, 2015); Pavee Point, *Submission on Ireland's Examination at the 111th Session of the Human Rights Committee, 7th–25th July 2014 (UN International Covenant of Civil and Political Rights)* (Dublin: Pavee Point, 2014); Pavee Point, *Submission to the Department of Justice and Equality: Framework Convention for the Protection of National Minorities, Fourth Monitoring Cycle* (Dublin: Pavee Point, 2014); European Commission against Racism and Intolerance, *ECRI Report on Ireland Fourth Monitoring Cycle* CRI (2013) 1, 2013.

28 Pavee Point, *Policy and Practice in Ethnic Data Collection and Monitoring*.

29 Pavee Point, *Traveller Proofing: Within an Equality Framework* (Dublin: Pavee Point, 2001).

30 Irish Human Rights and Equality Commission, *Public Sector Equality and Human Rights Duty*, ihrec.ie/our-work/public-sector-duty/, accessed 4 February 2019.

Sectarian legacies and the marginalisation of migrants

This chapter examines the role that political division and power-sharing has played in impeding a focus within social policy and politics on the needs of recent immigrants and longer-established black and ethnic minority groups (such as British Asians and Chinese) living in Northern Ireland. The organisation of political parties along sectarian lines in Northern Ireland, and a power-sharing system designed to represent only those who identify as 'green' or 'orange', inevitably work to exclude immigrants.

Drawing on policy debates and on interviews with Northern Ireland civil servants, politicians and key stakeholders in immigrant ethnic minority and community organisations, this chapter explores how marginalisation is reinforced through institutional structures, the local conceptualisation of 'good relations' and social cohesion, and the pitfalls of integrating into a post-conflict society where culture and ethnicity have been central to division. These interviews took place in 2011 during the consultation period for a new 'good relations' policy and the re-constitution of the Race Equality Forum to draft the 2015 Racial Equality Strategy; during a time when reflection on 'good relations', identity and integration was of high political importance in the Province.

Since the end of the violent conflict referred to colloquially as 'The Troubles', Northern Ireland has seen a significant increase in the number of immigrants and ethnic minorities. This demographic change brings with it the need to re-examine aspects of social welfare policy development and service provision, and thus necessitates a deeper understanding of the needs and experiences of new migrant communities. Northern Ireland is a small, sparsely populated country under the jurisdiction of the UK. It shares a land border with the Republic of Ireland and has been the centre of an ethno-political conflict between those who identify as British Protestant and those who identify as Irish Catholic for several decades. During this period of sustained violence, more than 3,600 people were killed, many of them civilians. The ceasefire in 1997, followed by the Good Friday Agreement in 1998, brought the conflict to an official end and established a forced power-sharing Executive. However, the region remains plagued by ethnic division and the socio-economic scars of the conflict. Housing, schools and many social and cultural activities remain segregated. More than 108 'peace walls' create physical divisions between majority Protestant and Catholic neighbourhoods, most of which were erected after the ceasefire.

A period of relative political and social stability, coupled with the expansion of the European Union in 2004–2007 (A8 and A2 accession), have led to a resurgence of immigration to Northern Ireland. In the mid to late 2000s, migrant workers from Eastern Europe arrived at a rate previously unseen in the region.[1] The increase in migrants living in Northern Ireland from this part of Europe was dramatic; going from 250 people in the 2001 Census to 32,400 in the most recent Census of 2011.[2] At its peak in 2007, following the expansion of the European Union, Northern Ireland experienced the sharpest rise in the rate of immigration of any region of the UK,[3] as migrant workers from Eastern and Central European countries took up employment in the meat packing and agricultural sectors across the region. While there have been significant changes to demographic trends since the late 1990s, there are some ethnic groups who are not new to the island. Jewish, Chinese, Indian and Pakistani communities have had a notable presence in Northern Ireland since the 1960s – their migration only stalling upon the beginning of the Troubles.

While there is some evidence that migration rates to the region have slowed since the economic downturn,[4] net migration has been on the increase for three consecutive years,[5] rates of births to non-UK- or Irish-born mothers are remaining steady,[6] and school registrations of children for whom English is not the first language continue to increase.[7] Yet this growing population continues to be discussed in isolation from the wider community, and usually in the context of immigration control, integration and criminal justice. There is little public debate about the political and social inclusion of individuals who do not define themselves as white Irish or white British. Cultural discussions centre on British (expressed as Unionism or Loyalism) or Irish (expressed as Nationalism or Republicanism) cultures. Even as identification with the superordinate identity of 'Northern Irish' becomes more prevalent – with nearly half of the electorate selecting this identity in the 2011 Census[8] – there is no sense that this change necessarily indicates a distancing from British-ness or Irish-ness. Despite it being held up as an emergent middle ground, the majority of those who self-identify as Northern Irish continue to vote for political parties based on religious or national identity.[9] Debates on minority languages refer to Irish and Ulster Scots, in spite of Polish being the second most commonly spoken language in Northern Ireland. This fact was the subject of political remarks during talks on an Irish Language Act, where the First Minister flippantly suggested it would be more appropriate to have a Polish Language Act than an Irish one.[10] Discussion of the first languages of first- and second-generation migrants features only in the context of translation services and associated costs.[11]

Institutional barriers to inclusion of minorities

There are a number of constitutional and institutional issues which make the recognition and inclusion of identities which fall outside of Irish/British difficult or secondary in the region. These relate to citizenship restrictions in the context of tightening immigration policies across the UK, top-down governance which leaves much of the decision-making affecting public services in non-governmental public bodies outside of local government, and the construction of political parties around the concept of national identity. Many of the things which characterise governance in Northern Ireland (consociational governance arrangement, political designation, the influence of sectarian issues on decision-making and the grappling of elected members with a burgeoning democratic process replacing years of Direct Rule) have made policymaking difficult in the region more generally.[12]

These common issues facing groups pushing for policy change in the jurisdiction are also a significant concern for policy relating to ethnic minorities and migrants. The following section is informed by a series of interviews with civil servants – primarily from the Racial Equality and Social Cohesion Units of the then Office of the First Minister and Deputy First Minister (OFMDFM), Members of the Legislative Assembly (MLAs) and Members of Parliament (MPs) from the main political parties including both community designations, and leaders of the black and minority ethnic, and migrant voluntary and community sector. The semi-structured interviews took place between 2011 and 2012, during the pre-consultation period for a new social cohesion strategy (the now defunct Cohesion, Sharing and Integration Strategy) and the new Racial Equality Strategy. They describe the institutional and legislative context in which minority identities are often overshadowed in favour of a 'two communities' narrative. Respondents identified several key areas in which minority interests are stifled: forced coalition government and entrenched division; poor interdepartmental working and failure to mainstream minority issues; poor data collection and monitoring; and the conceptualisation of 'good relations' and 'social cohesion'.

Forced coalition and the entrenchment of ethnic division

In post-conflict societies where ethnicity has been central to community division, ethnicity becomes the singular defining factor in identity, and all other components fall to the wayside. Often political leaders are the most unwilling to relinquish the importance of ethnicity. It is in their interest to maintain an emphasis on this identity in order to appeal to constituents along those lines.[13] While Northern Ireland has had (except during periods of Direct Rule from London) a government based on proportional representation, often held up as the model for post-conflict governance and inclusion of minority identities, this can also lead to stagnation and conflict management rather than political progress. In the Northern Irish Assembly, all political parties are effectively required to designate as being aligned to the unionist or nationalist blocs. The stipulation under the Good Friday Agreement that all significant legislation must be approved by a majority from both 'camps' in turn can lead to entrenchment of the same ethnic bloc divisions which were so core to conflict.[14]

One argument for increasing examination of the marginalisation of immigrants and ethnic minorities, and for addressing their experiences of racism and discrimination, is that doing so might 'dilute' the potency of 'green' and 'orange' cleavages. However, it is also the case that concepts and debates related to human rights and racism have been mobilised in conflicts between the two main ethnic blocs. For example, concerns about human rights have been used by Catholic nationalists to criticise Protestant unionists in ways that might make it difficult for both blocs to agree on how the concept might be used to address inequalities experienced by immigrants and ethnic minorities.[15] Also, as examined in Chapter 3, policy responses to racism and hate crime affecting immigrants have come to be subordinated by a dominant focus on addressing sectarianism.

Research examining the relationships between nationalist and unionist political parties and immigrants and ethnic minority groups in Northern Ireland has found the latter worried that they could not participate in the political system without choosing sides.[16] The apparent unwillingness of immigrants and ethnic minorities to participate in politics in turn discourages political parties from seeking their support and from addressing issues that affect them. The manifestos of all the main political parties in Northern Ireland have acknowledged the existence of immigrants and the need to treat them fairly, but in practice have been either indifferent to immigrants or anti-immigrant. Some high-profile unionist politicians have made or defended anti-immigrant statements.[17]

Under the D'Hont system[18] which governs the means by which responsibility for individual departments in the Northern Ireland Executive are allocated, ministries are led by opposing political parties. This has implications for interdepartmental working; taking the common policy problem of siloed decision-making a step further as issues such as language and culture – key to many policies on integration and minority protection – are politicised through the historical conflict. Policymakers and voluntary sector leaders raise concerns around a lack of interdepartmental working specific to ethnic minority and migrant communities. One MLA described the wide scope of ethnic minority and migrant needs, and pointed out that with such a broadly defined community there is no way that one department could possibly meet those needs on its own. Failure to work cross-departmentally can also have implications for funding of services which directly impact on ethnic minorities.

Through the Racial Equality and Social Cohesion Units, the Executive Office has responsibility for driving equality strategies, but the inclusion of these principles across individual departments has little to no accountability attached. Yet these departments are responsible for the development and evaluation of the policies which touch residents' day-to-day lives. Some figures in the voluntary and community sector have concerns about whether or not departmental policies are effective in addressing the nuanced needs within immigrant and ethnic minority and migrant communities. Some interviewees observed that poor understanding of such communities and their needs can lead to unbalanced policy responses. One senior civil servant interviewee with an equalities brief stated that service providers and government departments lacked experience in addressing needs other than those of the two main ethnic communities. There were high levels of scepticism among most interviewees that this situation would change until immigrants became electorally important to the main political parties.

Lack of mainstreaming and poor interdepartmental collaboration

Mainstreaming ethnic minority issues into everyday policymaking is often deemed to be the most effective means of ensuring the long-term wellbeing of minority groups. However, as noted in the previous chapter with respect to Travellers in the Republic of Ireland, there are significant challenges in ensuring that marginal communities benefit from services to the same extent as other users without special initiatives aimed at redressing inequalities of access and outcome. These include consultation and engagement with communities at risk of marginalisation and policy targets aimed at redressing unequal outcomes.

In Northern Ireland, Section 75 of the Northern Ireland Act (which provides the constitutional basis for much of the public sector) compels all policy, legislation and public service development to consider the impact it will have on minority or marginalised groups and take action to promote equality. Section 75 identifies nine categories: religion, political opinion, age, sex, race, sexual orientation, disability, marital status, and those with/without dependants.[19] Section 75 outlines the statutory obligation of public authorities to promote equality of opportunity between people of different faiths, nationalities, races, sexual preferences, genders, disabilities, political opinions, ages, or marital status. It also obliges public bodies to promote good relations between groups. The guidance applies to government departments, agencies and non-departmental public bodies and should be used at all stages and levels of the policy process.[20] Section 75 should thus help to 'mainstream' equality issues throughout policy.

While Section 75 was intended to have a strategic impact on people's lives, there are no specific policy outcome measurements. Two independent reviews of public authority understanding of Section 75 found that the emphasis was on the establishment of a process rather than the outputs of that process.[21] In spite of the intention of promoting equality, the interpretation of Section 75 by policymakers has emphasised the identification of potential negative equality impacts.[22] Those public authorities which have been most successful in implementing the schemes are those with strong internal leadership on the issue, which have formal internal structures and which facilitate an environment of cooperation across sectors.[23] The failure to properly implement equality measures in policy development in Northern Ireland has the potential for negative impacts on ethnic minority and migrant communities, and research into the social mobility of minority ethnic groups shows that equality monitoring is largely ineffective in protecting them.[24] Given the low numbers of immigrants and ethnic minorities in the region, the scope for political influence is already limited. Protection as a minority group under equality frameworks is a crucial part of social inclusion for minority groups. If the measures are not properly implemented, or are used only as 'tick-boxes', there is a risk of minority issues not being given due consideration in decision-making.

Data collection and monitoring, and 'pigeon-holing' minority identities

A significant amount of administrative data is collected across the Province relating to protected groups (including on grounds of race and ethnicity). There is a statutory duty on all public sector organisations and service providers to collect information on these groups, and users of public services will be asked regularly to complete anonymous monitoring forms. While this has become commonplace for Northern Ireland residents, it can seem intrusive for newcomer groups; particularly where the purpose is not made entirely clear or for those groups (e.g. asylum seekers) who might find providing personal details to a public body suspect or threatening. Additionally, the manner in which data are collected and analysed often leads to data on those who do not identify as white being excluded or deemed inconclusive because the numbers are not high enough to generate statistical significance.[25] This is the case in many large-scale data sets, such as the National Crime Survey, where data on minority ethnic users are excluded as they do not make up a statistically significant proportion of the population. In an era of increasing reliance on big data to justify policy decisions and resource allocation, smaller ethnic and racial groups are easily overlooked.

Also problematic for minority groups is the tendency for political elites and service providers to identify 'ethnic minorities' or 'migrants' as a homogeneous group.[26] Ethnic minority communities, if they wish to be included in decision-making, are expected to present as a homogeneous community. The process of consultation creates the false impression of clearly defined, easily identified groups – 'corporate representation'.[27] It does not recognise ethnic minority groups beyond their ethnic identification. There is no scope for considering the ways in which migrant and ethnic minority groups share other characteristics with the dominant ethnic groups recognised in policy, which a lens of 'superdiversity' might bring. As previously stated, the classification of a group to facilitate their access to the political sphere limits the scope of their identification within the policy process. Bloomfield and Bianchi point out that 'corporate multiculturalism harbours the danger of entrenching a singular representation of a community that is itself pluralistic and thus excluding discordant voices, particularly of women and younger people'.[28] Defining communities solely on the basis of ethnicity leaves little room for specific needs – those of women and ethnic minorities for example. There is no protection which recognises multiple deprivation or intersectional identities/oppression. This reductive view of minorities is problematic in most contexts but is exacerbated by a post-conflict society in which there is little room for aspects of identity which fall outside of ethnicity and nationality.

Several policymaker interviewees stated that real change – including access to interpreters and cultural sensitivity in public services – would not happen for ethnic minorities and migrants in Northern Ireland until their numbers grew significantly, and that this pattern is likely to continue until the numbers are electorally significant. One senior civil servant relayed an occasion when he was asked what he would do to improve the situation of ethnic minorities in Northern Ireland. His response – 'only partly flippantly: "have lots more of them!"' One Unionist MLA interviewed in 2011 said that most marginalised groups are 'off the radar' for most politicians and attributed this to the sectarian nature of politics in Northern Ireland. Another elected representative, a Unionist MP, delivered a quote which drove home the importance of numbers to political prioritisation:

> The ethnic minorities are a smaller group, and there is a much bigger group out there. And whether you like it or you don't that crops up ... Where does it fit in in the process? It fits in. But it may not be at the top.

The conceptualisation of good relations and social cohesion

In addition to a failure to mainstream the wide range of needs of minority groups into policy on public services, there are significant problems with the social cohesion and racial equality strategies in the Executive. Under the first Assembly following the Good Friday Agreement, good relations and racial equality were governed by *A Shared Future* and *The Racial Equality Strategy* (2005) respectively. These interdependent documents reflected on shared space across the ethno-religious divide in the region and were the result of extensive community engagement. The process of consultation in the first Racial Equality Strategy was extremely inclusive, with multiple layers of engagement of a wide range of groups – resulting in a policy which was largely accepted, and even championed, by the groups most directly affected. However, once devolution was stalled, and Sinn Fein and the Democratic Unionist Party (DUP) were elected in the new Assembly, these strategies were shelved in favour of new policies developed under the newly formed Executive. The policies which replaced them are significantly less comprehensive, vague in language and intent, and have less clear lines of accountability.

The shelving of *A Shared Future* left a vacuum in good relations strategy for several years. The present strategy, *Together: Building a United Community (TBUC)* is the second attempt since devolution was restored in 2007. The first attempt, the *Cohesion, Sharing and Integration* draft strategy, was scrapped before a final version could be completed. During the most extensive consultation process in the history of the Assembly, lasting more than a year and involving more than two hundred individual responses, the strategy was slated as being too vague and exclusive of any identities outside of British and Irish, vilifying young people and having no clear objectives. Presumably to avoid a similar fate, *TBUC*, launched in 2013, was written by the Executive Office (then OFMDFM) and published without consultation with or the involvement of the rest of the Executive's political parties. It centres on children and young people, a 'shared community', a safe community and protection of cultural expression. It should be noted, however, that protection of cultural expression is defined in line with British and Irish national identities, and that race, ethnicity and intersectional identities are referred to only to state that they are the province of the Racial Equality Strategy. This clear and deliberate separation of good relations, social cohesion and minority identities creates a lack of accountability for ethnic minorities or migrants in good relations policy. This in turn impacts on the prioritisation of these groups in good relations at a local government level, as councils have a statutory responsibility for allocating resources to promote good relations locally.

The current Racial Equality Strategy 2015–2025 follows its 2005 predecessor, which was sidelined by the Northern Ireland Assembly dominated by Sinn Fein and the DUP. On paper the 2005 Strategy was ambitious, as is its successor. The 2005 Strategy 'mainstreamed' responsibility across government departments but there was little concrete implementation in the absence of monitoring of progress or any other system of accountability for action. This lack of accountability persists with the current policy.[29] Outcome measures are based largely on self-report public attitudes data, and by its own admission the policy lacks indicators which centre on minority ethnic and migrant experiences. The 2015–2025 Racial Equality Strategy has set the eradication of racism and racial inequality as an objective and it has proposed both immigrant and refugee integration strategies. However, there is no funding directly attached to meeting any of these goals. The Strategy instead instructs departments to consider how they will meet the objectives of the Strategy when designing their budgets (the 'mainstreaming' bit).

The complexities of immigration and integration in a divided society

Northern Ireland remains a deeply divided society. Schools are segregated along religious lines – with only 7 per cent of children being educated in integrated schools.[30] Residential segregation is just as common, particularly in social housing, where 90 per cent of all social housing tenants live in segregated communities.[31] While there is a commitment in *TBUC* to the elimination of the 'peace walls' by 2023, there is little evident progress to date. Policies and legislation which favour 'constructive ambiguity' and tolerance over acceptance serve to maintain the post-conflict status quo.

This deeply entrenched social division and normalised sectarianism promotes territorial attitudes towards public spaces and institutions, and a sense of 'us and them' which is easily translatable to other 'outsider' groups.[32] Sectarianism provides a language and cultural template for othering and for accentuating difference which also affects ethnic minorities and immigrants. In Northern Ireland those not local to an immediate area are referred to as 'blow-ins', and social networks and tight family connections make it difficult for those falling outside of these communities to feel they belong. The territorialism which has built up around the conflict has been identified as a contributing factor to incidents of racist attacks in Belfast.[33] While some have argued against conflating sectarianism and racism lest the adversity faced by minority ethnic groups be subsumed by old divisions, others highlight the natural connection between sectarianism and racism as two sides of the same coin.[34] These parallels are clear when examining overlap between self-reported sectarianism and prejudice against minority groups, and where perpetrators of racist and sectarian hate crimes overlap.[35] Large numbers of migrant workers reported experiencing sometimes quite serious abuse based on their ethnicity or nationality. Some Polish workers had themselves been caught up in sectarian violence or been the target of sectarian abuse – including incidents of arson and attempts to force them from neighbourhoods – because they were believed to be linked to Catholicism and therefore tied in with 'that community'.[36]

Where groups are competing for resources, and sectarianism is tied in with resource allocation, 'outsider' groups can become dragged into or become scapegoats for historical grievances or misperceptions. In Northern

Ireland, where cultural and political rights have been contested for generations, ceding entitlements becomes a zero-sum game, tied constantly to 'us
and them' politics. This is reinforced by the political parties for the sake of
their majorities. Historical territorialism and tribalism lead to a perception
that certain neighbourhoods belong to certain groups. This is upheld at the
most senior political levels, as evidenced in 2014 by then First Minister
Peter Robinson defending racist attacks on social housing by implying that
the perpetrators were protecting the area for 'local people'.[37]

Positive public attitudes towards migrants in Northern Ireland had been
on a steadily upwards trend since the early 2000s, but the 2015 attitudinal
research results showed a marked reduction in willingness to accept individuals from minority backgrounds as family through marriage for the first
time in several years. Attitudes were particularly negative towards Eastern
European and Muslim populations.[38] While close links between the indigenous population and minority groups are increasing, casual contact
between racial groups is declining, and only one-fifth of respondents believe
that attitudes towards minority groups will improve in five years.[39] Positive
perceptions of migrants decrease significantly when respondents are asked
about the impact of migrants on the public sector. More than half of respondents believe that migrants put a strain on schools and health services and
take jobs away from the local community.[40]

The impact of alienation on everyday life

Without the critical mass to make demands and set agendas through traditional political activities, and with diminishing representation in civil society
and public life, minority ethnic people and migrants in Northern Ireland
often face multiple deprivation, discrimination and institutional barriers
to accessing services, and limitations to social mobility. Research into the
experiences of ethnic minorities and migrants in Northern Ireland continues to uncover the difficulties in accessing quality services in the areas of
housing, healthcare, policing, education, English-language instruction, and
access to benefits and fair employment.[41] Many minority groups experience
low rates of employment or employment in low-wage jobs, and in-work
poverty and underemployment are common.[42] This is linked to poor recognition of non-UK qualifications and experience, problems associated with
English-language acquisition, and institutional or indirect discrimination.[43]
Reports examining the experience of health and social services in the region
highlight significant problems in the provision of services to these communities. Migrants face poor availability of appropriate translation services,
often leaving children and family members to translate. They experience
direct and indirect discrimination, poor understanding of cultural needs

and a lack of awareness of services. Because many minority groups live in low-income areas, the 'postcode lottery' of provision often leads to poorer-quality services.[44]

Minority groups continue to face a dearth of representation in public life and immigrant- and ethnic minority-led groups have received declining levels of institutional support. The most prominent exception, Anna Lo, a former chairperson of the Chinese Welfare Association and member of the Alliance Party, was elected to the Northern Ireland Assembly for Belfast South in 2007. In 2014 she was attacked by a loyalist mob and became the focus of online abuse.[45] In various interviews she stated that there had always been a degree of racist harassment of the Chinese community in Northern Ireland but that this had become worse in recent years. In 2014 she resigned, citing racist abuse and institutional discrimination as reasons for leaving public life.[46]

Northern Ireland is shifting from a Province focused on ethnic conflict and community polarisation to an increasingly diverse society. The scope for multiple or intersectional identities, however, is limited in the political sphere. Those who do not identify as unionist or nationalist are often unaccounted for in any meaningful way in policymaking and the electoral process. The social and institutional reinforcement of the two-community narrative inhibits integration and the mainstreaming of minority identity into public policy, which has a deleterious effect on provision of health and social care services, education, employment and social mobility for these groups. Newcomer communities, those in low-wage employment, Muslims and Travellers are particularly marginalised – with poorer socio-economic, educational and health outcomes, as well as having increased vulnerability to racial discrimination, abuse and attacks. Social deprivation policies are entirely silent on the needs of immigrant and ethnic minority populations in Northern Ireland.

The absence of a critical mass either in voter constituencies or in policy circles has translated to an absence of accountability on this issue. In this context the exclusion of immigrants and ethnic minority communities from political and policy systems remains a peripheral issue. Migration is still largely perceived as a temporary issue, yet settlement and integration are clearly not acknowledged by the political establishment in any material way. While newcomers to the island have been effective in organising in civil society, recent gutting of funding to the voluntary and community sector has left many groups without representation in the political sphere. To address the inequalities facing these groups, or to further integration (however this might be understood), the primacy of unionism and nationalism must be confronted in the public sphere. There needs to be more statutory support for grassroots organising and minority-led civil society to address this democratic deficit.

Notes

1 G. Fegan and D. Marshall, *Long-Term International Migration Statistics 2006–07* (Belfast: Northern Ireland Statistics and Research Agency, 2008), p. 3.
2 Northern Ireland Statistics and Research Agency, *Census 2011: Key Statistics for Northern Ireland* (Belfast: NISRA, 2012), p. 6.
3 Fegan and Marshall, *Long-Term International Migration Statistics*, p. 11.
4 Northern Ireland Statistics and Research Agency, *Long-Term Migration Statistics 2016* (Belfast: NISRA, 2017), p. 8.
5 Ibid., p. 8.
6 Ibid., p. 24.
7 Ibid., p. 28.
8 J. Garry and K. McNicholl, *Understanding the Northern Irish Identity*, Northern Ireland Assembly Knowledge Exchange Seminar Series (Belfast: Northern Ireland Executive, 2015), p. 3.
9 K. McNicholl, 'The "Northern Irish" identity is no new dawn', *The Detail*, 2017, thedetail.tv/articles/the-northern-irish-identity-is-no-new-dawn, accessed 22 March 2018.
10 G. McKeown, '"No desire" for a Polish Language Act in Northern Ireland', *Irish News*, 15 February 2017.
11 P. Ramsey and B. Waterhouse-Bradley, 'Cultural policy in Northern Ireland: making cultural policy for a divided society', in V. Durrer, T. Miller and D. O'Brien (eds), *The Routledge Handbook of Global Cultural Policy* (Abingdon: Routledge, 2018), pp. 195–211.
12 C. Knox, 'Policy making in Northern Ireland: ignoring the evidence', *Policy & Politics*, 36:3 (2008), 343–359.
13 S. G. Simonsen, 'Addressing ethnic divisions in post-conflict institution-building: lessons from recent cases', *Security Dialogue*, 36:3 (2005), 300–304.
14 Ibid., pp. 299–304.
15 B. Graham and C. Nash, 'A shared future: territoriality, pluralism and public policy in Northern Ireland', *Political Geography*, 25:3 (2006), 254–257.
16 P. Hainsworth, C. Gilligan and A. McGarry, *Elected Representatives/Political Parties and Minority Ethnic Communities in Northern Ireland* (Belfast: Community Relations Council, 2008), p. 44.
17 Robin Wilson, *Northern Ireland Peace Monitoring Report: Number Four* (Belfast: Community Relations Council, 2018), pp. 32–36.
18 The election of the Northern Ireland Executive is decided using the D'Hont System. The D'Hont System, also known as the 'highest average' system, is a method of allocating votes which divides the number of votes by the number of seats won. This allows parties which received smaller numbers of votes to be more successful as the larger party wins more seats. It is designed to deliver a more proportional distribution of seats.
19 R. Osborne, '"Evidence" and equality in Northern Ireland', *Evidence & Policy*, 3:1 (2007), 79–97, pp. 82–85.
20 Ibid., p. 80.
21 Reeves and Associates, *Assessing the Impact of Section 75 of the Northern Ireland Act 1998 on Individuals*, 2007 (Belfast: OFMDFM), p. 11; MMMA Consultancy, *Assessing the Roles of the Voluntary and Community Sectors in*

Contributing to the Effectiveness of Section 75 *of the Northern Ireland Act*, 2007 (Belfast: ECNI, 2006), p. 3.

22 Reeves and Associates, *Impact of* Section 75, p. 11.

23 Equality Commission Northern Ireland, *Keeping It Effective: Reviewing the Effectiveness of* Section 75 *of the Northern Ireland Act 1998* (Belfast: Equality Commission Northern Ireland, 2008), pp. 25–28.

24 J. Irwin, R. McAreavey and N. Murphy, *The Economic and Social Mobility of Ethnic Minority Communities in Northern Ireland* (York: Joseph Rowntree Foundation, 2014), pp. 23–33.

25 B. Waterhouse-Bradley and M. Kerr, *BME and Migrant Confidence in Policing and Criminal Justice in Northern Ireland: An Exploratory Exercise to Support the Community Safety Strategy* (Belfast: Northern Ireland Strategic Migration Partnership, 2014), pp. 16–19.

26 J. Crowley, 'The political participation of ethnic minorities', *International Political Science Review*, 22:1 (2001), 99–121, p. 100.

27 Y. N. Soysal, *Limits of Citizenship* (Chicago, IL: University of Chicago Press, 2007), pp. 65–69.

28 J. Bloomfield and F. Bianchi, 'Culture, citizenship and urban governance in Western Europe', in N. Stevenson (ed.), *Culture and Citizenship* (London: Sage, 2001), p. 106.

29 Wilson, *Northern Ireland Peace Monitoring Report*, pp. 111–112.

30 Department of Education, 'Integrated schools', *Education*, 2018. education-ni. gov.uk/articles/integrated-schools, accessed 22 March 2018.

31 A. Morris, 'Over 90% of social housing in NI still segregated', *Irish News*, 20 February 2016.

32 H. Donnan, 'Because you stick out, you stand out: perceptions of prejudice among Northern Ireland's Pakistanis', in P. Hainsworth (ed.), *Divided Society: Ethnic Minorities and Racism in Northern Ireland* (London: Pluto Press, 2018), pp. 197–221.

33 P. Connolly and M. Keenan, *Racial Attitudes and Prejudice in Northern Ireland* (Belfast: Northern Ireland Statistics and Research Agency, 2000).

34 McVeigh and Roulston, 'From Good Friday to good relations', pp. 10–12.

35 B. Fanning and L. Michael, 'Racism and anti-racism in the two Irelands', *Ethnic and Racial Studies*, 41:15 (2018), 2656–2672.

36 R. McVeigh, *Migrant Workers and their Families in Northern Ireland: A Trade Union Response* (Belfast: NI ICTU, 2006), pp. 50–51.

37 A. Rutherford, 'First Minister Peter Robinson in U-turn over "locals only" race row', *Belfast Telegraph*, 20 June 2014.

38 L. Michael, *Racism and Intolerance towards Minority Ethnic Groups in Northern Ireland: Research Update 112* (Belfast: ARK Northern Ireland, 2017), pp. 2–3.

39 Ibid., pp. 3–4.

40 ARK, 'NI Life and Times Survey – 2016: attitudes to minority ethnic people', *Northern Ireland Life and Times* [Online], 2018, ark.ac.uk/nilt/2016/Minority_Ethnic_People/, accessed 22 March 2018.

41 F. Murphy and U. Vieten, *Asylum Seekers and Refugees' Experiences of Life in Northern Ireland* (Belfast: Racial Equality Unit, Executive Office, 2018), pp. 24–93.

42 A. Wallace, R. McAreavey and K. Atkin, *Poverty and Ethnicity in Northern Ireland* (York: Joseph Rowntree Foundation, 2013), pp. 24–50.

43 Irwin, McAreavey and Murphy, *Economic and Social Mobility*, pp. 34–56.

44 K. Radford, B. Sturgeon, I. Cuomo and O. Lucas, '*Walking This Thin Line*': *Black and Minority Ethnic (BME) Experiences of Mental Health & Wellbeing in N. Ireland* (Belfast: Institute for Conflict Research, 2018), pp. 5–10.

45 H. McDonald, 'Only Chinese-born parliamentarian in UK to quit politics over racist abuse', *The Guardian*, 19 May 2014.

46 B. Fanning, *Migration and the Making of Ireland* (Dublin: UCD Press, 2018), p. 217.

3 Bryan Fanning and Lucy Michael*

Institutional responses to racism in both Irelands

The notable absence in the Republic of Ireland of far-right organisations and the rebuttal of far-right advances by paramilitary groups in Northern Ireland have made both jurisdictions unusual in the European context, but this has not meant an absence of violent and periodically organised racism.[1] In several high-profile cases of fatal assault in the Republic, racism is acknowledged as a motivating factor.[2] Racist incidents have been more prevalent in Northern Ireland and more prominently reported by the media. For example, in June 2009 east Belfast homes were attacked by a gang chanting slogans of British far-right group Combat 18 and making Nazi salutes. Twenty Roma families fled, most financed to leave Northern Ireland altogether by the Housing Executive.[3] Homes of other immigrants including non-Roma Romanians, have also regularly been attacked.[4] Leaflets calling for Chinese residents' expulsion were distributed in loyalist South Belfast in 2004.[5] Attacks orchestrated by the local Ulster Volunteer Force command, connected to Combat 18, forced Chinese, Zimbabwean and others to leave homes in south Belfast and local estate agents were warned not to rent to foreign nationals.[6] Symbolism employed in these attacks includes the flying of Nazi, Confederate and KKK flags.[7] Violence against white Polish and other Eastern European identities includes arson attacks on houses and businesses and burning of Polish flags on Twelfth of July bonfires.[8] Organised racist violence has thus been a distinct focus of interest for both the state and civil society in Northern Ireland in a way that is not the case in the Republic. However, the persistent pattern of organised racist violence in predominantly unionist areas has made this politically difficult to address in the context of shared government.

Various chapters in this book, including the two previous ones, highlight experiences of racism in both Irelands and address the consequences of institutional failures to respond adequately to experiences of racism, whether as experienced by Travellers or Roma, by immigrants and ethnic minorities, in social housing and in the labour market. Like the previous two chapters this chapter examines institutional contexts and practices that pre-dated the large immigration to both Irelands since the turn of the century.

Comparative institutional responses to racism

Legislation and state policies aimed at addressing racism have evolved differently in the two Irelands. In the Republic both grew out of anti-racist activism concerned since the 1980s with anti-Traveller prejudice and, as immigration rose, out of non-governmental organisation (NGO) pressure upon the Irish state to address its responsibilities under the UN Convention on the Elimination of Racial Discrimination. In Northern Ireland legislative and institutional responses to racism were informed by UK practices, particularly as NGO advocates of anti-racism were influenced by mainland UK norms and debates. However, responses were later and weaker than elsewhere in the UK as gridlock in Northern Irish politics imposed limits on progressive social policy.

The Republic's Prohibition of Incitement to Hatred Act (1989) emerged out of concerns about publication of materials in Ireland by racist organisations elsewhere rather than about home-grown racism. This resembled the England and Wales Incitement to Hatred Act (1965) which has applied in Northern Ireland since 1970. Efforts to invoke the Act, however, in cases of discrimination or criminal acts where racism was claimed as a motivating factor, have been largely unsuccessful. The Act was not designed to apply in such cases. Furthermore, the judiciary in the Republic of Ireland are not subject to sentencing guidelines imposing higher tariffs on racially motivated assaults. Because courts do not take into account racism as a motivating factor there has been little impetus for Gardaí (Police) to do so either. The Act remains significantly underused.

NGO pressure on the Irish state to comply with international treaty obligations, notably the UN Convention on the Elimination of All Forms of Racial Discrimination, resulted in the Republic of Ireland signing the Convention in 1968, and becoming obliged to make periodic reports detailing efforts to address racist discrimination. Under NGO-levered international pressure, the Irish government committed to establish the National Consultative Committee on Racism and Interculturalism (NCCRI) during the European Year Against Racism (1997) and, at the 2001 World Conference on Racism in Durban, to have the NCCRI draw up the first *National Action Plan Against Racism*. Inaugurated in 1998 with an explicit remit of addressing racism in Irish society, the NCCRI was funded by and under the control of the Department of Justice, Equality and Law Reform. Initiatives included the establishment of the anti-racism awareness programme *Know Racism* in 2001, as well as the preparation of *Planning for Diversity: The National Action Plan Against Racism 2005–2008*.[9]

In 2000, the Equal Status Act was introduced to prohibit discrimination in provision of goods and services on grounds including 'race' and 'membership of the Traveller community'.[10] It remains the most important legislation in this area to date. However, subsequent amendments reduced its effectiveness in relation to accommodation and entry to licensed premises, the latter the result of a targeted lobby against Travellers. The Act was accompanied by the establishment of the Equality Authority, a Quango with statutory responsibility for promotion of equality initiatives (since transferred into the Irish Human Rights and Equality Commission).

International scrutiny has been promoted by civil society organisations as a means of holding the Irish state to account for its unwillingness to address racism. In submissions to the United Nations Committee on the Elimination of Racial Discrimination (CERD), Traveller organisations and other NGOs have repeatedly presented a united front, collectively and consistently criticising the Irish state's failure to address racism. These criticisms include denial of Traveller ethnicity, inaction over institutional barriers in health and education, treatment of asylum seekers in Direct Provision and lacunae in criminal law addressing racist offences.

The reluctance of the Irish state to acknowledge racism, even as it promoted 'interculturalism' became obvious when in 2008 it effectively dismantled the key institutional mechanisms for addressing racism under the guise of 'austerity'. The NCCRI was abolished in 2008, and the National Action Plan Against Racism discontinued. The Equality Authority budget was cut by 43 per cent, while other state-funded bodies received only minor cuts. Niall Crowley, the Authority's Chief Executive, resigned, arguing that budgetary reductions were a deliberate effort to hobble a body critical of government policy. The Authority had, in 2006, supported a case taken by a Traveller family against the Commissioner of An Garda Síochána, the Director of Public Prosecutions, a District Justice *and* the Attorney-General, challenging Public Order legislation on grounds of disproportionate and discriminatory impact on Travellers because of accommodation needs. In 2007 67 per cent of Equality Authority cases filed under the Equal Status Acts related to allegations of discrimination of people availing of public services. Crowley argued that government and senior civil servants experienced these allegations as a threat.[11]

The NGO Alliance Against Racism, a coalition of some thirty faith community, Traveller and immigrant-led bodies, labelled the cuts 'an attack on the human rights infrastructure of the State'. Its 2011 report to CERD argued that the Irish state now lacked the means for strategic responses to racism, a focal point for anti-discrimination and anti-racism measures, and a forum for national debate on these matters. The NGOs argued that the Irish state had deliberately sabotaged efforts to address racism and to meet its UN obligations. The impact of this shift in the state's approach has continuing significance today.[12]

In Northern Ireland, as noted in the previous chapter, leadership on anti-racism has been more consistently offered by an umbrella organisation representing ethnic minority-led groups and led by members of these. The Northern Ireland Council for Ethnic Minorities (NICEM) emerged during the 1990s out of a campaign involving Traveller, Chinese and Indian groups, with trade unions and statutory organisations, to enact anti-racism legislation similar to that elsewhere in the UK. The Race Relations (NI) Order 1997 is the key piece of legislation protecting Northern Ireland's ethnic minorities, and its passing partially addressed the gap in race equality legislation between Northern Ireland and the rest of the UK. This legislation was seen as an important part of the process of transitioning to a society which could not be simply conceived of as two communities. As a result of the legislation, NICEM took on a statutory role in challenging racism. In 2007, its chairperson Anna Lo was elected as the first ethnic minority Member of the Legislative Assembly. In this position, NICEM dominated ethnic minority representation for the next two decades, continuing to operate as an umbrella for small ethno-specific groups, professionalising advisory and research functions, but maintaining its powerful position by partnering with statutory agencies to provide specialist services.

A strong commitment to non-discrimination was contained in Section 75 of the Northern Ireland Act 1998, which required public authorities to have due regard to equality in their functions and practices, but this did not extend to the full range of public functions (including policing). When the Race Relations Amendment Act 2000 was introduced in Britain to address institutional racism in public bodies, it was not extended to Northern Ireland, and the 1997 Order had been introduced without taking account of criticisms that followed the 1976 version in England and Wales. A protracted period of consultation by the Equality Commission for Northern Ireland on revising the 1997 Order ran from 1999 to 2004 but came to nothing.[13] There was no political appetite for a formal review, particularly given suspension of the Northern Ireland Assembly between 2002 and 2007. The sole legislative development during this period was the Race Relations Order (Amendment) Regulations (NI) 2003 which implanted the EU Employment Equality Directive (2000/43/EC of 29 June 2000).

From the early 2000s, the policy discourse on race relations across the UK was shifting, and this was to have significant impact in Northern Ireland. The publication of the Cantle Report (2002) in response to the 2001 disorders in England prompted the shift from multiculturalist policy to 'community cohesion', and this influenced race relations development in Northern Ireland.[14] While there were hopes that expansion of ethnic diversity in Northern Ireland could decentralise the sectarian divide, it could not do so if ethnic minorities were excluded from Northern Ireland's civic life. *A Shared Future*, the policy document guiding this area from 2005, crucially distinguished between 'community relations', which referred specifically to divisions between the Protestant and Catholic communities, and 'good relations', referring to relations between persons of different religious belief, political opinion or racial group. A range of agencies and branches of government were required to develop and be accountable for 'good relations plans' but mostly these did not explicitly acknowledge racism.[15]

Civil society and political contexts

In Northern Ireland the influence of wider UK debates and norms is evident but conflicts and disputes within the Province, its legislative autonomy and the priority given to managing legacies of sectarianism have impeded the introduction of legislation from Great Britain. Civil society actors came to be co-opted within institutional processes that were designed to govern the Province during the Northern Ireland conflict. Immigrant ethnic minorities, unlike the main Protestant and Catholic ethnic groups, did not constitute a politically significant bloc. Their demands for measures to address racism using legislation introduced elsewhere in the UK were not politically influential.

In the Republic much of the infrastructure to address racism also preceded large-scale immigration and owed much to the efforts of civil society actors who led campaigns for Traveller rights and then became employed by state bodies such as the Equality Authority and the NCCRI. These bodies were undermined by the prevalence of anti-Traveller political populism and the state's failure to contest discrimination against Travellers. Campaigns to address racism more generally were driven by the same small group of now-institutionalised actors and ceased when these became marginalised in 2008.

Perhaps the main difference between both Irish cases and what has emerged since the 1960s in the British case has been the absence of the kind of anti-racist politics and social movements that led to increased black and ethnic minority political representation in the UK. In both Irish cases, significant levels of equivalent immigrant or ethnic minority-led activism have yet to emerge. In the Republic, for example, a number of African-led organisations have focused on providing services and promoting integration rather than on anti-racist activism. Similarly, African candidates in local government elections have not stood on anti-racist platforms although many privately acknowledge racism as a key issue.[16] In the absence of political clout, anti-racism activists have tended to call for the diffusion of good practice from other jurisdictions and adherence to the principles and practices emanating from international agreements on racism and to directives/agreements.

In both jurisdictions, 2009 marked an important turning point in institutional and civil society responses. In the Republic, the closure of the

NCCRI removed an important racist incident reporting system which offered data to facilitate review of statutory response systems within police and other state agencies and highlighted key areas for attention. NGOs which had built relationships with the NCCRI and the Equality Authority were forced to reassess their relationship with the state and find new channels of influence. Post-2008 efforts to promote anti-racist policy and legislation have mostly emanated from NGOs and immigrant-led groups working under the umbrella organisation European Netwok Against Racism (ENAR) Ireland. Other key actors have been the Immigrant Council of Ireland and Migrant Rights Centre Ireland (both also ENAR network members), neither of which are immigrant-led organisations. This collective activism has had little influence upon legislation or public policy, although it has kept racism in the public eye. Working relationships have often been fraught and characterised by mutual antipathy. In this context, critical insiders, typically former NGO leaders who worked for Department of Justice-funded bodies with an anti-racism remit, walked 'a tightrope', as one put it, between being co-opted and being shut down.[17]

Civil society responses to institutional intransigence in the Republic have been particularly constrained by the financial environment and the refusal of the Irish state to move forward on many areas of discrimination, including in public services. Increasingly, strategic litigation is seen by the main NGOs as a means of pushing the state to enact appropriate legislation to safeguard rights while they continue to call on international bodies to hold the state to account, for example through the European Parliament's investigative powers. The power of the Irish Human Rights and Equality Commission to report directly to the Irish parliament and to operate with some independence promises some progress in this area.

Civil society responses to racism in both jurisdictions have varied significantly. In the Republic, these are largely shaped by organisations specifically focused on racism or immigrant experiences, with notable international lobbying activities, but with few led by ethnic minorities. The Department of Justice, Equality and Law Reform became responsible for coercive responses to asylum seekers as well as for drafting legislation and developing policies aimed at challenging racism in Irish society. The Department has viewed migration primarily as a security issue while NGOs and other civil society actors have mainly been concerned with migrant rights, sometimes to the exclusion of older ethnic minority groups.[18] The introduction of the International Protection Act 2015 demonstrated the limited agency both of the dominant NGOs acting for migrants, and migrants themselves, and saw those NGOs sharply criticised by activist groups – particularly by the Movement of Asylum Seekers in Ireland, a group that supports those living in direct provision – for doing too little to support asylum seekers.[19] In contrast, in Northern Ireland responses have been dominated by NICEM, complemented by a range of migrant-focused projects in community development NGOs, and relations with the Executive are facilitated through a range of state-established consultation fora. In this, cooperation with the state in Northern Ireland resembles local modes of consultation elsewhere in the UK more closely than state–civil society relations in the Republic. Yet repeated delays in progressing legislation and enacting effective policies against racism have undermined the potential of this infrastructure.

In Northern Ireland, the 2009 Roma expulsions in Belfast prompted a bifurcation of the governance of racist violence and narratives of inclusion. An emerging policy gap became visible when the updated policy framework *Cohesion, Sharing and Integration*, immediately following the expulsions, *reduced* obligations on councils to address the impacts of racism, including educational and health inequalities and racist hate crime, even as the Executive and Police Service of Northern Ireland (PSNI) devoted additional resources to the latter. Increasingly, racist violence was incorporated into a hate crime framework, similar to elsewhere in the UK.[20] A non-legislative response in the form of the first *Unite against Hate* campaign was led by the Northern Ireland Office and Office of the First Minister and Deputy First Minister with the PSNI, the Equality Commission and the Community Relations Council, to raise awareness of hate crime among the general public and encourage reporting to the PSNI. When the PSNI pulled out of *Unite against Hate* in 2011, the partnersh ip lapsed. A more recent partnership arrangement between the PSNI, Victim Support NI and NICEM to support racist incident reporting addressed ethnic minorities as victims but had no awareness-raising function.

It became apparent that the PSNI (and Home Office), rather than the Executive, were driving responses to racist violence. The PSNI partnerships accelerated reporting of racist incidents, already steadily increasing from 1999 onwards, although clearance rates remain extremely low. Nonetheless there was no effective Executive response to the problem of racist violence or racial inequality. The Executive allowed the Racial Equality Strategy to lapse without replacement, and local councils continued to implement good relations strategies in piecemeal fashion. Notably, the Executive was urged by both the Advisory Committee on the Framework Convention for the Protection of National Minorities (2011) and the UN Committee on the Elimination of Racial Discrimination (2011) to amend the race equality legislation. Despite this, the revised good relations strategy, *Together: Building a United Community*, launched in 2013, did not explicitly address experiences of hate crime or discrimination.[21]

In the absence of political commitment (a theme addressed in Chapter 3) NGO calls for accountability to international commitments have had little lasting impact on Northern Ireland government policy. The coordinated approach of politicians, the civil service, equality bodies and ethnic minority-led NGOs (contrasting with the arm's-length relationship in the

Republic) has been essential in the face of sectarian division and in the context of the community relations agenda, but since the mid 2000s their ability to effect change has been depleted in the face of rising racist violence. The closure of NICEM in 2016 has left a vacuum. In the absence of this umbrella group, immigrant and ethnic minority-led groups have become increasingly overshadowed by larger white-led community development organisations when it comes to seeking representation in decision-making and in obtaining funding. The groups formally represented through NICEM now find their influence diluted within institutional debates about anti-racism.

NGO appeals to international bodies have had limited influence on state responses to racism. Northern Ireland, as a region within the UK, is not within the remit of CERD, which responds to UN member states. The Republic, though directly accountable to CERD, has tended to disregard its recommendations. The impact of British policy and legislative debates on Northern Ireland's responses to racism since 1997 has been relatively weak. For example, Northern Ireland is still exempt from the UK's Equality Act 2010. Indeed, there is evidence that the legislation introduced in Northern Ireland has produced more unequal results as a consequence of importing legislation from Westminster without adequate account being taken of existing critiques and implementation difficulties. This was the case both for the Race Relations (NI) Order 1997, and the Race Relations Order (Amendment) Regulations (Northern Ireland) 2003, both criticised by CERD. Civil society efforts have been focused on arguing for the adoption, and subsequently for the amendments, of these and other similar pieces of legislation in line with the wider UK legislative framework.

The limits of benevolence

Understandings of and responses to racism in Northern Ireland have been influenced by political priorities of addressing sectarianism. And, as noted in Chapter 3, sectarian politics make cross-community consensus on how to define racism almost impossible. Simply put, nationalist politicians support definitions of racism which include unionist sectarianism, a perspective that has been supported by the predominant literature on racism in Northern Ireland.[22] The problems produced by such a position are illustrated by the report to CERD in 2011 by the Northern Ireland Human Rights Commission which noted that 'Sectarianism in Northern Ireland frequently continues to be treated as something other than a particular form of racism.'[23]

The persistent hold of sectarianism in the region has meant that anti-racist campaigns have often been characterised by partisanship and failure to translate into cross-community engagement.[24] Sectarianism has even been read as a means of supporting civil society responses to racist violence, with diversion of funding away from minority ethnic groups to white settled community groups to address racism as part of good relations. Migrants have found it difficult to resist identifying upon and being identified upon sectarian lines.[25] The conceptual relationship between racism and sectarianism has therefore had significant impacts on the effectiveness of state and civil society responses to racism in Northern Ireland. The focus of state and civil society actors, including the Community Relations Council and various academics, on this relationship (particularly in explaining racist violence), has however distracted attention from wider structural forms of racism. Northern Ireland has also struggled to place the problem of racism in the context of a large population of white Catholic Polish recent immigrants, who have experienced both xenophobic and sectarian violence, and who have consequently been the focus of much anti-racism work by the state and civil society. Some of this work has aligned with militaristic sectarian sentiment, such as recent projects to emphasis Polish and British cooperation in the Second World War, prompting questions about the impact of anti-racist work in this context.

Yet longstanding concerns about sectarianism in the North have created some political space for a focus on racism through criminal justice measures. One outcome can be seen in a focus on hate crime. An area of positive impact has been in policing, where recent reorganisation of the PSNI has aligned its work on hate crime with forces across the UK, and responsibility for hate crime with key leadership positions in the PSNI. This has had an impact on the ability of the force to record and encourage reporting of racist crimes, although the effectiveness of the PSNI and other criminal justice agencies in processing these is still in question due to historically low trust[26] and slow improvement in prosecutions.[27]

In the Republic, the impetus to acknowledge and address racist crime has been considerably less. At the NCCRI's instigation, the Garda Síochána established an Intercultural Office, appointed ethnic liaison officers in each division and created a system to record racially motivated offences. However, since the closure of the NCCRI and the end of the *Know Racism* campaign there has been a policy leadership vacuum in institutional responses to racism at a national level. A hiring freeze from 2008 lasted several years and only a handful of Gardaí from immigrant community backgrounds have been recruited. The Intercultural Office has had little influence on operational policing including responses to racist incidents and crimes.[28] There has been little focus in monitoring racist offences and responses to these.[29] An Garda Síochána failed even to properly record racist incidents, despite adoption of the MacPherson definition (1999) and offers of cross-border assistance from experienced PSNI officers.

On both sides of the border there has been little political push to take racism seriously. An imbalance of power prevails in which black, ethnic minority and immigrant communities are politically marginalised and in both jurisdictions are dependent upon the goodwill of a civil society that is influenced by transnational anti-racist norms and which speaks on behalf of rather than represents those experiencing racism. Immigrant-led organisations in the Republic remain marginal within civil society. They are mostly unfunded by the state and have not been co-opted into institutional consultation processes to the same degree as has occurred in Northern Ireland. However, the focus on hate crime in Northern Ireland has been primarily a legacy of longstanding sectarian conflicts rather than motivated by a desire to address racism. By contrast, in the Republic the absence of hate crime legislation and institutional efforts to address it may be interpreted as a reflection of the ongoing denial of the state of the experience of ethnic minorities of racism and discrimination.

Notes

* This chapter is based on B. Fanning and L. Michael, 'Racism and anti-racism in the two Irelands', *Ethnic and Racial Studies*, (2017), DOI: 10.1080/01419870. 2017.1403641.

1 S. Garner, 'Ireland and immigration: explaining the absence of the far right', *Patterns of Prejudice*, 41:2, 109–130.

2 L. Michael, *Afrophobia in Ireland: Racism against People of African Descent* (Dublin: ENAR Ireland, 2015).

3 'Only two Roma from 114 remain after Northern Ireland race shame', *Belfast Telegraph*, 27 June 2009.

4 'Two racist attacks every day in Northern Ireland's race-hate crime surge', *Belfast Telegraph*, 21 April 2014.

5 E. McKeever, R. Reed, S. D. Pehrson, L. Storey and J. Christopher Cohrs, 'How racist violence becomes a virtue: an application of discourse analysis', *International Journal of Conflict and Violence*, 7:1 (2013), 108–120.

6 B. Rolston, 'Legacy of intolerance: racism and Unionism in South Belfast', *IRR News*, 10 February 2004.

7 'Racists fly Ku Klux Klan flag in east Belfast', *Belfast Telegraph*, 1 July 2004; P. Ghosh, 'Poles in Northern Ireland complain of "racism" and discrimination: white-on white hate crime?', *International Business Times*, 19 July 2012.

8 'Polish concern over rise in racist attacks in Northern Ireland', *Irish Times*, 14 April 2015.

9 Department of Justice, Equality and Law Reform, *Planning for Diversity: The National Action Plan against Racism 2005–2008* (Dublin: Stationery Office, 2005).

10 The Equal Status Act (2000) addressed discrimination on nine grounds: gender, civil status, family status, age, race, religion, disability, sexual orientation and membership of the Traveller Community.

11 N. Crowley, *Empty Promises: Bringing the Equality Authority to Heel* (Dublin: A & A Farmer, 2010).

12 NGO Alliance Against Racism, *Shadow Report in response to the Third and Fourth Periodic Reports of Ireland under the UN International Convention on*

the *Elimination of All Forms of Racial Discrimination* (Dublin: NGO Alliance Against Racism, 2011).

13 E. Meehan, 'The experience of a single Equalities Commission in Northern Ireland', *Scottish Affairs*, 56:1, 35–56.

14 Independent Community Cohesion Review Team, *The Cantle Report – Community Cohesion* (London: Home Office, 2002).

15 Equality Commission for Northern Ireland, Section 75 *of the Northern Ireland Act 1998: Promoting Good Relations – A Guide for Public Authorities* (Belfast: ECNI, 2007).

16 B. Fanning and N. O'Boyle, 'Immigrants in Irish politics: African and East European candidates in the 2009 local government elections', *Irish Political Studies*, 25:3 (2010), 417–435.

17 B. Fanning, *Racism and Social Change in the Republic of Ireland* (Manchester: Manchester University Press, 2012), p. 236.

18 L. Michael, *Afrophobia in Ireland: Racism against People of African Descent* (Dublin: ENAR Ireland, 2015).

19 D. Landy, 'Challengers in the migrant field: pro-migrant Irish NGO responses to the Immigration, Residence and Protection Bill', *Ethnic and Racial Studies*, 38:6 (2015), 927–942.

20 J. Todd, J. Ruane and M. Dunne, *From 'A Shared Future' to 'Cohesion, Sharing and Integration': An Analysis of Northern Ireland's Policy Framework Documents* (York: Joseph Rowntree Foundation, 2010).

21 R. McVeigh, *Good Relations in Northern Ireland: Towards a Definition in Law* (Belfast: Equality Coalition, 2014).

22 R. McVeigh and B. Rolston, "From Good Friday to good relations: sectarianism, racism and the Northern Ireland state". *Race and Class*, 48:4 (2007), 1–23.

23 UN Committee on the Elimination of Racial Discrimination, *Consideration of reports submitted by States parties under article 9 of the Convention: [concluding observations of the Committee on the Elimination of Racial Discrimination]: United Kingdom of Great Britain and Northern Ireland* (Geneva: CERD, 2011), p. 7.

24 P. Geoghegan, 'Multiculturalism and sectarianism in post-agreement Northern Ireland', *Scottish Geographical Journal*, 124:2–3 (2008), 185–191.

25 A. Lee, 'Are you a Catholic Chinese or a Protestant Chinese? Belfast's ethnic minorities and the sectarian divide', *City*, 18:4–5 (2014), 476–487.

26 K. Radford, J. Betts and M. Ostermeyer, *Policing, Accountability and the Black and Minority Ethnic Communities in Northern Ireland* (Belfast: Institute for Conflict Research, 2006).

27 F. Haughey, *Racism in Northern Ireland: The Racial Equality Strategy from Policy to Practice. Summary Report of Main Findings* (Belfast: NICEM, 2014).

28 B. Fanning, B. Killoran and S. Ní Bhroin, *Taking Racism Seriously: Migrants' Experiences of Violence, Harassment and Anti-Social Behaviour* (Dublin: Immigrant Council of Ireland, 2011).

29 L. Michael, 'Anti-Black racism: Afrophobia, exclusion and global racisms', in A. Haynes, J. Schweppe and S. Taylor (eds), *Critical Perspectives on Hate Crime: An Irish Perspective* (London: Palgrave Macmillan, 2017); L. Michael, *Reports of Racism in Ireland: 13th+14th Quarterly Reports of iReport.ie, July–December 2016* (Dublin: ENAR Ireland, 2017).

African asylum seekers and refugees in both Irelands

On 3 January 2018, the story of a violent attack in Dundalk, County Louth began to circulate in the Irish media. A young Japanese man lost his life, violently, as he walked home from a night-shift. Stabbed and left for dead, Yosuke Sasaki had only been living in Ireland for a year. That morning, two other young men were also attacked, but both survived their injuries. For Yosuke Sasaki, it was catastrophic. The media ran with stories that intimated the possibility that this was Ireland's 'first' terrorist attack. The alleged attacker, Mohammed Morei, a young eighteen-year-old man was quickly captured and taken into custody. Racist and angry comments were thrown at Mohammed as he was detained at Dundalk court. Public responses to the event were stark. Mohammed was thought to be an asylum seeker. It was reported that he had had his asylum application rejected somewhere in Great Britain; that he took the ferry to Belfast and crossed into the Republic of Ireland – sleeping rough in an abandoned site in Dundalk. Claims were also made that Mohammed travelled to Dublin but then returned to Dundalk, where on 3 January he carried out this brutal attack. Debates ensued about the motives for the attack – was he a member of ISIS? Could this in fact be the first terrorist act of this type in Ireland?

More salient, however, to the focus of this chapter were the questions about how Mohammed had so easily crossed to the Republic of Ireland, having had his asylum application rejected in the UK. Critiques of both the UK and Irish asylum processes abounded, as did criticisms of policing and security across the island, particularly with respect to the border. In the midst of debates about Brexit and the possibilities of the reinstatement of a hard border on the island these questions have had a particular resonance. In the days after the attack, racist posters began to appear in various spots around Dundalk.

Different layers of racist discourse became evident through the media coverage of this murder: Islamophobia – anti-Muslim racism (the asylum seeker, Mohammed) and the murder of another non-white other (Yosuke) were the key dichotomies. This particular story evinces the notion that ideas of whiteness and the plurality of racisms have to be more carefully scrutinised in the context of non-white newcomers to Ireland (and indeed, elsewhere). Both implicitly and explicitly, this is one of the goals of our work and in the broader collection as a whole.

This chapter focuses on the everyday life experiences of African asylum seekers and refugees on the island of Ireland in order to consider different notions of belonging, 'racisms'[1] and integration at play. Key to our thinking herein is the fact that asylum seekers' and refugees' experiences in Northern Ireland and the Republic of Ireland are differently fashioned through two distinct immigration systems, as well as two distinct national, historical and socio-economic contexts.[2] We also want to highlight how practices of racism come to be differently shaped through local contexts. While both parts of the island share much in terms of historical experience, there is little doubt that Northern Ireland and the Republic of Ireland have come to be differently shaped.

At the time of writing this chapter in 2018, the lack of certainty of how Brexit will further reconfigure the relationship between the two contexts still features large. This is significant for any further consideration of the experience of asylum seekers and refugees as well as any reflection on the variant articulations and intersections of 'racisms' in Europe.[3] Engagements with notions of integration and anti-racism have also been differently articulated on both parts of the island, and this is also key to how asylum seekers and refugees experience life in both places.

Herein, we shall explore the ways in which sectarian community divisions in Northern Ireland frame the everyday experiences of asylum seekers and refugees. We also reflect comparatively on the ways in which refugees in the Republic of Ireland have engaged with the growth of racism in the context of an austerity Ireland through their own sense-making mechanisms (in particular, religion). We argue that hegemonic whiteness and institutional racisms shape the experiences of African asylum seekers and refugees in ways that go beyond the legal divide as far as the two jurisdictions are concerned.[4]

We draw on two distinct and original sets of empirical data. Research in Northern Ireland was commissioned for the Racial Equality Unit in Stormont. It took place in 2016 and 2017 and was conducted predominantly in Belfast and Derry/Londonderry. The second was a qualitative research project informing the development of a refugee integration strategy for Northern Ireland. Currently, Northern Ireland is one of the few jurisdictions in the UK which does not have one.[5] For this research, we conducted semi-structured interviews with forty-eight asylum seekers and refugees from ten different countries, as well as fifty members of the NGO/Charitable sector and service providers (health, education, labour and housing) in Northern Ireland.

Our second data resource is an ongoing longitudinal ethnographic project which started with an Irish Research Council-funded project entitled *After Asylum: Refugee Integration in Ireland* (Principal Investigator, Mark Maguire). For this project, one of the co-authors of this chapter and a researcher on this project (Fiona Murphy) focused predominantly on Nigerian and Congolese refugees who had mostly been through the Direct Provision system. Ethnographic research was conducted in Dundalk, Drogheda and Dublin for a period of two years. With this chapter, we thus contribute to a critical debate on how ethnic identity, religion and race as visible differences play out in distinct ways across the island of Ireland.

Asylum and refuge in Northern Ireland and the Republic of Ireland

The asylum experience on the island of Ireland differs dramatically depending on whether one might seek asylum in Northern Ireland or the Republic of Ireland. Two distinct systems of migration management operate, both highly problematic.[6] Northern Ireland is a complex space through which to consider immigration law. Immigration law comes from Westminster and Northern Ireland must implement this accordingly. However, Northern Ireland is outside of the UK policy of asylum seeker dispersal, so asylum seekers come to Northern Ireland in three distinct ways: either independently, as programme refugees or through family reunification programmes. Northern Ireland has responsibility for integration as a devolved matter. Asylum seekers are housed in dedicated asylum housing managed by the Housing Executive but this is also governed by Westminster. The growing commercialisation of asylum seeker housing has seen a gross deterioration in housing conditions for asylum seekers. Added to this is the growing issue of homelessness and destitution of asylum seekers and refugees in the UK.

With the British referendum vote to leave the European Union (Article 50 triggered on 29 March 2017) Northern Ireland's particular situation, unlike any other region in the UK, has captured international attention – underlining its complex relationship, history and future.[7] Sharing a spatial border with another EU country – the Republic of Ireland – underlines the frictions, contradictions and tensions of an unresolved colonial past and the way sectarian conflict impacts the everyday lives of people in Northern Ireland (in particular for those living close to the border).

Before the EU referendum in 2016, the city of Belfast featured in international news signposting a significant rise in race hate crimes in Northern Ireland. The recent interest in more thoroughly recording hate crime, sectarian and racist violence is an expression of the transformation of the social fabric, seeing a rise in immigration since the end of the 1990s, for example with the Good Friday Agreement in 1998. This also means that since the 2000s the number of asylum seekers in Northern Ireland has increased. At the time of writing, under the Vulnerable Person Relocation scheme, approximately eight hundred Syrian refugees and others from countries including Somalia have arrived to make new lives in Belfast and Derry/Londonderry. Wider Northern Ireland has also received people with refugee status from Somalia and other countries. In 2018, there were approximately seven hundred asylum seekers living in Northern Ireland (mostly residing in Belfast), with an average of 200–300 new applications per year.[8] While this represents less than 1 per cent of the overall UK figures, the accommodation of asylum seekers and refugees and the 'integration' of the latter nonetheless pose challenges for state policy, social institutions and employers in Northern Ireland, particularly given Northern Ireland's status as a post-conflict/divided society.

In the Republic of Ireland, immigration law is closely governed by national and EU directives. Currently, asylum seekers are kept in Direct Provision, a system of open detention, where people are housed together communally without the ability to cook or live independently. People have spent very long periods of time waiting in Direct Provision for their asylum application to be processed. The McMahon Report (2015) detailed the dehumanising living conditions of Direct Provision, and since its publication there has been widespread protest aimed at ending this system.[9] At the time of writing, debates about giving asylum seekers the right to work have figured large, and limited plans to adhere to the EU reception directive are afoot. Sites such as Dundalk and Drogheda were chosen for the *After Asylum* research project because at the time of research they had a high number of refugees due to their proximity to one of the larger Direct Provision centres, Mosney. Dundalk was also chosen due to its particular proximity to the border with Northern Ireland and its long, complex relationship with Northern Ireland. Dublin, as the capital city, also became a key site due to the numbers of refugees living in different parts of the city – we spent much of our research time in Clondalkin and Tallaght. In general, the numbers of asylum seekers in Ireland on a yearly basis have tended to be between two thousand and three thousand (figures for 2016 show a decline in applications).[10] Ireland has had a poor history in terms of accepting and processing asylum seekers, due in no small part to the system of Direct Provision. Integration strategies and engagements have also been piecemeal at best, with, until recently, little examination on how such processes are shaping and have been shaped by those seeking asylum in the Republic of Ireland.[11]

Northern Ireland: a white ethno-religious place, worlds apart?

The focus of our research on asylum seekers and refugees was on their everyday experience of Northern Ireland, and so the topic of Northern

Ireland's complex history of conflict and division was often brought up by our research participants. Over the course of our work, we encountered many stories of how this history impacts on their relationship with Northern Ireland. One of our participants, a young man from Kenya, told us that articulations of sectarianism were an issue for many asylum seekers and refugees as they go about their daily lives. He put it thus:

> It does affect me because, especially because now for me, I have a child with an Irish woman ... because she wouldn't go to Protestant areas, which limits my movement with my daughter, to wherever I want to go and definitely, it affects me too much, because I used to and I stay in a lot. Like if I go looking for a house now, she's not happy because of where I'm going to take, do you know what I mean? Because, not because she wants to tell me which place I should go and get housing, she's worried when my daughter comes in there, it's going to affect her. It does affect me because I just find it very very wrong, do you know? (Kenyan refugee, interview 2016)

Fear of sectarianism – and here, with respect to moving within or to a more Protestant neighbourhood – overrides other fears of racism. The right to move freely in the city (e.g. Belfast) and near the Irish border is particularly problematic for African asylum seekers and refugees. Many are not aware of the legal consequences of moving across the national border, but also their visibility makes them vulnerable to police checks and sectarian violence in particular parts of the city. Racism and sectarianism in Northern Ireland have been little discussed.[12] McKee looked at Eastern Europeans, Muslims and a third category of 'other ethnic groups' in her 2015 study focusing on an analysis of the *2013 Northern Ireland Life and Time Survey*. She found 'partial support for the sectarianism hypothesis, with those most accepting of mixed marriages more willing to accept all three groups, although the effect was largest with Muslims and, in general, the coefficients were somewhat smaller than with social contact or economic self-interest'. She concluded that more research and discussions of 'racism alongside sectarianism' are needed.[13] It has been argued that equating sectarianism with a propensity towards racism is far too facile. However, Neil Jarman and Rachael Monaghan make the following argument:

> As sectarian residential segregation has continued to increase it is likely that some people have identified the minority communities as the new 'other' and turned their attentions away from the Protestant or Catholic minority towards the Chinese and Indian communities who are beginning to create new interfaces in some working class communities. This is not to argue that racism and sectarianism are exactly the same thing but that they have common roots in a society which does not tolerate difference, which is focused in upon itself, is insecure and which accepts violence and abuse as a broadly legitimate form of expression.[14]

While segregation patterns in Northern Ireland are lower in the 2011 Census compared with 2001 there are many studies which claim that spatial segregation continues to be a barrier to successful integration processes.[15] Further, the statement by the UN Advisory Committee on the Elimination of Racial Discrimination (2011) and Council of Europe (2011) on racism and sectarianism is worth considering in this regard. They state that '[treating] sectarianism as a distinct issue rather than as a form of racism [is] problematic, as it allows sectarianism to fall outside the scope of accepted anti-discrimination and human rights protection standards'.[16]

Critical to this chapter is also the fact that the conflict in Northern Ireland has not been properly considered in UK policy thinking on racism. In line with this argument, we posit that the different notions of ethnicity and race that are used across the UK need more attention in the context of the island of Ireland: ethnicity in a UK (GB) context 'defines ethnicity primarily in terms of "colour" – 98 per cent of Northern Ireland residents are defined solely as "white"'.[17] Thus, in the British context, ethnicity is primarily identified with non-whiteness.

It is important to mention that Northern Ireland also has a more recent history of combating the negative imprint of sectarianism and racism. A number of anti-racism groups (in particular at the grassroots level) are in operation, for example the West Against Racism Network in Belfast. The Equality Authority, Human Rights Commission and the Racial Equality Unit also work to find ways to eliminate racism and discrimination in Northern Ireland. Likewise, many members of the Northern Ireland voluntary sector provide anti-racism training (such as the Northern Ireland Council for Ethnic Minorities and CRAICNI). However, the view that sectarianism is the business of the two dominant political ethno-religious communities and less of newcomers is difficult to change, as our research data indicate.

Our research participants frequently equated racism and sectarianism when speaking about housing, schooling and employment; the three areas of their daily concern. In that sense, the impact of sectarianism was felt in most areas of their everyday lives. One female refugee from Zimbabwe when talking about employment referred to the specific religious sectarian context of Northern Ireland:

> I practise Catholicism. It's not a problem for me to have loads of friends from other communities, so it doesn't bother me at all. But I would be a bit careful when I'm saying to another person my religion. Or if I'm applying for work, I must be like should I say it, should I not. (Interview 2016).

As a newcomer to Northern Ireland society she felt anxious about societal codes and felt a lack of certainty in manoeuvring group boundaries, which impacted on her confidence.

The spatial complexities of Northern Ireland are compounded by its history. As most of this research was undertaken in Belfast, it makes sense to comment on how Belfast as a city with high levels of spatial segregation can be a complex place for asylum seekers and refugees to live and settle in. The areas in which asylum seekers and refugees are housed impact on their access to employment and health services, as well as broader social networks with the host community and other members of the asylum-seeking and refugee community. Often asylum seekers and refugees are housed in lower-quality housing in underprivileged areas with high levels of segregation. In the context of Belfast, where there are higher levels of asylum accommodation, South Belfast has become something of a hub for asylum seekers and refugees and also a number of civil society sector organisations supporting them. In particular, the spaces around the Queen's University district are vibrant and mixed, with an international community. In our interviews, research participants expressed a preference to live in this area. Given the pressures on the housing system, this is not always possible and so asylum seekers and refugees find themselves living right across the city. When asked whether the history or legacy of the Troubles posed any specific problems in their lives, our research participants answered with very mixed responses. A number suggested that they just treat everyone the same and don't like to think about the divide specifically, but others engaged with the issue and its impact on their daily lives.

There is very little research extant to substantiate the links between religiously segregated places and racism.[18] The media, however, have drawn a number of links between divided areas and an increase in racism. This means that some asylum seekers and refugees are fearful about being housed in certain areas even without ever having visited them. One research participant told us 'I am too scared to get to know my neighbours, I just stay in my house you know, getting depressed' (Somalian asylum seeker, interview 2016). The perception that these areas are much more challenging to live in means asylum seekers and refugees sometimes feel anxious about receiving housing in these areas. This is an idea perpetuated by host community members as much as anyone else. As one research participant articulated it:

We had a friend actually who was saying, who lived in North Belfast, his dad was really old. And he was saying to me if my area was okay for you, I would have given you my daddy's house for the time being until you get a permanent home, which was very kind of him. But then he said people might not receive you around there so I don't want to cause you problems. So he couldn't give us that house. And also he had a landlord who had a nice apartment in North Belfast which was manageable. Their rent was reasonable. But I did not want to change the school. And then he said the colour might cause a problem when the children come back from school. The colour of the uniform. Maybe nowadays it has improved a bit. But still people will ask you, I want to go

and rent a house at this area, do you think I'll be safe? People will be concerned where they go because they will know some areas might not be as
friendly as others. (Sudanese refugee, interview 2016)

The complex entanglements of sectarian divisions and racisms highlight
how challenging Northern Ireland can be for black asylum seekers and
refugees to live in. Our research participants, many of whom were content
to remain in Northern Ireland, nonetheless concluded that the particulari-
ties of life there exposed them to a much stronger sense of feeling like an
outsider. While much of this is perception, it is important to note that
many of those we interviewed also felt a kind of security with respect to
being outside of extant sectarian divisions. The logic of who is inside and
who is outside in the context of Northern Ireland is thus magnified due to
unresolved historical tensions, further compounded in 2018 by the politics
of Brexit.

The Republic of Ireland: black believers and white (Catholic) secular Ireland

In the Republic of Ireland, the experiences of asylum seekers and refugees
are differently shaped primarily due to a different asylum system as well as
a different state approach to migration and integration. The landscape of
anti-racism also differs. In a previous study undertaken with Mark Maguire
from 2009–2011, one of the co-authors of this chapter (Fiona Murphy)
engaged with questions of integration as they existed in relation to issues
of education, politics, the labour market, second-generation African youth
and religion. Over the duration of the project from 2009 onwards, debates
about racism on the taxi ranks in Ireland's towns and cities loomed large
in the media.[19] In 2000, the Irish taxi industry was deregulated in order to
facilitate open competition for fares and this greatly contributed to acri-
mony on the taxi ranks between full-time and part-time drivers, and ultimately engendered hostility towards migrant taxi drivers.[20] We (Maguire
and Murphy) conducted very close ethnographic research on taxi ranks in
Dublin, Drogheda and Dundalk at a time when, particularly in Dundalk
and Drogheda, African taxi drivers had become the target of violent racist
abuse. During this time, Ireland had also entered a period of deep economic
recession and austerity, and African taxi drivers as a visible other became
victims and targets of racism and prejudice anchored in a putative discourse
of employment shortage.[21]

In the same period, we were also conducting research in African Pentecostal churches in the same towns, and this crisis of racism and prejudice
was a recurrent topic at many of the services attended.[22] A strong theme in
many of the church services was an attempt to make sense out of these

increasingly hostile racisms by linking them to economic recession and austerity. Interviewing African taxi drivers, sitting with them in their cars while people passed them by in favour of a white taxi driver, and attending Pentecostal services (where the challenges of living with racism were often discussed) unequivocally demonstrated the challenges of everyday life for African refugees in austerity Ireland. Pastors and even some of the taxi drivers that were interviewed attempted to fashion a moral ledger in which an Ireland pre-austerity was recalled as a more welcoming, less racist place. However, while austerity might have accelerated racism and resentment, this claim has to be interpreted alongside a longer history of state and institutional racisms.

Gabriel, one of the research participants in this project, was both a taxi driver and a Pentecostal worshipper and often spoke about his concerns at being a black taxi driver in a small Irish town. Over the years we got to know him and his family, it was clear that he was becoming increasingly alarmed at having to drive taxis in the small town in which he lived. He worried incessantly that one day the verbal abuses he regularly suffered would culminate in violence. He felt deeply angered by his experiences but worried that this anger would impact on his young children. Accompanying him and his young family one Sunday to a Pentecostal service, we heard him openly pray for an austerity Ireland to find recovery, because by doing so he believed that the racism he was experiencing might lessen. Another driver, a friend of Gabriel, explained it to us in these terms:

> On Saturday, I went to the rank. I was there for two hours. When I got to the rank there was only two cars, one in the front and me. So the one in the front took a run while I was there, and another car pulled behind me, which is a white guy. When the customer came he took the white one. That one went and come back again, and he took about four runs when I was in number one. So he made me mad, he made me feel bad as hell. I can't blame God for making me a black man, you know? It frustrates me, you feel bad, am I not a human being? (Interview 2010).

For many of the taxi drivers we met Pentecostalism offered a different space through which to interpret their encounters with racism within their everyday lives. As another driver, Michael explained:

> It is racism, FACT!! People can call it whatever they like, but it is pure racism when someone looks at you and say, 'Oh it is a black driver', and then goes behind you and finds a white driver ... It is humiliating, degrading ... Is it I am a subhuman being? But I refuse to accept this kind of theory that I am a subhuman being. No! ... I always tell myself that God can give me the courage to accept the things I cannot change and the wisdom to change the things I can. I can't change this. (Interview 2010)

Pentecostal sites of worship exist in Ireland in the margins, or the zones of invisibility, hidden in plain sight in industrial warehouses. After a violent confrontation between African taxi drivers and white taxi drivers in the carpark of a Louth radio station, and inspired by a broader movement of Pentecostal spiritual mapping and the Great March for Jesus which started in London in 1987, a number of Pastors from various Pentecostal denominations decided to organise a 'Jesus Walk' through Drogheda. In common with the Great March for Jesus and the subsequent emergence of thousands of similar marches, the Jesus Walk intended to spread the message of Jesus and to let the people of Ireland know about the existence of African Pentecostalism. It was a mobile performance of faith, a kind of spiritual warfare on an Ireland deep in the recesses of recession and caught, as the Pastors saw it, in the binds of racism. Central to the organisers' aim was the intention of praying Ireland out of economic crisis in order to remedy many of the experiences of their worshippers. Initially, the organising committee had hoped that members of the mainstream, dominant churches in Ireland would also participate but it attracted only the interest of Charismatic Catholics practising in the area.

Akin to the March for Jesus in the UK, this Irish 'Jesus Walk' through Drogheda plotted a religious geography which intersected with some key Irish institutions and historical sites. For the Pastors and other participants on the walk that gloomy Saturday morning, the walk was an attempt to show the people of Drogheda that they could perhaps collectively find and share in a better life. Critical emphasis was placed on praying Ireland out of the recession and addressing their own often unequal presence in Ireland. Ritualistically sprinkling oil at significant sites such as the police station, hospital and court was both an attempt to imprint their religious identities on and reshape local place. As the town slowly moved out of its Saturday slumber, street cleaners, market stall holders, passengers in cars, and busy doctors and nurses glared at the group of praying walkers. No one asked to join in, no one stopped and prayed in solidarity and the group, it seemed, remained marginal, isolated somehow from the mainstream.

On returning to the church, Pastor Femi announced his hope that both the town of Drogheda and Ireland would eventually be awash with hope and success, with a sense that they had been prayed for. The walk, then, was an attempt to 'enchant' the Irish landscape, to engender a symbolic geography of Pentecostalism near sites of Irish historical and societal significance. In a town, however, with a recent history of racial conflict (particularly in the taxi industry), the desire to ignite a response to Pentecostal idioms of being was met only with silence. Nonetheless, for the participants of the walk there was a sense that day and in discussions afterwards that the Jesus Walk, as the first of its kind in the town, birthed some form of recognition. It said very simply, we are here, we want to protest exclusion and racism, we want to belong. The pastor described it thus:

We have an adage from Nigeria that says, well you want to put a bucket on your head, and you are calling for help, you don't leave it for the person helping you, you also support with the hand and both of you put it on the head. You know a lot of immigrants have come here, probably they need help, prob they have been subjected to all kinds of attacks problems and so on, they also have a part to play in developing where they are. For me, I find everywhere you are is a home, and wherever is a home, you have to make it very good for yourself. So we try to tell them and let them know what have you to contribute to the society. (Interview 2010)

In redrawing the town in a spiritual frame, the Pastors and congregation were beginning the process of reconstituting their sense of belonging and home. While the Jesus Walk is open to multiple interpretations, it can be seen primarily as a means by which Pentecostal refugees living in Drogheda and its surrounds attempted to weave an alternative tapestry of meaning, which embraced new ways of becoming, belonging and integration. It publicly expressed a multiplicity of belonging that served as both a reminder of and protest against exclusion and racism.

Ultimately, the Jesus Walk was an attempt to create new solidarities not only in response to the experiences of many of the African taxi drivers in the area, but also to address issues of exclusion and racism more broadly. What happens in African churches in terms of responses to these issues is just one example of what is a very robust anti-racist movement in Ireland. Since 2010, there has been a steady growth of grassroots organisations which attempt to combat racism and exclusion, such as the Anti-Racism Network Ireland and MASI (Movement of Asylum seekers in Ireland), complementing the professional anti-racism and migrant support organisations in the NGO sector. The previous chapter examined how there has been an ongoing failure on the part of the Irish state to deal with hate crime and racism in a meaningful and responsive fashion. The challenge of doing so is now an urgent one, as the voices and lives of our research participants evince – living in Ireland in 2018 as an asylum seeker or refugee means navigating a very fraught terrain of acceptance and tolerance.

Conclusion

Mohammed, the asylum seeker and alleged murderer, and Yosuke, the Japanese victim of Mohammed's vicious attack, introduced at the beginning of this chapter, cannot be regarded as clear-cut examples of non-white victimhood and white racist hate crimes. Nonetheless, the tragedy of this entanglement of violence and institutional failures ties into a more endemic situation where violence on the street has become instrumental in enacting rage and even trauma. The links between the sense of alienation and marginalisation that the experience of racism and prejudice engenders and the challenges of fully integrating into society were frequently mentioned by our research participants in both Northern Ireland and the Republic of

Ireland. Asylum seekers and refugees in Northern Ireland feel very ambivalent about the place they live: regarding themselves as outsiders being highly dependent on their current living conditions and future prospects of being granted legal status. Being in a legal and social limbo thus undermines their feelings of belonging. This is of course true of asylum seekers everywhere. The everyday life experiences of asylum seekers and refugees are however affected by the ongoing tensions in Northern Ireland; in particular being confronted with spatial segregation. This results in no-go areas, or as far as housing and neighbourhoods are concerned also produces anxieties for asylum seekers and refugees. Though spatial division clings to ethno-national tensions it intersects prominently with religious, intra-Christianity sectarianism, thus impacting on the wellbeing and life of newcomers to the society. Our research participants repeatedly highlighted how the complexities of this context engendered a sense of alienation and, sometimes, fear. With great irony, however, some commented that being outside of such divisions could also be a source of security. Such is the challenge of being a newcomer in a society still coming to terms with a very troubled history. Making connections between sectarianism and racism, beyond the academy, is however a relatively sensitive and emotive issue. In the context of our work with asylum seekers and refugees in Northern Ireland, we engaged with many NGOs, charities and service providers working in this sector. There are evident disagreements in this sector over the mooted connections between conflict/post-conflict, sectarianism and racism, in spite of some robust academic work emerging on this topic. Our ongoing work in this area calls for a more radical acceptance of the impact of post-conflict divisions in the lives of newcomers to such a society.

In the Republic of Ireland, Direct Provision continues to impact on the mental health and wellbeing of asylum seekers and refugees. While there is growing public support to end the system of Direct Provision, at a political level there is still little being done to restructure the current approach to asylum processes. The story of racism and exclusion in the Republic of Ireland is, like anywhere, however, a complex one. Broadly, there has been a failure on the part of the Irish state to deal with the complexities of racism and integration. Economic crisis and austerity measures created a new excuse to ignore the weakness in the Irish state's approach to asylum seekers and refugees. Direct Provision continues in spite of ongoing criticisms and campaigns, and recent attempts to achieve the right to work have been met with a very limited interpretation of this right. The intersections of austerity and economic recovery with some of this have also challenged progress in these areas. So too have constructions of Ireland as post-Catholic in spite of an ongoing relationship between state and the Catholic Church in many spaces, in particular education. In the context of our research in the Republic, many African research participants were practising Pentecostals. Faith – Pentecostalism – shapes the feeling of belonging particularly for some African asylum seekers and refugees in the Republic. This figured large in our research encounters – especially with respect to understanding the dynamics of integration and racism.

Because of the limitations of living life in Direct Provision, asylum seekers struggle with everyday life in Ireland, even after achieving refugee status. Articulations of belonging are highly connected to these experiences and many research participants continue to point to how their experiences in Direct Provision have negatively impacted on their relationship with Ireland.

Examining Northern Ireland and the Republic of Ireland in tandem in the context of asylum seekers' and refugees' everyday life experiences shows the plurality of racist practices on the island of Ireland. In Northern Ireland, our research participants equate their sense of feeling to be outsiders to the complexities of living in a post-conflict setting, Brexit, and a poor state response to hate crime and integration. In the Republic of Ireland, our participants equally reflect on state failures in response to hate crime, racism and also to the asylum system more generally and Direct Provision in particular. In the Republic, the complexities of austerity and economic decline and the growing housing crisis were also flagged as fuelling resentment towards asylum seekers and refugees. While the refugee crisis (or border crisis, as we prefer to call it) has evoked more empathy/sympathy in both contexts, state responses remain weak. Inherent in this too is the danger of racist practices becoming banalised in political and media discourses which further contributes to weak responses to these very urgent issues.

The comparative study of asylum and refugee experiences in Northern Ireland and the Republic of Ireland, as two quite different contexts on the same island, evince the urgency of addressing the complex intersections of poor asylum processes, racism and exclusion. The tragic story of Mohammed, a young asylum seeker, and the murder of a young Japanese man in Dundalk, is evidence of the urgency of needing to work in a more cohesive and collaborative way on these issues across the island of Ireland.

Notes

1 S. Garner, *Racisms: An Introduction* (London: Sage, 2010), pp. 1–19.
2 F. Murphy and U. M. Vieten, *Asylum Seekers and Refugees Experiences of Life in Northern Ireland* (Belfast: Stormont and Queen's University Belfast, 2017), pp. 10–20.
3 U. M. Vieten, 'Tackling the conceptual order of multiple discrimination: situating different and difficult genealogies of race and ethnicity', in D. Schiek and A. Lawson (eds), *European Union Non-Discrimination Law and Intersectionality – Investigating the Triangle between Racial, Gender and Disability Discrimination* (Farnham: Routledge, 2011), pp. 63–76.
4 J. Bourne, 'The life and times of institutional racism', *Race & Class*, 43:2 (2001), 7–22.

5 Murphy and Vieten, *Experiences of Asylum Seekers and Refugees.*
6 M. Maguire and F. Murphy, *Integration in Ireland: The Everyday Lives of African Migrants* (Manchester: Manchester University Press, 2012), pp. 1–16.
7 D. Schiek, '"Hard Brexit" – how to address the new conundrum for the island of Ireland?', Working paper of the Jean Monnet Centre of Excellence – Tensions at the Fringes of the EU (Belfast: Centre for European & Transnational Legal Studies, School of Law, Queen's University Belfast, 2017), pp. 1–8.
8 Murphy andVieten, *Experiences of Asylum Seekers and Refugees.*
9 B. McMahon, *Working Group Report to Government on Improvements to the Protection Process, including Direct Provision and Supports to Asylum Seekers – Recommendations of the Working Group Department of Justice and Equality* (Dublin: Department of Justice and Equality, 2015), pp. 1–392.
10 Asylum Information Database, *Asylum Statistics: Republic of Ireland*, www.asylumineurope.org/reports/country/republic-ireland/statistics, accessed 21 January 2019.
11 Maguire and Murphy, *Integration in Ireland*, pp. 1–16; C. Murphy, L. Caulfield and M. Gilmartin, *Developing Integration Policy in the Public Sector: A Human Rights Approach* (Maynooth: Maynooth University Social Sciences Institute, 2018).
12 C. Gilligan, *Northern Ireland and the Crisis of Anti-Racism – Rethinking Racism and Sectarianism* (Manchesterl: Manchester University Press, 2017).
13 R. McKee, 'Love thy neighbour? Exploring prejudice against ethnic minority groups in a divided society: the case of Northern Ireland', *Journal of Ethnic and Migration Studies*, 42:5 (2015), 777–796.
14 N. Jarman and R. Monaghan, *Racist Harassment in Northern Ireland* (Belfast: Institute for Conflict Research, 2003), p. 21.
15 C. A. Malischewski, *Integration in a Divided Society? Refugees and Asylum Seekers in Northern Ireland* (Oxford: Refugee Studies Centre, 2012), pp. 3–23.
16 C. Bell and R. McVeigh, *A Fresh Start for Equality? The Equality Impacts of the Stormont House Agreement on the 'Two Main Communities' – An Action Research Intervention* (Dublin: Equality Coalition, 2016), p. 24.
17 Ibid., p. 24.
18 R. McVeigh and B. Rolston, 'From Good Friday to good relations: sectarianism, racism and the Northern Ireland state', *Race & Class*, 48:4 (2007), 1–23.
19 Interview data in this section of the chapter are also published in Maguire and Murphy, *Integration in Ireland*. Permission has been given to republish these data herein with acknowledgement.
20 M. Maguire and F. Murphy, 'Neo-liberalism, securitization and racialization in the Irish taxi industry', *European Journal of Cultural Studies*, 17:3 (2014), 282–297.
21 Ibid., p. 287.
22 M. Maguire and F. Murphy, 'Ontological (in)security and African Pentecostalism in Ireland', *Ethnos: Journal of Anthropology*, 4 (2015), 1–23.

5 Philip J. O'Connell*

African non-employment and labour market disadvantage

Employment is central to the process of economic integration and social inclusion. The Organisation for Economic Cooperation and Development (OECD) notes that 'Jobs are immigrants' chief source of income. Finding one is therefore fundamental to their becoming part of the host country's economic fabric.'[1] Employment leads to financial independence and allows a person to contribute to society and avoid the risk of poverty and social exclusion in their host country. Through employment, immigrants can build social networks, develop their language skills and increase participation in society. Job loss may be associated with poverty, psychological distress and more general social exclusion.

Less than 40 per cent of adult African nationals in Ireland are employed, far less than the average for Irish 'natives' or for other immigrant groups.[2] They also suffer much higher rates of unemployment than the national average. The pattern is similar in other European labour markets. This chapter explores the underlying reasons for African disadvantage in the Irish labour market.

Previous research has generated a substantial body of evidence suggesting that immigrants tend to fare less well than 'natives' in host-country labour markets. This is attributed to the tendency for immigrants to possess characteristics associated with lower productivity (including lack of familiarity with language and local networks, and little possession of relevant human capital) and perhaps also information deficits or discriminatory behaviour on the part of employers. But there is also evidence of variation within immigrant populations, with ethnic minorities experiencing higher unemployment and receiving lower wages. Moreover, immigrants may experience lower employment or wages than naturalised citizens because they are less well integrated in host societies and economies and less likely to participate in the full range of rights in the labour market enjoyed by natives and citizens.

Research undertaken in the United States during the 1970s found that, soon after their arrival in the US, foreign-born men earned substantially less than the native-born with similar characteristics, although their earnings increased more rapidly than those of native-born men. This narrowing of the wage gap was believed to be related to their acquisition of knowledge of the language and labour markets as well as training relevant to jobs in the US.[3] Research published in 1997 found that foreign-born ethnic minorities in the UK had higher unemployment rates than UK-born minorities but found no evidence that UK-born minorities fared worse than white UK-born individuals, suggesting that the key factor here was immigration rather than ethnic minority status.[4] However, another UK study (from 2001) found that both white and non-white immigrants had a lower probability of being employed, compared with white UK-born individuals, and while the disadvantage decreased over time for white immigrants it persisted among non-white immigrants.[5] A 2003 study of labour market performance of immigrants in the UK found that individuals of minority ethnic groups, particularly those from Asian, Caribbean and African communities, were significantly less likely to be employed than the white native-born population in the UK, as were white individuals from former Eastern Bloc European countries.[6] An analysis of data on employees in Sweden found large and significant differences in unemployment during the period 1992–1995; the unemployment rate among non-Europeans was twice that among natives, with the rates among European and Nordic groups lying between the two extremes.[7] Other papers also show that labour market outcomes of immigrants, in both the United States and the United Kingdom, varied by country of origin.[8]

In Ireland, research based on Labour Force Survey data found that non-nationals were significantly more likely to be unemployed than natives in Ireland in 2004, controlling for other factors such as age and education. Black Africans showed the highest rates of unemployment, but the unemployment risk was also higher for immigrants from non-English-speaking countries.[9] An examination of differences in labour market outcomes and respondents' interpretations of those differentials concluded that there is 'hierarchical racial order in Ireland with Whites at the top, Blacks at the bottom'.[10] Immigrants in Ireland were also found to be less likely to be in high-level occupations, immigrants from the New Member States of the EU (NMS) had the lowest occupational attainment, and there was little evidence of improved occupational attainment over time among the latter group.[11] More recent work has shown that black Africans suffer particular labour market disadvantages: they had less than one-third the chances of being employed, and more than four times the probability of being unemployed, compared to white Irish natives in 2010, even after taking account of differences in gender, age, education and other factors that can affect individual labour market outcomes.[12] That study also found that black Africans were much less likely to be in privileged managerial or technical occupations or to be in high-income-earning groups, although these disadvantages were shared with other immigrant groups, particularly those from the new EU member states.

There are three broad categories of factors that are held to influence how immigrants fare in labour markets compared with natives. The first set of factors relates to the personal characteristics of immigrants. Such characteristics can include education, experience, age and gender. In many countries, immigrants tend to have lower levels of education than natives, and this can give rise to lower employment, higher unemployment and lower occupational attainment of immigrants as a group. Mobility itself can also hamper success in the labour market, at least for a time. New entrants to a country may lack local knowledge and networks, their qualifications may not be well recognised and they may be less fluent in the language of the destination country. All of these factors can influence labour market success. Much of the research on the labour market integration of immigrants in Ireland has attempted to take account of such factors in order to identify the specific effects of immigrant status.[13]

A second group of factors relates to the behaviour of natives and others in the labour market. A particular focus here is on employers, who may engage in discriminatory hiring practices in favour of natives against immigrants, either because they consider that immigrants as a group may be less productive or because they prefer to hire from within their own national or ethnic group. Employees, either incumbent or potential, may also engage in discriminatory practices in order to reduce competition with immigrants. Discrimination is difficult to detect in data depicting labour market outcomes: if a minority group has a high unemployment rate, is this due to the characteristics of the group or to unobserved discrimination? As noted above, most studies of immigrants' outcomes in the labour market in Ireland take account of differences in relevant factors, such as gender and education, so the question remains as to whether unexplained residual differences in outcomes between natives and immigrants can be attributed to discrimination or to other unobserved factors. One approach is to ask survey respondents about their experiences of discrimination and analyse the relationship between these subjective experiences and objective labour market outcomes. A study that adopted this approach in the Irish context found that the black African national–ethnic group is much more likely than either Irish natives or other immigrant groups to have experienced discrimination while looking for work. Black Africans were about seven times more likely to report having experienced discrimination while looking for work than their Irish counterparts, even when other influential factors were taken into accounted.[14] This experience of discrimination was far more severe than for any other national–ethnic group, and while the overall rates of discrimination experienced by minority groups declined between 2004 and 2010 in Ireland, high levels of discrimination reported by black Africans persisted. Earlier survey research found that black Africans experienced the most discrimination of a range of national and ethnic groups surveyed, including in the work domain, in public places, and in pubs and restaurants, as well as experiencing institutional racism and discrimination.[15] A field experiment designed to directly measure the extent of discrimination in recruitment found that candidates with an obviously African, Asian or German name were half as likely as Irish candidates to be called for a job interview, although they detected no evidence of additional discrimination against Africans or Asians compared with Germans.[16]

A third set of factors that influences immigrants' labour market prospects consists of state policies that regulate access to the labour market as well as the bundle of rights that can be exercised by different groups. One example of such regulation is that all nationals of the European Economic Area (EEA), which includes all EU nationals, may migrate to Ireland and take up employment without restriction. Non-EEA nationals are subject to managed migration policy that is designed to meet labour needs from within the EU and to rely upon the Employment Permit system to meet identified skills shortages, most in highly skilled occupations. The Employment Permit system has been revised on several occasions, most recently in 2014, but a continuing feature has been that most work permits restrict mobility between employers, often requiring immigrants to secure jobs before their arrival and requiring them to obtain a new permit should they wish to change employers. Many permits require an intra-EU labour market needs test before a non-EEA immigrant can be recruited, and many restrict family reunification of spouses and dependants. These regulations put non-EEA immigrants at a disadvantage relative to EEA nationals as well as to Irish citizens.

A further restrictive policy pursued by the state relates to the treatment of those seeking international protection in Ireland. Up to June 2018, asylum seekers awaiting decisions on their applications for refugee status were denied the right to work in Ireland. Asylum seekers are accommodated collectively in Direct Provision centres and receive small allowances and are effectively excluded from participation in the Irish economy and society. Previous research suggests that the severe disadvantages suffered by black Africans may be due in part to the fact that many black Africans in Ireland are refugees and would have spent an extended period of time excluded from the labour market as asylum seekers in the Direct Provision system, leading to a scarring effect on their future employment prospects.[17] However, it is also necessary to consider the low labour force participation rates among Africans and to examine their characteristics (including gender, education and household structure) and barriers to labour force participation associated with those characteristics. Most Africans in Ireland would have found themselves on the wrong side of one or other of these state policies at some stage during their residency.

Table 5.1 Population by region of birthplace, 2011

	Number	Per cent
Ireland	3,745,350	82.5
UK	302,370	6.7
Old EU13[1]	60,670	1.3
New EU12[2]	218,880	4.8
Africa	55,750	1.2
Asia	79,990	1.8
Nth America, Australia, New Zealand	49,360	1.1
Rest of world	26,200	0.6
All	4,745,350	100.0

Notes:
1 The old EU15 minus the UK and the ROI, pre-2004.
2 The new EU10 plus Bulgaria, Romania and Croatia, 2004.
Source: Census of Population 2011, Minnesota Population Center.

This chapter draws on nationally representative data from the 2011 Census of Population to examine the labour market outcomes among Africans in Ireland in some detail, and compares them with the experiences of other immigrant groups.

Table 5.1 shows the distribution of population by region of birthplace in 2011. Over 82 per cent of the population of Ireland were born in Ireland. Almost 800,000, or 18 per cent of the population, were born abroad. It should be noted that about 85 per cent of the population are Irish nationals as many born abroad to Irish emigrants claim Irish nationality, and some immigrants had naturalised by 2011. The single largest group of immigrants came from the UK, over 300,000, or almost 7 per cent of the total population. Almost 56,000 were born in Africa, just 1.2 per cent of the population in 2011.

Table 5.2 presents the rates of employment, unemployment and activity for those aged 15–64 years by region of birth recorded in Census 2011. The employment rate is measured as the proportion of working adults in the working age population. The unemployment rate is the number of unemployed expressed as a proportion of the labour force, which is the number employed plus unemployed. The rate of economic inactivity is the proportion of working age adults in the population who are not engaged in the labour force.

On average almost 58 per cent of the working age population are employed but there are important differences in employment and economic activity between immigrant groups. Europeans tend to show higher employment rates, mainly because most of them came to Ireland to work. Non-Europeans tend to have lower employment rates, partly because many of

Table 5.2 Employment, unemployment and economic inactivity by region of birth, 2011

	Employed %	Unemployed %	Inactive %
Ireland	57.6	18.6	29.3
UK	55.9	21.2	29.1
Old EU13	65.1	11.7	26.2
New EU12	66.6	23.0	13.6
Africa	44.0	34.7	32.7
Asia	54.8	19.2	32.2
Nth America, Australia, New Zealand	55.2	14.1	35.8
Rest of world	52.0	27.1	28.6
All	57.8	19.3	28.4

Source: 2011 Irish Census.

these tend to be students. The African group stands out with an employment rate of only 44 per cent, far lower than any other group of immigrants, and an unemployment rate of 33 per cent, far higher than any other group. We can draw on the Census data to examine whether these striking discrepancies are related to the characteristics of the African population in Ireland. The 2011 Census was collected in the midst of a deep and prolonged economic crisis with mass unemployment. Immigrants in general were hit hard by the Great Depression in Ireland, with substantially higher unemployment rates than Irish natives. However, the African disadvantage indicated in Table 5.2 has been a persistent feature of the Irish labour market before, during and after the recession.[18]

Table 5.3 shows employment and unemployment by sex. The African disadvantage is evident for both men and women. About 50 per cent of African males are employed, more than ten percentage points lower than the average employment rate. African women are even more disadvantaged: their employment rate, less than 38 per cent, is seventeen percentage points below the average female employment rate. The gender gap in employment is also higher among Africans. The average employment gap between men and women is about six percentage points, but the employment rate among African women is twelve percentage points lower than that of African men. A substantial gender gap is also found among immigrants from the residual 'Rest of weorld' group, but at much higher rates of employment.

Africans are also distinctive with respect to unemployment. In general, female unemployment is lower than male unemployment in Ireland. This is partly due to the impact of the Great Recession, which entailed far greater job losses among men than women, partly because it centred on a property

Table 5.3 Employment and unemployment rates by sex and region of birth

	Employment		Unemployment	
	Male %	Female %	Male %	Female %
Ireland	60.3	54.9	22.6	13.7
UK	59.7	52.2	24.9	16.5
Old EU13	70.7	60.3	11.8	11.6
New EU12	70.1	63.0	24.0	21.9
Africa	50.2	37.8	32.9	36.9
Asia	58.6	50.6	21.1	16.7
Nth America, Australia, New Zealand	59.8	51.5	15.3	12.9
Rest of world	57.8	47.1	26.9	27.3
All	60.8	54.8	22.8	15.0

Source: 2011 Irish Census.

crisis in the male-dominated construction sector (although higher male than female unemployment rates have long been a feature of the Irish labour market, in contrast to other European countries).[19] Higher male unemployment rates prevail to a greater or lesser extent across all of the immigrant groups excluding the 'rest of the world' category. However, the African female unemployment rate is extraordinarily high at almost 37 per cent compared with the male rate of 33 per cent. Some of the discrepancy between Africans and other immigrant groups might be due to compositional differences. This could occur, for instance, if there were substantial differences in the distribution of educational qualifications or ages, between the various immigrant groups.

Figure 5.1 shows the highest level of educational attainment by region of birth, and there is little here to suggest that African underemployment is related to education. About 16 per cent of Africans had lower secondary education or less, compared with over 32 per cent of Irish natives and 27 per cent of those born in the UK, but, as we have seen in Table 5.2, both of these groups had much higher employment rates, and lower unemployment rates, than Africans. At the upper end of the educational distribution, Africans appear to be a relatively well-educated group: almost 45 per cent of Africans had a third level of education, compared with 30 per cent of those born in Ireland and 36 per cent of those born in the UK. This is consistent with in-depth accounts of African migration to Ireland which suggest that Africans, particularly Nigerians, the largest African nationality in Ireland, are characterised by middle-class chain migrants seeking opportunity in Ireland.[20] The proportion of Africans with higher education did fall well

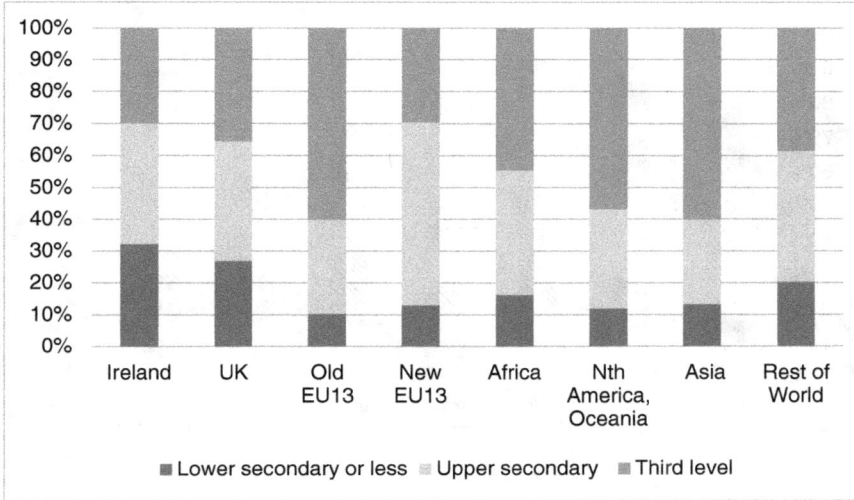

100% 90% 80% 70% 60% 50% 40% 30% 20% 10% 0%

Ireland   UK   Old EU13   New EU13   Africa   Nth America, Oceania   Asia   Rest of World

■ Lower secondary or less   ■ Upper secondary   ■ Third level

Figure 5.1 Educational attainment by region of birth
Note: EU 13 = all post-2004 new member states.
Source: Derived from P. O'Connell, 'Why are so few Africans at work in Ireland?
Immigration Policy and Labour Market Disadvantage', UCD Geary Working
Paper Series: WP2018/16 (Dublin: UCD, 2018).

below the proportion of those from Asia and from the new settler countries of North America and Oceania with third-level education, but both of these latter groups had comparatively high employment rates.

Part of these educational differences may relate to age. Given patterns of educational expansion, younger people tend to have higher educational profiles, and most migrants are young. Figure 5.2 shows the distribution of age groups in each of the regions of birth.

There is nothing in the comparative data on age groups to account for the low employment rate among the African group. Over 80 per cent of Africans are in the prime working age groups, 25–59 years, compared with just 73 per cent of Irish-born and 75 per cent of those born in the old EU member states, both of which groups have higher employment rates. Analysis of Census data indicates that African women are more likely to have relatively large families: 27 per cent of African-born women had three or more children in 2011, compared with about 14 per cent of Irish-born and 16 per cent of UK-born women. This could reduce the employment rate of African women, compared with their Irish-born counterparts. However, this would be unlikely to account for employment rate differences between males from the different populatiaon sub-groups.

Given that there are substantial compositional differences between the various country-of-birth groups, in factors that may influence labour market

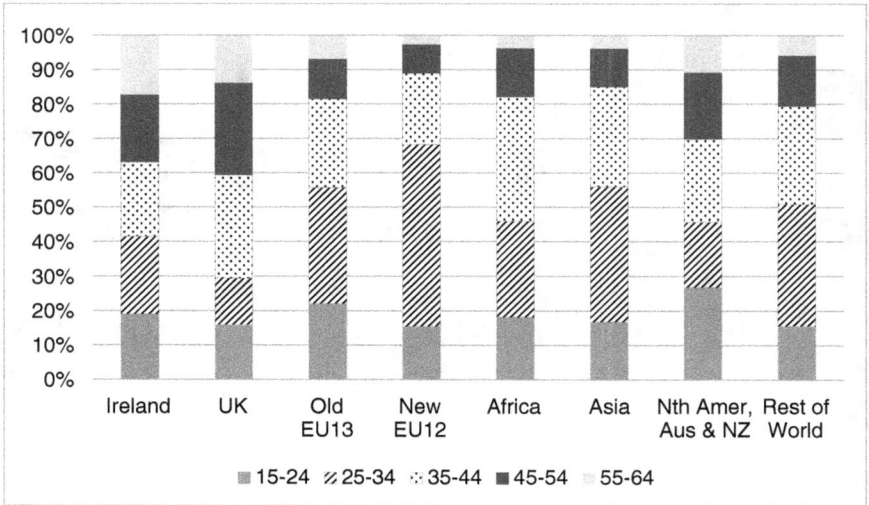

Figure 5.2 Age group by region of birth
Source: Derived from P. O'Connell, 'Why are so few Africans at work in Ireland?
Immigration Policy and Labour Market Disadvantage', UCD Geary Working
Paper Series: WP2018/16 (Dublin: UCD, 2018).

outcome, it would be useful to employ a multivariate framework that allows us to compare those outcomes while controlling for relevant covariates in order to isolate the specific effect of region of birth. A recent paper adopts such a multivariate approach to the analysis of the 2011 Census.[21] The paper develops models for both employment and unemployment, which are estimated separately for men and women, given the substantial gender differences in labour market behaviour and outcomes. With respect to employment, education is found to have a strong positive influence on the odds of being employed; so does being married or in a partnership, strongly so for men. The number of children in the household tends to increase the employment rate of men, but it strongly reduces the employment rate of women. Men and women aged 35–44 tend to have higher employment rates than younger or older age groups. These are conventional findings in statistical models of employment. However, the Census also collects information on two variables specifically related to migration: timing of residence in Ireland and fluency in the English language. Including these migration-related variables, the models show that relatively recent immigrants, who arrived in Ireland after 2001, are less likely to be employed than those who arrived earlier, consistent with the theory that recent arrivals find it more difficult to settle into new labour markets. Fluency in English is very important: those with fluent English are more likely to be employed than those who responded to the Census that they spoke the language 'well', who in turn are more likely to be at work than those with poor English.

So, when the influence of all these individual characteristics and migration variables is controlled for, does this eliminate the effects of difference between regions of birth? Clearly not: Figure 5.3 shows odds ratios of employment by region of birth, controlling for other relevant influential factors. The odds ratios are relative to Irish, whose odds would be 1, so British men and women are about three-quarters as likely as their equivalent Irish counterparts to be at work, while males from the old pre-Enlargement EU countries are 1.7 times more likely to be at work than their Irish counterparts. The Africans stand out: an African man is only about 40 per cent as likely as an Irish male with the same profile to be employed and an African female half as likely to be at work as her Irish counterpart. This analysis shows that the employment chances of Africans actually fall relative to those of the Irish-born when we take account of their personal characteristics. If the observed African disadvantage were due to personal characteristics, such as education, age or family structures, then we would expect that controlling for these factors would narrow the gap between

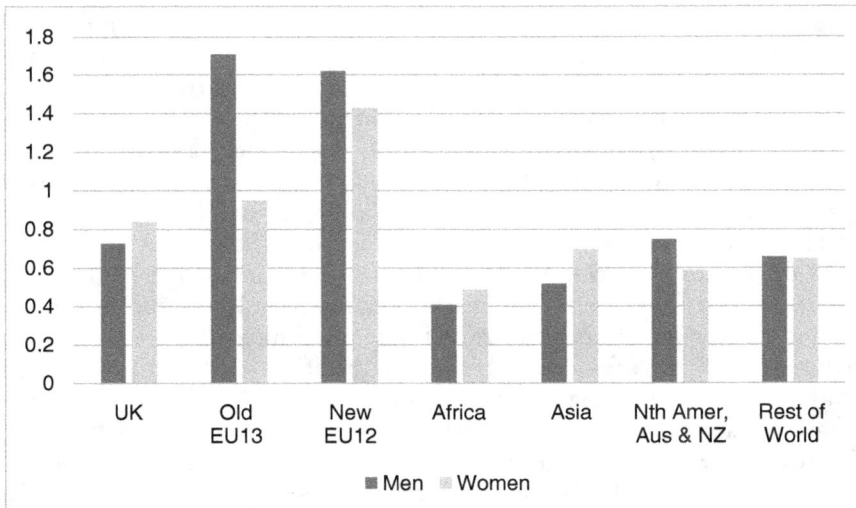

Figure 5.3 Odds ratios of employment by region of birth, controlling for other relevant factors,[1] compared with native-born Irish
Note: The models for the population aged 25–64 years control for marital status, number of children, age, education, time of arrival and fluency in English.
Source: Derived from P. O'Connell, 'Why are so few Africans at work in Ireland? Immigration Policy and Labour Market Disadvantage', UCD Geary Working Paper Series: WP2018/16 (Dublin: UCD, 2018).

African and Irish employment chances. So, the African group has an exceptionally low employment rate *despite* its relatively favourable characteristics (e.g. in terms of education and age) rather than because of disadvantageous characteristics. Figure 5.3 also shows that the employment odds of several other groups – from Asia, from North America, Australia and New Zealand, and from the Rest of the World group of countries – are substantially lower than those of Irish people after controlling for individual characteristics.

It is clear that Africans remain severely disadvantaged: they are much less likely to be employed than either native Irish or other immigrant groups. Asians also show poor labour market outcomes, although not to the same extent as Africans. Previous research has suggested that some of the African disadvantage may be due to discrimination or to the policy of excluding asylum seekers from the labour market in the Direct Provision system. As it happens, Africans and Asians consistently feature in the list of 'top six' countries of origin among asylum applicants in the Irish system.[22]

The Census does not record whether individual immigrants have ever claimed asylum in Ireland, although it does record information about specific country of origin. However, my paper develops a new approach to capturing the potential impact of the Direct Provision system on the labour market prospects of immigrants by matching data published by Eurostat on the number of asylum seekers by country of origin to the individual-level country information in the Census to create an 'Asylum:Population Ratio' indicator that measures the ratio of the number of asylum seekers from each country to the population from that country resident in Ireland in 2011.[23] The Asylum:Population Ratio can be assigned to each individual in the Census. That analysis shows that individuals who come from a country with a high Asylum: Population Ratio in Ireland are less likely to be employed than those who come from countries with a low Asylum:Population Ratio.

The Asylum:Population Ratio indicator captures the probability for each individual of experiencing the Direct Provision regime and thus of having been excluded from the labour market for an extended period of time in Ireland. Inclusion of the asylum ratio in the employment models also reduces the impact of region of birth, and the effect was most pronounced among Africans and Asians, who together accounted for over 90 per cent of asylum seekers in the Direct Provision system at the time of the 2011 Census. These results are consistent with the idea that Direct Provision has lasting negative effects on the employment prospects of asylum seekers in Ireland, and that this is reflected in the poor labour market outcomes observed particularly among Africans and, to a lesser extent, among Asians.

The paper also estimates models for unemployment. Here, the African disadvantage is even more stark. After taking account of individual characteristics, English-language fluency and time of arrival in Ireland, African men are two-and-a-half times more likely to be unemployed than native-born Irish men (Model A in Table 5.4) and African women are three-and-a-half

Table 5.4 Odds ratios of unemployment by region of birth, controlling for individual characteristics and for the Asylum:Population Ratio, compared with native-born Irish

Models control for:	Men		Women	
	Model A: Individual characteristics[1]	Model B: Asylum population[2]	Model A: Individual characteristics[1]	Model B: Asylum population[2]
	Odds ratios	Odds ratios	Odds ratios	Odds ratios
UK	1.45[3]	1.45	1.27	1.27
Old EU13	0.57	0.57	0.88	0.88
New EU12	0.88	0.88	1.04	1.04
Africa	2.52	1.82	3.59	2.76
Asia	1.96	1.64	1.44	1.37
Nth America, Australia, New Zealand Oceania	1.28	1.28	1.93	1.94
Rest of world	1.95	1.57	2.08	1.83

Notes:
1 Model A: Controls for marital status, number of children, age, education, time of arrival and fluency in English.
2 Model B: Includes Asylum:Population Ratio in addition to variables specified in Model A.
3 All odds ratios in bold are statistically significant.
Source: Derived from P. O'Connell, 'Why are so few Africans at work in Ireland? Immigration Policy and Labour Market Disadvantage', UCD Geary Working Paper Series: WP2018/16 (Dublin: UCD, 2018).

times more likely to be unemployed than Irish women with the same profile. In general, non-Europeans show higher rates of unemployment than the Irish and those from other EU countries, reflecting, at least in part, the effects of the Employment Permit system on the labour market prospects of those from outside the EEA. The Asylum:Population Ratio also significantly increases an individual's odds of being unemployed.

Table 5.4 also shows that inclusion of the Asylum:Population Ratio reduces the effect of region of birth: among African women, taking account of the risk that an individual might have been exposed to the Direct Provision system reduces the odds of being unemployed from 3.6 to just under 2.8 times those of an Irish woman. Among men the odds of unemployment are reduced from 2.5 times the Irish to 1.8 times the Irish risk. We can see a similar pattern among Asians, another group with a substantial number of people in the asylum system, although the effects here are much more muted. Taking account of the Asylum:Population Ratio has little impact on the odds of unemployment of the other regional group.

The research reviewed in this chapter suggests that even when we try to adjust for all the factors that we can measure, however inexactly, it is clear that Africans continue to be very severely disadvantaged in the labour market, with substantially lower employment rates and higher unemployment rates. In international research, the persistence of unequal outcomes after adjustment for other relevant factors is commonly attributed to discrimination.[24] Such an interpretation would be consistent with previous Irish research that has employed different methods to assess discrimination in the labour market and found that black Africans are a great deal more likely than either Irish nationals or other national–ethnic groups to report discrimination in both looking for work and in the workplace.[25]

Conclusion

This chapter set out to explore why African immigrants have poor labour market outcomes in Ireland, with very low employment and exceptionally high unemployment rates. The analysis draws on a 10 per cent sample of the 2011 Census of Population, which provides us with an unusually large data set to examine underlying differences of experience and of composition between different groups of immigrants.

I used those data to address two broad explanations for why Africans might fare so poorly in the Irish labour market. The first explanation relates to the composition of the African-born in the Irish population: the idea that the distribution of factors that influence employment and unemployment may be unfavourable for the African group relative to Irish natives and/ or other immigrant groups. Thus, for example, if Africans as a group tend to be less educated or older than other groups then this might help to explain why they display lower employment and higher unemployment. In fact, however, we find that Africans are a relatively well-educated group and are concentrated in the prime working age groups. When we draw on research that adjusted a range of individual characteristics and migration-related variables in statistical models of employment and unemployment, we find that the disadvantages associated with belonging to the African immigrant group intensify. This suggests that if African immigrants had a less favourable profile than they do, then their membership of the African group would have led to even lower employment and higher unemployment than that observed. Thus, for example, if African-born women shared the same characteristics as Irish-born women, in terms of age, marital status, number of children, education and fluency in English, then their odds of unemployment would be five times that of their Irish counterparts. Given the findings of similar increases in employment and unemployment penalties among Asian immigrants when personal characteristics are taken into account, we must conclude that such characteristics do not provide an explanation as to why Africans, and to an extent Asians, but not other immigrant groups, fare poorly in the Irish labour market. This is important because it precludes any arguments that might suggest that the disadvantages experienced by Africans in the Irish labour market are somehow due to their personal disadvantages or failings.

We then turned to an alternative explanation that seeks to take account of the experience of at least some African and Asian immigrants in Ireland. Previous research has suggested that some of the African disadvantage may be due to the policy of excluding asylum seekers from the labour market under the Direct Provision system. While the Census does not record whether immigrants have ever claimed asylum in Ireland, it does record information about specific country of origin. I draw on recent research that develops a new approach to capturing the potential impact of the Direct Provision system on the labour market prospects of immigrants by expressing the number of asylum seekers from a country to the total number of immigrants from that country resident in Ireland. That asylum to population ratio, which provides a rough measure of the risk of an individual, does have significant impact on labour market outcomes: it reduces an individual's likelihood of being at work and increases their probability of being unemployed. Importantly, that asylum population ratio also reduces the effect of belonging to the African and Asian immigrant groups. The asylum ratio is intended to capture the probability of being at risk of experiencing the Direct Provision regime and thus of having been excluded from participating in the labour market in Ireland for an extended period of time. Its inclusion in the employment and unemployment models had the most pronounced effect among Africans and Asians, who together accounted for over 90 per cent of asylum seekers in the Direct Provision system at the time of the 2011 Census. These results are consistent with the idea that Direct Provision has lasting negative effects on the employment prospects of asylum seekers in Ireland, and that this is reflected in the poor labour market outcomes observed particularly among Africans, and, to a lesser extent, among Asians.

In May 2017, a Burmese man who had spent eight years in Direct Provision won his appeal against the legal ban preventing him from working, with the Supreme Court determining that, in an international protection system with no temporal limits as to when the application process will be concluded, an absolute prohibition on the right to work for persons in the protection process is contrary to the right to seek employment under the Constitution. The Court adjourned consideration of its Order for six months to enable the state to consider its response. An intergovernmental task force recommended that the best option available to the state to comply with the judgment would be to opt into the EU (recast) Reception Conditions Directive which lays down standards for the reception of international protection applicants.[26] In June 2018 the Government announced that asylum seekers would be allowed to work from nine months after their application for asylum is lodged if they have not received a decision on their case. Hopefully, this may help to bring to an end a grudging approach to the treatment of asylum seekers looking for protection in Ireland, a policy stance that this chapter demonstrates has had lasting negative impacts on their labour market prospects.

The analyses reviewed above do not account for all of the African disadvantage. Even after we take account of individual characteristics, migration-related variables and the asylum system, Africans still stand out as severely disadvantaged in the Irish labour market: African women are three times as likely to be unemployed as their Irish counterparts, African men, more than twice as likely. In this they differ from other immigrant groups when the range of influential factors is controlled for. In seeking to account for this remaining unexplained African disadvantage, we can take note of the previous research findings that black Africans in Ireland are a great deal more likely than any other immigrant groups to report having experienced discrimination while looking for work. This would suggest that the disadvantages experienced by Africans in the Irish labour market appear to be due to a combination of restrictive policies on the part of the state and discriminatory practices on the part of employers.

Notes

* My thanks to Pierce Parker for careful and systematic research assistance with the data analysis.

1 OECD, *International Migration Outlook 2015* (Paris: OECD, 2015), p. 79.

2 P. O'Connell and O. Kenny, 'Employment and integration', in A. Barrett, F. McGinnity and E. Quinn (eds), *Annual Monitoring Report on Integration 2016* (Dublin: ESRI, 2018), pp.18–21.

3 B. Chiswick, 'The effect of Americanization on the earnings of foreign-born men', *Journal of Political Economy*, 86:5 (1978), 897–921.

4 D. Blackaby, S. Drinkwater, D. Leslie and P. Murphy, 'A picture of male and female unemployment among Britain's ethnic minorities', *Scottish Journal of Political Economy*, 44:2 (1997), 182–197.

5 M. A. Shields and S. Wheatley Price, 'Language fluency and immigrant employment prospects: evidence from Britain's ethnic minorities', *Applied Economics Letters*, 8:11 (2001), 741–745.

6 C. Dustmann, F. Fabbri, I. Preston and J. Wadsworth, *Labour Market Performance of Immigrants in the UK Labour Market*, Home Office Online Report

05/03 (London: Research Development and Statistics Directorate, Home Office, 2003).

7 M. Arai and R. Vilhelmsson, 'Unemployment-risk differentials between immigrant and native workers in Sweden', *Industrial Relations: A Journal of Economy and Society*, 4:3 (2004), 690–698.

8 D. G. Papademetriou and A. Terrazas, 'Immigrants and the US economic crisis: from recession to recovery', in D. G. Papademetriou, M. Sumption and A. Terrazas (eds) with C. Burkert, S. Loyal and R. Ferrero-Turrion, *Migration and Immigrants Two Years after the Financial Collapse: Where Do We Stand?* (Washington, DC: Migration Policy Institute, 2010), pp. 22–46; M. Sumption, 'Foreign workers and immigrant integration: emerging from recession in the United Kingdom', in D. G. Papademetriou et al., *Migration and Immigrants Two Years after the Financial Collapse*, pp. 47–65.

9 P. O'Connell and F. McGinnity, *Immigrants at Work: Ethnicity and Nationality in the Irish Labour Market* (Dublin: Equality Authority and ESRI, 2008).

10 E. Joseph, 'Whiteness and racism: examining the racial order in Ireland', *Irish Journal of Sociology*, 26:1 (2018), 46–70, p. 46.

11 A. Barrett and D. Duffy, 'Are Ireland's immigrants integrating into its labour market?', *International Migration Review*, 42:3 (2008), 597–615.

12 G. Kingston, P. O'Connell and E. Kelly, *Ethnicity and Nationality in the Irish Labour Market: Evidence from the QNHS Equality Module 2010* (Dublin: Equality Authority and ESRI, 2013).

13 See, for example, Barrett and Duffy, 'Are Ireland's immigrants integrating into its labour market?'; Kingston, O'Connell and Kelly, *Ethnicity and Nationality in the Irish Labour Market*; O'Connell and McGinnity, *Immigrants at Work*.

14 G. Kingston, F. McGinnity and P. O'Connell, 'Discrimination in the labour market: nationality, ethnicity and the recession', *Work, Employment and Society*, 29:2 (2015), 213–232.

15 F. McGinnity, P. O'Connell, E. Quinn and J. Williams, *Migrants' Experience of Racism and Discrimination in Ireland* (Dublin: ESRI, 2006).

16 F. McGinnity and P. Lunn, 'Measuring discrimination facing ethnic minority job applicants: an Irish experiment', *Work, Employment and Society*, 25:4 (2011), 693–708.

17 Kingston, O'Connell and Kelly, *Ethnicity and Nationality in the Irish Labour Market*.

18 Ibid.; P. O'Connell, 'Migration', in W. Roche, P. O'Connell and A. Prothero (eds), *Austerity and Recovery in Ireland: Europe's Poster Child and the Great Recession* (Oxford: Oxford University Press, 2017).

19 P. O'Connell, 'Unemployment and labour market policy' in Roche, O'Connell and Prothero (eds), *Austerity and Recovery in Ireland*.

20 B. Fanning, *Migration and the Making of Ireland* (Dublin: UCD Press, 2018), pp. 179–199.

21 P. O'Connell, 'Why are so few Africans at Work in Ireland? Immigration Policy and Labour Market Disadvantage', UCD Geary Working Paper Series: WP2018/16 (Dublin: UCD, 2018).

22 See, for example, Office of the Refugee Appeals Commissioner, 2011, *Annual Report 2011*, Dublin.

23 O'Connell, 'Why are so few Africans at work in Ireland?'.

24 D. Pager and H. Shepherd, 'The sociology of discrimination: racial discrimina-
     tion in employment, housing credit and consumer markets', *Annual Review of
     Sociology*, 4:1 (2008), 181–209.
25 Kingston, McGinnity and O'Connell, 'Discrimination in the labour market'.
26 Department of Justice and Equality, November 2017: www.justice.ie/en/JELR/
     Pages/Access_To_Work_for_International_Protection_Applicants, accessed 23
     January 2019.

6 Pablo Rojas Coppari

The lives of Filipino-Irish care workers

This chapter examines Filipino migration to Ireland through the lens of the care industry, informed by the experiences of migrants in a range of occupations and with varied legal statuses. It draws on semi-structured interviews with migrant domestic and care workers, observations of the Domestic Workers Action Group and the work conducted by the Migrant Rights Centre Ireland (MRCI) in this sector. Filipinos in Ireland have often been heralded as an example of successful integration, the example of those in the nursing profession frequently being cited. This assumption obscures the reality of a large number of Filipinos, engaged as domestic workers, child-minders, cleaners and carers; they often find themselves unable to progress in the labour market due to discrimination and are often exposed to the exploitation and isolation of low-paid caring occupations.[1] Exclusionary labour migration and family reunification policies have resulted in many remaining undocumented in the state, adding another layer of vulnerability to many of them.

Data for this chapter come from twenty qualitative interviews of Filipino workers in the domestic and care sector. They took place between January and March 2017 and were carried out as part of a broader research project on labour market precarity and migration in Ireland. The sample comprised nineteen women and one man, and all but one of them held work permits for the sector. Participants were recruited with the help of the MRCI, and most of them had engaged in advocacy or campaigning with the organisation. Most interviewees arrived in Ireland soon after 2001. With the exception of two cases the initial work permits were issued for employment in private homes; the employment of domestic household personnel had never been a common practice in Ireland and developed with the simultaneous rising cost of childcare and elderly care. Recruitment was mainly informal and based on recommendations, benefiting from the presence of the newly established Filipino community in the country. By 2003 rumours had spread about forthcoming changes in immigration policy, resulting in more people taking the opportunity to move to Ireland.

Fourteen of those interviewed had become Irish citizens and four had secure long-term residency status. One participant held a work permit and one was undocumented in the state. Nine worked to provide care for the elderly, eight provided childcare, one worked in both areas and two worked with patients in a hospital setting. Thirteen worked in private homes while seven provided care in an institutionalised setting (a hospital, nursing home or childcare facility). The analysis of the data obtained through the interviews was supplemented with observations of the Domestic Workers Action Group and the Justice For the Undocumented campaign group, both of which are migrant-led initiatives supported by the Migrant Rights Centre Ireland and facilitated by its resources.

Labour migration from the Philippines is structured and best understood as a consequence of the changing nature of the globalised economy which led to the liberalisation of trade, increased reliance on foreign direct investment among developing nations and overall economic interdependence. These resulted in what theorists have argued constitute a 'new international division of labour'.[2] In 1974, former Filipino president Ferdinand Marcos initiated a programme to encourage overseas migration for the purposes of labour in order to curb increasing unemployment and to counteract the deterioration of the national economy. Four national agencies were created with the purpose of addressing the issues related to the employment, welfare and reintegration of returning overseas Filipino workers. The Philippines economy quickly became dependent on the remittances of migrant workers, which in 2014 represented 8.4 per cent of national GDP.[3]

The global demand for cheaper labour and increased pressure for women to enter the labour market led to the feminisation of migration, where women from the Global South migrate to take on roles in reproductive labour in developed countries, thus allowing the local women to participate in the primary labour market. Large numbers of Filipinas left, and continue to leave, to find work as nurses, caregivers and domestic workers. This process has been conceptualised as part of an 'international division of reproductive labour' and later theorised as part of an emergent global care chain field within which those who might take on caring roles in sending countries are displaced and instead engage in providing care to host societies sustaining in those societies a productive labour force.[4]

Filipino migration across the care industry is now a global reality: it has transformed the lives of Filipino families and reshaped social structures by positioning women as active agents of upward social mobility, while also changing how caring roles in receiving countries are perceived, understood and commodified. In between these two realities, carers struggle to find the transnational spaces where they can exercise agency both as professionals and heads of families, having to perform the docile and invisible roles expected from them by immigration systems and segmented labour markets.

Migration to Ireland

The number of Filipinos in Ireland grew quickly between the late 1990s and the early 2000s, to become one of the larger immigrant communities in the country. Just two hundred or so Filipinos lived in the Republic of Ireland in 1997. By the time of the 2002 Census this number had grown to around 3,900. Many of the initial arrivals were nurses sourced through recruitment drives abroad; these were subsequently joined by domestic workers, carers and those employed in other sectors. It is believed that up to 60 per cent of Filipino migrants were nurses in the early 2000s, with this number falling as a percentage over time as they were joined by dependent family members and other categories of migrant workers.[5]

Nurses were admitted through the Working Visa Authorisation Scheme, a labour migration system for the highly skilled sector which contrasted with the Work Permit scheme, a temporary migration system for lower-skilled workers. The latter afforded limited rights and tied migrant workers to the employer, who applied for a permit on their behalf. This became the main avenue for the admission of domestic and care workers as well as Filipinos working in the manufacturing, food, and accommodation and restaurant industries.

Filipinos are believed to constitute the largest community of undocumented migrants in the state.[6] A growth in the undocumented Filipino population took place as a result of an abrupt shift in Irish immigration policy in October 2003. Before then, the system had fast-tracked applications for certain categories of skilled worker from non-EU countries, and was, in theory, more restrictive in other cases. In practice, a laissez-faire system operated until 2003 when a new Employment Permits Act was introduced, which granted free access to the Irish job market to people from the new EU member states (from 1 May 2004). Now unable to obtain work permits, some Filipinos arrived in Ireland as visitors, taking advantage of the established presence of family and friends in the country. Many found employment but were unable to regularise their residency status.[7]

According to the 2016 Census, the size of the Filipino community now stands at 14,725, with as many as 3,500 individuals now holding dual Filipino and Irish citizenship. It is not clear how many of an estimated 8,500 undocumented Filipino adults have been identified by the Census. Filipino women account for 59 per cent of the community. Around two-thirds of the Filipino population live in the greater Dublin area, the rest dispersed around the country with larger pockets present in bigger towns and cities.

The Migrant Rights Centre Ireland has consistently exposed the issues affecting documented and undocumented workers in precarious sectors of employment. Undocumented Filipinos are overrepresented in caring roles, particularly in a domestic context where their working conditions can be very poor, resulting from isolation and a lack of enforcement of employment rights. Others work in informal sectors such as cleaning and maintenance where cash-in-hand payment is prevalent.

Working conditions in the care industry

Most of the twenty interviewees were employed under 'live-in arrangements', whereby employers provided meals and accommodation in the house, in exchange for a deduction of up to €54.13 weekly from the salary. Such arrangements, where care workers depend on their employer for a place to live, have been found to facilitate workplace exploitation.[8] One participant described how the blurred lines between work and personal time led to live-in workers being taken advantage of, so that they felt on call far beyond their working hours:

> If they [employers] want to go out they don't really worry about it, because you are there. It seems like not but you work there twenty-four hours inside the house ... when you are living in, even though your job is finished in eight hours when you are inside the house you still feel like you are working. The children are coming in your room, they are going to call you, you know something like that.

It is difficult for domestic care workers to assert their rights because they are often isolated. Fifteen participants in the study reported exploitation in one or multiple employments. Until 2011, labour inspections in the private home were not permitted, and since then only in circumstances where the employer is agrees to being inspected, making it very difficult for workers to report breaches and seek redress. Once workers secure residency or citizenship, they tend to favour *live-out* arrangements, which allow for greater control of their working time and employment conditions. However, live-in arrangements are often the only option for undocumented migrants, au-pairs and other categories of migrant who have limited choice in the labour market.Eleven of those interviewed were still working in private homes, where work conditions are generally poorer than in institutional settings. For instance, the average hourly rate for domestic care workers was €10.50 compared with €15.50 in public or private institutional settings. Work in the private home offers less security, contracts often being terminated as soon as caring roles are no longer needed; as there are no pay scales applicable in home care there is no recognition of previous experience and workers often start new jobs at rates of €10 per hour or less, losing any advantage acquired over time.

Yet, it is important not to paint work conditions in nursing homes and childcare facilities as ideal. Starting salaries are often below the low-pay threshold of €13.50 an hour and opportunities for wage increases are limited, particularly with privately run care providers. Workers complain of poorly managed facilities and are sometimes responsible for as many as fifteen patients; with very little support from management they often feel that quality of care is compromised. Nonetheless, this type of employment offers more security and participants often aimed at securing work with state-funded providers which were regarded as ideal employers, because conditions were better:

> I am thinking of getting into HSE [Health Service Executive] ..., sometimes people get 16 euro an hour and plus you have pension scheme, you know. When you retire some day you have something. We need to look after our future and not only this time because I am nearly in my fifties now.

The ability to make such career decisions is linked to a person's immigration status and mobility in the labour market. Undocumented workers, who comprise up to 29 per cent of those working in the care industry, have limited choice outside of private homes where their legal status can remain unchecked and they often report poor working conditions, such as working around the clock for as little as €4 per hour.[9] Their irregular status prevents them from accessing employment with better conditions, such as in residential settings, due to strict control on their right to work.

Living as transnational families

Determining the reasons why people migrate is not easy; often there are multiple factors taken into consideration which can seem to be contradictory. From the discussions with participants, three apparent themes emerged: to improve family conditions, to maximise income and to experience life abroad. Half of the participants had previous migration experience to countries in the Gulf Region or East Asia, often as domestic and care workers. These women acquired the role of breadwinners prior to migrating, often due to a change in family circumstances which led to a reconfiguration of gender and family roles, deviating from traditional expectations in Filipino society.[10]

Only five participants had dependants join them in Ireland but almost every single one of them had, and often continue to have, responsibilities towards family members. Definitions of family and kinship are traditionally more extended than those in Western societies, and those family members who migrate abroad play a key role in securing social mobility for their extended family members at home.[11] This responsibility towards extended family is stronger for those migrants who are not married, who are often expected to look after the welfare of the parents and help in the education of their siblings' offspring. Meeting such obligations has been a motivation for some of those who have come to Ireland. As one interviewee put it:

> I hope to create a better future for my family like helping my nieces go to college because some of my brothers they are struggling ... so those children still want to go to college and get a nice education and it's kind of like I am single and I had to help finance their college.

Eleven of the interviewees had children back in the Philippines – some cared for by extended family and others by partners – and providing financial support for these children continues to be the reason for working abroad and in the making of career decisions. Many interviewees talked about how difficult it was to have to leave their children in order to be able to afford a good secondary or tertiary education for them; one participant with young children back home poignantly describes her experience: 'The only regret in my life is the fact that I am minding other people's children, and my own child I cannot mind. This is the hardest part of my life.'

Ireland has not legislated rights for family reunification, and while in practice the procedure has been streamlined over the years, it continues to be determined by ministerial discretion and high income thresholds. Domestic workers living in private homes face additional barriers, as they cannot make applications for family reunification unless they can demonstrate their own place of residence. In two cases, care workers who had given birth in Ireland had no choice but to send the children to the Philippines to be cared for by relatives so that they could continue to work in Ireland. For workers in the care sector, who are often low paid, the cost of living, and particularly childcare, in Ireland makes life as a family impossible, as explained by the quote below:

> I have four children, it's very expensive here. Renting would cost €1,600 a month, I earn only €1,600 and I couldn't work because my children are so small. If I bring them here, I cannot mind them because I would have to work for the bills. If we live and work here it would just be enough for us. It's better to send money.

Some Filipino migrant workers make immense sacrifices to contribute to the upward social mobility of family members at home. Financial remittances may be used to provide private education or to buy property. Although their lives in Ireland may be impoverished, being able to provide for their families at home gives them influence as heads of family from afar. For undocumented workers, the gulf between Ireland and home can be significantly more painful. There are documented cases where migrants have spent more than ten years away from their families. Several interviewees described the sense of providing for their families as the only thing that kept them going. Yet they often missed key events in the life of their children, such as graduation ceremonies and weddings, and the funerals of parents and relatives. These absences put strain on personal and family relationships.

Social isolation, entrapment and precarity

Leah Vosko's conceptualisation of precarious employment is useful to understand the entrapment experienced by care workers in Ireland; this emphasises two elements which affect the position of Filipino migrants in the Irish labour marker.[12] The social context relates to the value put by state and society in the work carried out, and social location relates to the interaction between employment and other social relations, such as gender and citizenship. In the employment of migrant care workers in Ireland we find arrangements typical of precarious work: temporary contracts, low pay, forced self-employment, over-reliance on employment intermediaries such as employment agencies, and part-time and unsecured hours. This work is often carried out under the framework of a precarious migrant status which limits access to social welfare and political rights, and is situated in a context of state divestment from the provision of care, which as a result is devalued.

Filipino care workers who have permanently settled in Ireland experience the consequence of several years of precarious employment: low pay results in income poverty, lack of progression leads to career entrapment, and different expressions of isolation manifest as social exclusion. The prohibitive and rising cost of housing was a recurrent theme discussed with participants: housing costs had always been a significant expense in their monthly budget, but costs have soared since 2015 to reach an all-time high. House ownership was very limited and only two participants owned their house; in order to afford rental costs, most participants had to resort to house-sharing. Even among families with children house-sharing among co-ethnics was common, since this allowed them not only to reduce costs but also to circumvent the growing problem of discrimination in accessing housing. It allowed them to split childcare duties but resulted in reduced contact with the wider community.

This combination of low income and high cost of living as well as financial obligations in the Philippines left very little disposable income; many migrants grew isolated from the communities in which they lived, unable to socialise even after years of living in Ireland. As one participant describes, once she has met her remittance obligations and paid her bills, she has very few options to treat herself: 'right now we are renting our own place, it's very hard. Even during our day off, you know, Filipinos we just go somewhere and order coffee and stay there. After some time we go in and we are told that we are not allowed anymore.'

Access to social protection payments is conditioned by the immigration status of the person. Undocumented workers and those on work permits, for example, are precluded from accessing most payments, which leaves them excluded from important safety nets. Even those who qualify tend to be cautious before applying for payments – they are afraid that it may jeopardise a future citizenship application or visa sponsorship for relatives. This leaves care workers over-reliant on the income secured from their employment, making it harder to leave when they encounter exploitative conditions, especially if they have acquired debt or have dependants:

> It would be difficult for a mother who has children back home to leave, even though she is exploited, she will think first, 'if I leave this job ... what money am I going to send home?' The typical mother is going to sacrifice herself just to gain the money to provide for the children back home, especially if she is the only breadwinner for the family.

Experiences of discrimination in and outside of work are common features of the lives of participants after they arrive in Ireland. Many victims of discrimination at work felt their complaints were not being taken seriously by the management, whom they often described as 'white European' or 'exclusively Irish'. In one case, a carer reported physical abuse by patients to the management but not only was her report ignored, but she was subsequently singled out and harassed by colleagues sympathetic to the patients perpetrating the abuse: 'It was really bad. You just feel you are not from here, just get out of here. It was that type of bullying.' Another care worker in a nursing home described how the management gathered all Filipino workers and told them that the problem with cockroach infestation in the premises was due to them, 'Asians eating their rice all the time.' Sadly, most of these experiences were interiorised and rationalised as being exceptional rather than structural in nature; often perpetrators of aggression were dismissed as being 'just some troublemakers' and incidents went largely unreported, with the victims assuming they just 'had to avoid them'.

Trying to live and belong in Ireland

Despite the hyper-precarity[13] generated by the intersection of precarious employment and precarious migrant status, the story of Filipino workers in the care industry is one of resilience and endurance; from the interviews with participants it became clear that a number of coping strategies were used to counteract exclusion and to minimise or exit precarity.

Mobility in the labour market was perceived as essential in order to access better employment conditions. Workers who were in the Work Permit system had to complete sixty months of legal residency before they could acquire such mobility; in this period workers often had to endure higher risk of exploitation before being 'set free' from work permits and the corresponding dependence on their employer for immigration purposes. Once the workers gained secure residency status, they were able to apply for employment in places which would not accept work permit applications, such as nursing homes and hospitals.

Many of the interviewees had worked at low rates of pay since arriving in Ireland, with thirteen still earning less than the €13.50 living wage threshold. To compensate for the lack of increments and stagnant wages, many relied on additional part-time and casual jobs in their free time to increase their income. These jobs generally included house and office cleaning and childminding, and were paid cash in hand, with typical hourly rates of €12 to €15 free of tax deductions. Participants worked between eight and fifteen additional hours a week on average, but it was not uncommon to hear of workers who also did extra hours during the week, worked seven days a week or had up to three sources of employment. These were risky practices for those still in the work permit system and for undocumented workers: the first were not allowed to work for more than one employer and if found working outside the terms of their immigration conditions could have their permission revoked. For the second group, multiple casual employments paid cash in hand facilitated their anonymity but created greater exposure and the possibility of being detected by the authorities. Needless to say, long working hours limited the ability to participate in activities outside of work, further isolating them from their communities.

The professionalisation of the care industry and the introduction of minimum requirements for the provision of child and elderly care opened up an opportunity for many workers previously employed in private homes to upskill in order to move into institutional care. While none of the participants reskilled out of the care industry or had their qualifications and previous professional experience recognised, many among them acquired professional qualifications. These qualifications were seen as an entry pass to better pay, security and improved working conditions – many participants had a long-term goal of joining HSE-administered care providers where conditions of employment are considered optimal and there is a possibility to contribute to a pension scheme.

Overall, the group demonstrated patterns of integration and assimilation. Among the participants only two had made plans to return to the Philippines in the near future; participants' perception of their own identities reflected the complexities of their lives and the transnational spaces in which their life investments were taking place. The rate of naturalisation among this group of long-term residents in Ireland was very high. While they clearly considered themselves Filipinos, with strong connections to their country of birth and usually frequented Filipino émigré community spaces and gatherings, their Irish citizenship was seen as a reflection of the efforts and contribution they have made to the country. They saw themselves as making important contributions to Irish society. As one interviewee put it:

> just don't discriminate me, you know because I am an immigrant and a carer. Hello I am a carer but I am doing a noble job. You don't want to care for your parents, I was the one caring for your parents so I think I am much better than you.

Many participants discussed plans to retire to the Philippines but two interviewees who had stopped working decided to continue to live in Ireland instead, explaining they found it difficult to readapt to full-time living in the Philippines. Many talked about wanting to spend time between the two countries but emphasised their commitment and belonging to Ireland. Doing so will be particularly difficult for undocumented carers. Many have established employment and community relations in Ireland but are at risk of deportation. For this reason, many have become involved in the Justice for the Undocumented campaign group, advocating for the implementation of a regularisation scheme. With years of separation and unable to visit home or leave Ireland, they have grown to identify as Irish and part of the new Ireland. As one of the campaign leaders eloquently put it:

> We refuse to be invisible any longer. All we need is a chance to fix our situations, just like the Irish undocumented in the US. After ten years working for Irish families and Irish businesses, I'm asking the Irish government – can you see me now?

Filipino care workers have contributed extensively to Irish society by looking after children, the elderly and ill people; yet their stories of integration are tainted with exploitation, exclusion and irregularity. The state's failure to recognise and regulate the care industry's need for migrant labour leaves workers vulnerable to precarious employment. Their experiences in the immigration system have left them at a disadvantage, forcing them to redefine their family relationships and how they interact with the society around them.

Yet the story of Filipino care workers is also one of resilience and commitment to Ireland and the people for whom they care; the high rate of naturalisation is evidence of how Ireland has shaped their own identities and of their intention to remain connected to Ireland. While most of them continue to show strong ties to the Philippines, they also identify as part of modern-day Ireland and are proud of their contributions as carers.

Notes

1 D. Sabenacio Nititham, *Making Home in Diasporic Communities: Transnational Belonging amongst Filipina Migrants* (London: Routledge, 2017), pp. 10–15.

2 F. Fröbel, J. Heinrichs and O. Kreye, *The New International Division of Labour: Structural Unemployment in Industrialised Countries and Industrialisation in Developing Countries* (Cambridge: Cambridge University Press, 1980).

3 S. Christ, '"You are supposed to treat them like your mum and dad": narratives about transnational family lives by middle-class Filipino children', *Journal of Ethnic and Migration Studies*, 43:6 (2017), 902–918.

4 R. S. Parreñas, 'Migrant Filipina domestic workers and the international division of reproductive labor', *Feminist Critical Theory*, 14:4 (2005), 85–101, p. 561.

5 J. Buchan, T. Parkin, J. Sochalski and World Health Organization, *International Nurse Mobility: Trends and Policy Implications*, WHO/EIP/OSD/2003.3 (Geneva: World Health Organization, 2003).

6 Migrant Rights Centre Ireland, *Ireland is Home: Survey and Policy Paper on the Lives of Undocumented Migrants in Ireland* (Dublin: MRCI, 2015).

7 B. Fanning, *Migration and the Making of Ireland* (Dublin: UCD Press, 2018), p. 200.

8 B. Anderson, 'A very private business: exploring the demand for migrant domestic workers', *European Journal of Women's Studies*, 13:3 (2007), 247–264.

9 Migrant Rights Centre Ireland, *Ireland is Home*.

10 Christ, '"You are supposed to treat them like your mum and dad"'.

11 F. V. Aguilar, 'Brother's keeper? Siblingship, overseas migration, and centripetal ethnography in a Philippine village', *Ethnography*, 14:3 (2013), 346–368.

12 L. Vosko, *Precarious Employment: Understanding Labour Market Insecurity in Canada* (Montreal: McGill-Queen's Press, 2006).

13 H. Lewis and L. Waited, 'Asylum, immigration restrictions and exploitation: hyper-precarity as a lens for understanding and tackling forced labour', *Anti-Trafficking Review*, 5:1 (2015), 49–67.

7 Marta Kempny

Polish spaces in a divided city

Polish people currently form the largest ethnic minority in Northern Ireland. Like those in the Republic of Ireland, most Poles currently in Northern Ireland migrated following the accession of Poland to the EU in 2004, peaking around 2006–2008.[1] In this chapter, the experiences of Polish migrants in Northern Ireland are critically examined through social relations in the neighbourhood and migrants' construction of space in the city. The aim of this research was to shed light on everyday experiences of exclusion and inclusion and how the perceptions of Polish settlers have shifted over time. It also endeavours to address the reactions of interviewees to changes in social and political attitudes in the UK in the wake of the Brexit vote.

There are about thirty thousand Polish nationals in Northern Ireland, the majority residing in Belfast. These Polish migrants were usually young adults when they arrived in Northern Ireland, and they have been economically active since the very beginning of their stay. Although migration is not a new phenomenon in Northern Ireland, it has for a long time experienced less inward migration compared with many other parts of the UK. The specific historical context of Northern Ireland, namely the legacies of sectarian conflicts, was mostly unknown to Polish migrants before their arrival. However, sectarian divides within Northern Irish society have affected how Poles have felt included and excluded in local communities.[2]

Belfast is a city entrenched with social divisions, along lines of religion, ethnicity and class. Here, urban spaces have traditionally been polarised between Catholic and Protestant parts.[3] Earlier migrant groups have found themselves unable to avoid identification along neighbourhood sectarian lines in many cases,[4] although they have been largely more mobile within Northern Ireland and the city of Belfast than non-migrants. Polish migrants have settled in a range of different parts of Belfast, but many of them have chosen East Belfast in which to live, due to relatively low rent prices. East Belfast is a traditionally loyalist working-class area and the introduction of Polish Catholics into this Protestant locality adds an additional layer of complexity to the social geographies of Belfast. The housing market thus channels migrants to specific locations that are not necessarily welcoming.[5] North Belfast, too, offers affordable housing prices, in a mixed Protestant/ Catholic part of the city, and is the second preferred option for migrants to settle in. The third most popular location for Polish migrants is South Belfast, mainly the Ormeau Road and Lisburn Road areas. These latter parts of the city are predominantly inhabited by middle-class individuals from mixed ethno-religious backgrounds, and many immigrants choose to reside here. Polish ethnic 'places' (such as grocery shops, bistros and hair-dressers) are readily visible in the urban cartography of North, East and South Belfast, and they are important ways in which claims of migrant belonging are made in the city and Northern Ireland at large. East Belfast in particular can be seen as a Polish enclave, with the largest number of these places of belonging.

Most Poles are Catholic. Yet, paradoxically, West Belfast, a predominantly Catholic area, was viewed by many interviewees as an undesirable area in which to live. This may have been due to the monocultural character of the area, with Poles unwilling to live where there were few other Polish immigrants.[6]

The focus of this chapter is on perceptions of inclusion and exclusion among Polish migrants in Belfast. I draw on longitudinal data from fifteen Polish participants from two waves of data collection in 2008 and 2017, the first involving in-depth interviews, and the latter using interviews with the same informants undertaken while walking around parts of the city that had meaning for them ('walking interviews'). The sample consisted of seven males and eight females who were in their thirties and forties in 2017, maintaining class and gender balance. While half of my interviewees felt that they did not speak English well in 2008, in 2017 all said they had a good grasp of English. At least some had intended to return to Poland in 2008, but all were still in Northern Ireland in 2017.

Despite the fact that the English skills of my interviewees have improved, all of them have remained in the same kinds of job they had in 2008 (mostly blue-collar jobs with some few exceptions, such as a call centre agent, interpreter, clerical assistant and pharmacist). Polish migrants have a very high level of economic activity as a group but structural and economic factors (including the global recession from 2008 and levels of English-language fluency) have prevented many from progressing to better jobs than those they were able to obtain initially.[7]

Longitudinal studies allow social scientists to understand life development and social change as an ongoing process in which structure and agency interact, and in which individuals and cultures are always 'processes of becoming'.[8] They enable researchers to obtain a more nuanced understanding of the complexity of people's worlds and lived experiences, which are contingent and contextually moulded. I built relationships with my participants that continued beyond the field research period. Although this study captured perceptions of respondents at a particular time, it was not possible to ignore changes in the lives of participants in the research that had taken place since they arrived in Northern Ireland. The essence of a longitudinal perspective is one of ongoing contextualisation.[9] A longitudinal perspective enables researchers to go beyond a snapshot of time and grasp the dynamic interplay of temporality, contextuality and relationality.[10] Walking interviews are a research tool that seeks to understand a sense of place as understood by the interviewee. They draw out connections between the body, landscape and memory.[11] During walking interviews I asked my informants to show me around places in Belfast that were significant to them. I invited them to take photos of important sites. I paid attention to the intimate geographies of location (e.g. places of belonging, places of avoidance), to the importance of 'neighbourhood infrastructure' (e.g. shops, cafes, parks, etc.) and to the local geographies of social networks (e.g. neighbours, friends and familiar strangers). Different kinds of mobilities engaging different body rhythms were combined in this research, as some of my informants had cars and drove me to their favourite places, where they parked to take a stroll along areas of Belfast. Interviews were conducted in Polish and were audio recorded. They were then transcribed and translated into English. Particular attention was paid to how the Polish migrants made sense of spaces 'in between', which included streets, alleyways, sidewalks, bus stops, parks and open spaces.

Migrant placemaking

When migrants come to new places in the receiving countries, they engage in the practices of placemaking. In its simplest definition placemaking involves transforming abstract, unfamiliar space into a familiar and meaningful place.[12] In this way, through everyday life practices, new locations become meaningful to their inhabitants and become places.[13] 'Place' in this respect is an analytically powerful concept, as it transforms 'space' understood as a generic idea into 'place' through the actions and experiences of individuals.[14] Place provides a ground through which identity is developed and negotiated. Charles Tilley upholds that 'personal and cultural identity is bound up with place; a topoanalysis is one exploring the creation of self-identity through place. Geographical experience begins in places, reaches out to others through spaces, and creates landscapes or regions for human existence.'[15] Space can be considered as embracing a network of places, which are a combination of a location (the answer to the question 'where?'), a locale (the material setting) and a sense of place (subjective and emotional attachment to place).[16] Social bonds between people in a space might be more important than a bond to a place in people's lives.[17]

This suggests that 'the attachment comes from people and experience, the landscape is the setting'.[18] Placemaking, so understood, can give migrants a sense of belonging to a new community, and deal with alienation, isolation and difference.[19]

Studies of Polish communities in British cities illustrate how they often carve out their own spaces of belonging in multi-ethnic neighbourhoods. Migrants often transplant close and intimate relationships from their home country into their new locations in the UK.[20] Polish nationals often were reunited with family members and close friends in the UK. These transplanted relationships may limit migrants' integration in the longer term.[21] Placemaking may however also equally involve emphasis of ethnic difference and the drawing of rigid boundaries between 'us' (the migrants) and 'them' (local community). Recent Polish migrants in Birmingham have, for example, experienced alienation from earlier Polish community institutions based on ethnic identifications that emphasise Catholicism and have been unable to respond to the diversity of recent migrants.[22]

Existing studies however leave scope for more longitudinal work, particularly focusing on how place might be reconceptualised by migrants over time. This chapter seeks to fill this gap by examining how perspectives of Poles living in diverse environments in Belfast have changed over the course of a decade. In the following sections I shall explore the particular experiences of four female participants, first of sectarian segregation in the city, and then of living in multi-ethnic neighbourhoods.

Inclusive spaces in a segregated city

Belfast's sectarian divisions shape both choices about residency and experiences of placemaking for Polish migrants. A key theme emerging from the interviews in determining insider/outsider status was how participants made sense of those divisions. This was particularly interesting in the case of migrants who lived in North and East Belfast, in the Protestant parts of the city. Migrants' senses of place were in these contexts multifaceted and dynamic, and their accounts offer an insight into the impact of the sectarian divide on day-to-day lives and how this has changed over a decade. Each case is specific and contingent on people's personal circumstances, experiences and life histories.

In what follows I shall contrast two different stories. Ania's walking interview revealed how her perception of Belfast's urban space has changed in a positive way, while Ola's walking interview revealed a shift from positive to negative imaginings of the city.

Ania arrived in Belfast in 2005, and at the time of the first interview in 2008 she was expecting her first child as a single mother. Like many other Polish migrants, she was drawn to affordable private sector housing in East

Belfast, and rented a single room there. She later moved to North Belfast, where she acquired accommodation from the Housing Executive. She is now married to a Polish husband and has two children. She is employed by a pharmaceutical company. She has a wide network of Polish and Northern Irish friends, whom she became acquainted with through her workplace and her daughter's school.

In 2008, Ania told me that she relied on knowledge that other migrants shared about Belfast. Back then, certain perceptions of Belfast circulated among Polish nationals, and for newcomers they often served as cultural repertoires that informed migrants how to navigate the city. East Belfast was twice as popular among this group as North or South Belfast. Ania believed that loyalist areas of the city were exclusive and preferred to stay away from them, but her view has since changed:

> At the beginning when I came here, I believed in different legends. For example I was living in East Belfast and I would stay away from places such as Donegal and Shankill Road. And see now I'm living in Tigers Bay!

Ania stayed away from Donegal and Shankill Road specifically as these were considered unsafe by the Polish community. Collective imaginings of the city strongly influenced Ania's individual choices at that time.

For Ania social networks are important in fostering a sense of community and feelings of belonging to both Poland and Northern Ireland. As we were leaving her house, she pointed at a neighbouring building, saying 'My neighbour Billy worked with me and he is nice. He comes to my house for a cuppa. I have no problem living in North Belfast.' Ania's Protestant neighbour Billy was employed as a cleaner in the pharmaceutical company where she worked. They first knew each other as neighbours and later discovered they worked together. They have since become friends and Ania receives Christmas cards and presents for her children from Billy.

She also has a Polish network in the neighbourhood. 'I have some Polish friends across the street and I used to babysit their children. We meet on different occasions such as birthdays. We went to Funky Monkeys together.' Funky Monkeys is an indoor softplay centre, used by many migrants to hold birthday parties for their children or simply spend afternoons together. These examples highlight the importance of both bridging and bonding capital in migrants' lives. Development of bridging capital relates to maintaining links between individual group members and people from outside the migrant community. It allows migrants to build bridges with the members of the local community and enhance feelings of belonging as insiders to Northern Ireland. Accumulation of bonding capital refers to maintaining relations with the other members of the Polish community, which may make migrants feel more like they are in Poland.

Ania took me for a drive to public parks at Waterworks, Cavehill and Hazelbank that she had come to enjoy visiting. For example, referring to Hazelbank, which is a park situated on the shores of Belfast Lough, she said:

> Where I come from in Poland, there is nothing. The landscape is flat, greyish and gloomy. And here the colours are nice, there is sea. We walk around, or I run. Kids play in the playground. We collect seashells and make mudpies. When it is warm we take a blanket and a basket with some goodies and have a picnic.

Ania's perspective on parts of Belfast, often portrayed as unwelcoming to Polish immigrants, was a positive one. Through their day-to-day experiences and everyday life mobilities migrants like her participate in the production, alteration and creation of the meanings attributed to spaces and places.

There are other aspects to her sense of belonging. Ania has recently applied for a British passport and feels that she is a member of Northern Irish society. She told me, 'I see no difference in my treatment between Protestants and Catholics.' However, Brexit has influenced her political views. Ania, driving past Sinn Fein local governmental election posters, said that she will vote for Sinn Fein because 'I need to take these Protestants down a peg.' She also added, 'I won't vote for the DUP-ę' (*dupę* meaning 'ass' in Polish). Politically, she has identified with Catholic nationalism in Northern Ireland because she has felt treated as an outsider by unionists following the Brexit vote.

Nevertheless, Ania's story documents a shift from negative to positive perceptions of the Protestant parts of the city. Her political leanings (towards Sinn Fein) have not undermined her positive perceptions of predominantly Protestant parts of Belfast. Her political attitudes did not shape her perceptions of Belfast's spaces and places.

Ola's story is different. Whereas in 2006, she considered herself more of an insider to the local community, she now considers herself an outsider. There was a visible shift in her representations of her local neighbourhood in East Belfast, from convivial and welcoming to hostile and segregated.

Ola arrived in Belfast in 2006. She has been employed as a cleaning lady since then and lives with her older son and a Polish friend in East Belfast, in a predominantly loyalist working-class area. Her English is intermediate and she prefers to use Polish interpreters when possible. At the beginning she lived in a street around Woodstock Road and then moved a couple of streets further away.

Ola in 2008 represented East Belfast as a nice place to live, and said that, based on the advice given by other Polish migrants, she would avoid areas such as Shankill and Donegal Road. She took me to the street where she had previously lived, just a couple of blocks away:

> We lived on this street and till this day I speak to these people and have good relations with them. For example there was an elderly man and lady who

lived there and they would knock on our door around 11 at night to ask us if we could help to fix their car. Here it is different. There were working professionals, no one was reliant on benefits.

In her new neighbourhood she has experienced incidents of hate crime, including arson damage to her car, arson attempts on her home and harassment. Police were not able to resolve the issue due to a lack of evidence. Instead, local paramilitary organisations have resolved this problem, in the end forcing Ola's neighbours to move out. East Belfast throughout 2014 and 2015 was the subject of much scrutiny when organised harassment of Polish families and an arson attack on a Polish beauty salon prompted fears about their safety. By 2017 her opinion of the area had thus changed. She said:

> East Belfast is a massacre. Here it is a mix of everything, Protestants, Catholics, people were resettled from Shankill and Donegal. There was a lot of social malaise there and now it is all centred here.

This links back to the point that I made earlier, that often migrants no longer seem to perceive Belfast as simply divided into Catholic/Protestant communities, but include other factors such as social class in the ways they imagine and reimagine their spaces of belonging.

As we walked, Ola took me to places that weren't there in 2008. She showed me two large and well-known Polish food and general stores, Polita and Karolina. These shops are very popular among migrants and constitute spaces of belonging, which play a significant role in creating a sense of 'home away from home'. They are also spaces where migrants can evoke embodied memories of their homeland.

Ola also took me to the local GP practice where a Polish doctor works. As a Polish–English interpreter I had heard of this doctor on many occasions, and it appears that indeed many Poles in East Belfast register with this particular practice to avail of medical services provided by their compatriot. It is clear that a large number of Poles distrust local doctors and when possible get medical treatment back home or, as in this case, seek Polish medical staff, who they believe are more competent or helpful. Ola also showed me a place in East Belfast where her former hairdresser 'Szalone nozyczki' ('Crazy Scissors') used to be. Since the place closed she gets her haircuts in Poland.

Ola's experience illustrates that East Belfast life for Polish migrants is one of both inclusion and exclusion. It is an inclusive social space, as it has accommodated Polish migrants' diverse needs. However, this also leads to creation of areas of self-segregation, consequently contributing to migrants' social exclusion and isolation.

Superdiverse neighbourhoods

South Belfast offers us the opportunity to explore Polish migrants' experiences of multi-ethnic neighbourhoods. South Belfast is the most ethnically diverse part of the city. There are people from black, Asian and minority ethnic groups, Eastern Europeans, people from other European countries such as Spain and Italy, and people from other countries (e.g. USA and Australia). Ethnic shops and restaurants are also readily available in this area of Belfast, and there are a high number of these due to a steady student and visitor population. Although there are lower numbers of Poles living there than in East or North Belfast, it was selected as the site for a new Polish consulate in 2017.

In other British cities, according to Philimore and Pemberton, migrants from countries including Poland which joined the EU in 2004 have reported difficulties living within superdiverse urban environments, as they were not accustomed to visible difference and could not relate to it.[23] They felt they did not fit in within communities with large numbers of black or Asian migrants. Philimore and Pemberton noted tensions between different ethnic groups living in diverse areas. For example, one of their Lithuanian interviewees stated that she had bad experiences with Polish people and a Polish respondent in the same study noted that 'all the Polish people' complainedthat there were a lot of black people.[24] These observations are relevant to this chapter as I noticed similar attitudes among my informants.

According to Philimore and Pemberton, 'super-diverse neighbourhoods are demographically "layered", accommodating both old ("established") and new ("more recently arrived") immigrants from multiple countries of origin, as well as long-standing non-migrant populations'.[25] I shall specifically compare and contrast Ala's and Ewelina's ideas about these contact zones. Ala's and Ewelina's cases present two different ways in which migrants imagine such superdiverse environments. Whereas for Ala South Belfast provides a safety net, where minority cultures can thrive, Ewelina sees South Belfast as too diverse, which made her feel uncomfortable to such an extent that she moved out to North Belfast.

Ala was a PhD graduate in South Belfast who at the time of the city walk lived in the Ormeau Road area. She arrived in the city in 2006 to pursue her career dreams. She is now working as a Polish–English interpreter and teaches a couple of hours a week. She has a Polish husband whom she met in Belfast. She has a couple of Polish friends and several international and Northern Irish friends but still feels isolated from mainstream society. This is mainly due to the nature of her precarious work which makes it difficult to make contacts.

Ala has always lived in South Belfast and never moved to another part of the city. She commented: 'I like South Belfast and I would never move to another part of the city. I wouldn't feel comfortable say in East Belfast or North Belfast. The community here is mixed, you have students, working professionals, some working-class people. I have a friend on Shankill but I'm reluctant to walk there. There are working-class people and may not like foreigners. Same goes for West Belfast.' Her fear restricted her likelihood of exploring the city beyond South Belfast. Ala showed me around her favourite places, emphasising the diverse and multicultural character of South Belfast:

> I like Botanic garden, it is beautiful in the summer time when everything blossoms up. You get a cosmopolitan feel here, think about a Chinese community mural that used to be here, Chinese people practising tai-chi, many Spaniards sitting on the grass on the sunny days, Mela festival.'[26]

She also commented:

> I like Botanic Avenue because you have many small bars and cafes. Many tourists stay here. I feel comfortable here. You have Boojum and Kurrito [ethnic-style restaurants] next to each other, cultural mix and match!

As the walk continued, Ala took me to Asia supermarket, a large store in South Belfast selling mostly Asian foodstuffs, although some Caribbean, Latin American and Eastern European products are also available there. She said,

> Everyone comes here. My Polish friends get chickens here, whereas my Mexican friends used to get chilli here. Although it is supposed to be an Asian supermarket it is readily available to people from diverse ethnic backgrounds.

When in order to probe her level of exposure to other cultures I asked Ala whether she participated in multicultural events in South Belfast, she mentioned that she attended the Mela festival every year, and went to an International Friendship Club's gatherings at a local cafe. South Belfast offers far more opportunities for mixing with a range of ethnic groups than other areas, both at special events and in everyday interactions.

These examples show that for Ala spaces of inclusion encompass super-diverse environments where she is able to mingle with members of other nationalities. This is where she feels comfortable and at ease. She told me that being able to partake in a multi-ethnic society compensates her longing for home.

It is worthwhile mentioning here that Ala has maintained a strong sense of Polishness, despite her exposure to other cultures. As Kymlicka aptly put it, 'That we learn from other cultures, or that we borrow words from other languages, does not mean that we do not still belong to separate societal cultures, or speak different languages.'[27]

Ala expressed her fear that the UK leaving the EU may mean that post-Brexit it becomes less diverse. In this context, she expressed her appreciation towards the Republic of Ireland, and emphasised that she did not exclude moving there in the future. When I asked her why she felt this way, she responded that she wanted to live in an EU country, but also added 'Irish people are more relaxed, this is my impression. They are welcoming towards foreigners. It would be probably easier to live in a country with a Catholic majority.' This is an interesting point, and in my research to date I have come across some individuals who highlighted the links between Poland and Ireland, emphasising the unifying role of religion in migrants' attempts to integrate within the host society. Seen from this angle, Ala can be seen as an outsider within. She considers herself a member of multicultural society but not quite the same as the mainstream society. Due to social isolation, precarious employment and lack of social networks, Ala's perceptions of urban spaces in Belfast remained vastly unchanged since 2008.

Ewelina's experience offers a contrasting perspective. Ewelina is a law graduate who came to Belfast in 2008. She has two daughters and a Polish husband. She originally lived in South Belfast and then moved to North Belfast. Most of her friends are still Polish, although she speaks fluent English. When she moved to Northern Ireland through chain migration, her friends suggested that she stayed in South Belfast, as this is a good area for newcomers. Back in 2008, Ewelina seemed to be happy, just like Ala, in South Belfast, which provided her with a safety net of living in a multi-ethnic environment. She then said 'everyone here is from outside NI, so we are all in the same shoes.' She felt at ease living in a superdiverse context and she pointed to the commonality with members of other ethnic groups, to whom she could relate, given their similar migration experience.

However, since 2008 Ewelina's views have changed significantly. During our city walk, shesaid that she moved from South Belfast to North Belfast to avoid 'overpopulation', saying that she was not used to so many people of colour. She said that Botanic Garden was 'doing her head in':

> Every time I went there I saw these Muslim women sitting on the grass with these cloths over their heads, and could not understand how they could live their lives like this, having time fly through their fingers, just looking after their kids, nothing else. Or look at the Holylands, these Roma Gypsys living together like sardines.

Before Ewelina became pregnant with her first daughter, she and her husband decided to move to North Belfast in order to purchase a house on mortgage. As she recalled:

> 'When we have arrived here we followed other people's advice and settled in South Belfast. But now we were ready to make our own conscious choices. We weren't sure what parts are safe, and where the troubles are, so we asked our estate agent, and he said that this part was quiet.'

Ewelina decided to move out from South Belfast in order to look for new experiences, and was happy to accept advice from a local estate agent rather than fellow migrants. This suggests that as Ewelina felt more secure in Northern Ireland, she started considering herself as more an insider to the local community than members of other ethnic groups. One can see here a visible attempt to draw rigid boundaries based on race. In this sense Ewelina's approach towards multiculturalism is in stark contrast with Ala's attitudes towards 'the other'. It also suggests that there are good reasons why Catholic Polish migrants might choose to assimilate with sectarian unionist traditions across Belfast, becoming less visible within the local population, despite earlier fears about organised racism against them in Protestant areas. There are too emerging projects aimed at cementing common values and traditions between Poles and unionists in Northern Ireland, although anti-racism or intercultural projects have sometimes emphasised militaristic themes popular with loyalists which might be considered exclusive of nationalist communities, such as murals erected on the Shankill Road in 2015 commemorating Second World War Polish pilots who fought with Britain and continuing community workshops on this theme.

Conclusion

The decisions taken by the participants whose experiences were explored in this chapter demonstrate that the experiences of Polish migrants in Belfast are multifaceted and diverse, and the sense of insider/outsider status does not change in a linear way over time. Moreover, people's migration strategies may change over time as they decide to settle down permanently in Northern Ireland. This chapter took a life course/case study-oriented approach to tease out different nuances that exist with regard to processes of migrant inclusion/exclusion in Northern Ireland.

Polish migrants are insiders to the island of Ireland because of their specific situation. Many of them want to remain permanently in Northern Ireland and *nolens volens* they become immersed in the local society. They become immersed in Northern Irish society. They develop friendships with members of the local community. Many migrants have families here and they want to give a sense of local Irish/British belonging to their children.[28] As a result, Polish nationals settle down in different parts of Belfast, in both Catholic and Protestant areas. Whereas in early years post-migration they rely on cultural narratives from their fellow migrants for how they navigate the urban space of Belfast, as they become more insiders to the local community, their ideas about the city are often challenged and contested. Some of them become actively involved in local politics, taking sides in local sectarian traditions and conflicts.

Equally important is the fact that some Polish migrants may prefer to stay within safety nets of culturally diverse environments. They are open to novel cultural experiences and actively engage in various multicultural events, participating in the civic spaces of Belfast. On the other hand, some Polish migrants may consider themselves as more insiders to the local community than members of other ethnic groups, and I have come across instances of racism towards members of other migrant populations. There are also Poles who prefer to settle down in areas of high concentration of their compatriots, such as East Belfast. Sometimes this may lead to social isolation and exclusion where there is very limited contact with members of the local community, leading some Poles to live on the margins of Northern Irish society.

The experiences of Polish migrants in making sense of multi-ethnic neighbourhoods in Belfast cannot be interpreted outside the context of the divided city, but these experiences offer us some understanding of the contexts in which migrants make decisions about their residential mobility within the city. This offers a point of comparison for future studies of Polish migrant decisions about mobility elsewhere on the island of Ireland. It also offers a strong counter-narrative to suggestions that Poles in Northern Ireland might easily decide to move to the Republic post-Brexit.

Notes

1 I. Wardach, *Polish Residents in Belfast: Issues of Discrimination, Safety and Integration* (Belfast: Belfast Integration Project, 2016).
2 M. Kempny, 'Tales from the Borderlands: Polish migrants' representations of the Northern Irish conflict in Belfast', *Space and Culture*, 16:4 (2013), 1–12.
3 M. Svašek, 'Shared history? Polish migrant experiences and the politics of display in Northern Ireland', in K. Burrell (ed.), *Polish Migration to the UK in the 'New' European Union* (Farnham: Ashgate, 2009), pp. 129–149.
4 A. Lee, 'Are you a Catholic Chinese or a Protestant Chinese? Belfast's ethnic minorities and the sectarian divide', *City*, 18:4–5 (2014), 476–487.
5 C. Doyle and R. McAreavey, 'Possibilities for change? Diversity in post-conflict Belfast', *City* 18:4–5 (2014), 466–475.
6 Ibid.
7 Census 2011, 'Ethnicity, identity, language and religion – economic activity by main language', www.ninis2.nisra.gov.uk, accessed 26 January 2019.
8 E. Morawska, 'Studying international migration in the long(er) and short(er) durée', International Migration Institute Working Papers Series 44 (Oxford: International Migration Institute, 2011), p. 6.
9 K. O'Reilly, 'Ethnographic returning, qualitative longitudinal research and the reflexive analysis of social practice' *Sociological Review*, 60 (2012), 518–536, p. 521.
10 L. Ryan and A. D'Angelo, 'Changing times: migrants' social network analysis and the challenges of longitudinal research', *Social Networks*, 53 (2018), 148–158.
11 J. Evans and P. Jones, 'The walking interview: methodology, mobility and place', *Applied Geography*, 31 (2011), 849–858.

12 Yi Fu Tuan, *Space and Place – The Perspective of Experience* (Minneapolis, MN: University of Minnesota Press, 2001).

13 T. Creswell, *Place: A Short Introduction* (Hoboken, NJ: Blackwell Publishing, 2008); J. Rigg, *An Everyday Geography of the Global South* (New York: Routledge, 2007).

14 M. Crang, *Cultural Geography* (New York: Routledge, 1998); D. Massey, *Space, Place and Gender* (Oxford: Polity Press, 1994).

15 C. Tilley, *A Phenomenology of Landscape: Places, Paths, and Monuments* (Oxford: Berg, 1994), p. 15.

16 Cresswell, *Place*.

17 S. M. Low and I. Altman (eds), *Place Attachment* (London: Plenum Press, 1992).

18 R. Riley, 'Attachment to the ordinary landscape', in ibid., p. 19.

19 D. Phillips and D. Robinson, 'Reflections on migration, community, and place', *Population, Space and Place*, 21:5 (2015), 409–420.

20 E. Piętka, 'Encountering forms of co-ethnic relations: Polish community in Glasgow', *Studia Migracyjne – Prezeglad Polonijy Rok*, XXXVII Z.1:139 (2011), 129–152, p. 136.

21 P. Trevena, D. McGhee and S. Heath, 'Location, location? A critical examination of patterns and determinants of internal mobility among post-accession Polish migrants in the UK', *Population, Space and Place*, 19: 6 (2013), 671–687.

22 N. Gill, 'Pathologies of migrant place-making: the case of Polish migrants to the UK', *Environment and Planning A*, 42:5 (2010), 1157–1173.

23 S. Pemberton and J. Phillimore, 'Migrant place-making in super-diverse neighbourhoods: moving beyond ethno-national approaches', *Urban Studies*, 55:4 (2018), 733–750.

24 Ibid., p. 746.

25 Ibid., p. 734.

26 The Mela festival is an annual event celebrating the cultural diversity of Northern Ireland. The *Mela* transforms the park into a garden filled with the sights, sounds and smells of different ethnic minorities in Northern Ireland.

27 W. Kymlicka, *Multicultural Citizenship: A Liberal Theory of Minority Rights* (Oxford: Oxford University Press, 1995), p. 102.

28 M. Kempny, 'Between transnationalism and assimilation: Polish parents' upbringing strategies in Belfast, Northern Ireland', *Social Identities*, 23:3 (2017), 255–270.

8 Teresa Buczkowska and Bríd Ní Chonaill

Experiences of racism in social housing

This chapter focuses on social housing as a particular domain where exclusions of migrants and ethnic minorities are prevalent. Everyone has a right to feel safe[1] in their own home and neighbourhood yet, between 2013 and 2014, there was a noticeable increase in the number of reports of individuals and families in Ireland experiencing racism in housing, either in the home or in its vicinity. While offering insights into immigrants' experience of racism and racially motivated anti-social behaviour in social housing in the Republic of Ireland, it is argued in this chapter that the exclusion immigrants suffer is twofold: the immediate impact of harassment, and the insufficient institutional responses to it.

This chapter draws on research produced for the Immigrant Council of Ireland on the prevalence of racism in social housing, the type and severity of the racism experienced, and the resulting impact on the victims and their families.[2] An overview of the harassment and exclusion that immigrants experience is provided through an analysis of data gathered in 2013 and 2014 by the Immigrant Council's racist incidents support and referral service. The second part of the chapter concentrates on the migrants' responses to those exclusions as well as institutional responses to them. The reactions of local authorities and the Gardaí to the complaints shed light on the factors contributing to victim satisfaction with institutional responses. In addition to analysing policy and practice around racism in social housing, wider influences such as the legislative framework will be considered. It is argued that the limited response constitutes a second layer of exclusion experienced by immigrants suffering racism in social housing.

There is a close correlation between 'having a sense of home' and 'a sense of belonging and connection' and 'integration'.[3] Racism has been identified as one of the factors that impedes the process of integration.[4] The impact of racism is not just an issue for particular ethnic groups but also affects broader community relations with ramifications for integration and social cohesion.[5] The negative repercussions of racist crime feed into people's relationships with one another, particularly when the perpetrators are neighbours, ultimately impacting inclusion, social cohesion and integration. Racism in housing is thus an important area of concern.

In the 2016 Census, social housing units accounted for 8.4 per cent of the total occupied dwellings, with people self-identifying as non-Irish residing in 14 per cent of this housing stock.[6] Preliminary research conducted for the Immigrant Council in 2014 found that most of the reports brought to the organisation's attention were related to incidents at or near home. Within a two-year timeframe, we investigated 54 related cases mostly in the greater Dublin area; a total of 198 people in these households were affected by experiences of racial harassment, intimidation and violence. Of the 54 racist cases some 26 (48 per cent) occurred in social housing estates. A further 16 incidents happened in private rented accommodation and the remaining 12 incidents occurred in accommodation owned by the victims.

The focus of this chapter is on social housing, where support for victims of racism and harassment was potentially 'more accessible' than with respect to other forms of tenure.[7] In accordance with Section 35(3) of the Housing (Miscellaneous Provisions) Act 2009, local authorities are required to develop plans to tackle anti-social behaviour. The Criminal Justice Act 2006 defines anti-social behaviour as: '(a) harassment (b) significant or persistent alarm, distress, fear or intimidation, or (c) significant or persistent impairment of their use or enjoyment of their property'. This legislation provides a framework for responding to anti-social behaviour motivated by racism. However, the research found that victims of racist anti-social behaviour have been left without help, compounding their sense of being an outsider in Irish society.

During the two-year period studied, the largest group found to be experiencing racism in social housing was residents of black African descent (46 per cent), followed by those of Central and Eastern European (24 per cent) and those of Asian (12 per cent) descent. Seven per cent of victims were Roma and another 7 per cent of Muslim background. Four per cent were white Irish settled people who were attacked due to having an ethnic minority family member. In terms of gender, males and females were equally targeted. Of particular concern is the fact that children and young people under eighteen accounted for 42 per cent of the victims of racist harassment and discrimination in social housing. This percentage is five times higher than was found to be the case in other contexts where complaints of racism have been documented in the Republic of Ireland and Northern Ireland.[8]

In all cases where the nationality of the perpetrator could be determined (75 per cent) perpetrators were identified as white Irish. In 25 per cent of incidents the perpetrator was either unknown or only the gender or approximate age could be identified from the victim's or witnesses' description. In the case of racism in housing, perpetrators were easy to identify; most were neighbours of the victims or other people known to them. Children and young people under eighteen account for a significant proportion of the reported perpetrators. This is in keeping with the findings of research undertaken in 2011 on behalf of the Immigrant Council.[9] The fact that children and young people under eighteen are engaging in racially motivated anti-social behaviour in a similar manner to adults is a very worrying trend that merits further research. The data collected by the European Network Against Racism (ENAR) Ireland in the same period once again reflect the findings of this research.

The prevalence, severity and types of racist incident

In 2013, seventeen cases (21 per cent of all racist incidents reported to the Immigrant Council) occurred in housing, with a rise to thirty-seven cases (17 per cent) in 2014.[10] These figures reflect findings elsewhere. In 2015, ENAR Ireland also recorded incidents at or near home as being the highest proportion of reports to iReport.ie, with sixty cases.[11] Racism in housing emerged also as being more serious in nature, involving a higher number of incidents of violence and damage to property. Three categories have been used by the Immigrant Council to categorise cases:

- *Aggravated offences*: instances of verbal or written harassment that would fall under the Prohibition of Incitement to Hatred Act (1989). Any acts of physical violence that inflict injuries as well as property damage are also included in this category.
- *Persistent harassment*: instances of social isolation or other forms of racially motivated harassment that are persistent and prolonged in occurrence (e.g. daily verbal harassment, persistent exclusion from communal life).
- *Single incidents* of verbal and non-verbal harassment that have no criminal element (e.g. name calling, offensive gestures, inappropriate comments).

These categories were applied in this analysis of racially motivated anti-social behaviour in the twenty-six incidents reported in social housing. Comparing the classes of racist incident in social housing with the Immigrant Council's statistics of all racist incidents, Figure 8.1 shows that the percentage of aggravated racist incidents perpetrated on people is far higher in social housing than in the general statistics.

It is possible to further disaggregate the nature of racism in social housing. In these incidents, we use six categories to do so (Figure 8.2). Some incidents contain a range of elements and types of racist harassment, and for that reason there is some overlap between the various categories – for example, an individual who has been subjected to a physical assault could also experience property damage.

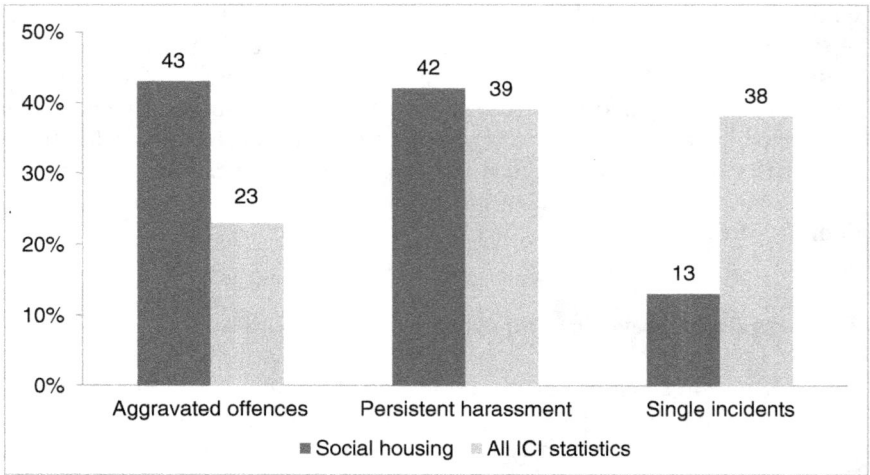

Figure 8.1 Classification of racist incidents reported to the Immigrant Council of Ireland (ICI): all incidents versus social housing incidents for 2013–2014
Source: B. Ní Chonaill and T. Buczkowska, *Taking Racism Seriously: Experiences of Racism and Racially Motivated Anti-Social Behaviour in Social Housing* (Dublin: Immigrant Council of Ireland, 2016).

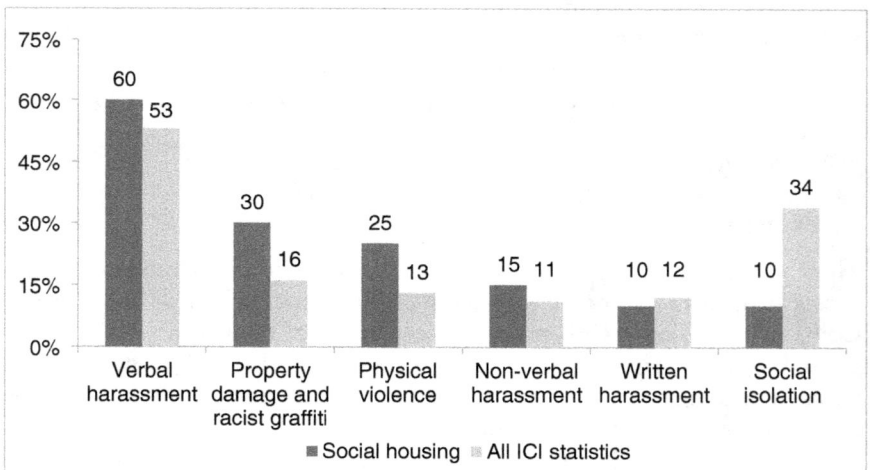

Figure 8.2 Nature of racist incidents in social housing versus all Immigrant Council of Ireland (ICI) statistics of racist incidents for 2013–2014
Source: B. Ní Chonaill and T. Buczkowska, *Taking Racism Seriously: Experiences of Racism and Racially Motivated Anti-Social Behaviour in Social Housing* (Dublin: Immigrant Council of Ireland, 2016).

Verbal harassment was reported by the vast majority of victims. Many stated that it was an everyday occurrence in their lives. Some incidents were very serious, involving threats of violence and even death. While incidents involving verbal harassment may seem to be trivial, incidents like this were repeated every day over a long period of time, having a serious effect on people's quality of life.

Property damage and racist graffiti were reported in one-third of incidents in social housing. In many cases the property damage was extensive or recurring up to eight times a year. People's family homes and their private or work vehicles were subject to vandalism, break-ins, arson and theft. Four victims reported that their house was set on fire. Sixteen families reported broken windows, including one incident where a child's bedroom window was shattered by a stone while the child was sleeping in the room.

Physical violence, which was reported in one-quarter of incidents, ranged from pushing, slapping and spitting to an assault that inflicted injuries which required medical attention. Incidents involving violence were targeted at children and young people under eighteen, and the perpetrators of the violence were both children and adults alike. Physical violence was also directed at victims' family pets.

Non-verbal harassment (15 per cent) rarely occurred on its own; usually it was layered with other forms of abuse. Offensive looks or gestures were frequently documented as part of bullying practices carried out by children. Examples included neighbours throwing bananas into the victim's back garden with their child's name on them (child of mixed Irish and African origin) and deliberate noise pollution (e.g. playing music very loudly).

Written harassment (10 per cent) involved letters or flyers expressing anti-immigrant hostility, some of them containing threats of physical violence and death. A family of Eastern European origin received a letter accusing them of being 'parasites on the welfare system' and ordering them to 'Get out while it's still safe'. A family of mixed Irish and African origin received anonymous text messages with racist content telling them that they 'are not welcomed in the town'.

Social isolation ranged from incidents where neighbours were not replying to greetings or not responding to questions or any attempts to converse, to instances where victims were being excluded from community life. A family of Polish origin reported that their children were the only ones who were not invited to children's birthday parties on the estate. All invitations to their children's birthday parties were also shunned by the residents of the estate.

Comparing the statistics of all racist incidents in Ireland gathered by the Immigrant Council with those in social housing, the latter are distinctive because they contain a higher percentage of property damage and physical violence. People subjected to racist harassment in their local authority housing estates are almost twice as likely to suffer from property damage and physical assault as someone subjected to racist harassment in other social settings.

The impact of racially motivated anti-social behaviour

Racially motivated anti-social behaviour had repercussions for the victims' identity, self-esteem and self-reliance. Most of the Immigrant Council's clients reported the following: sleep disturbance, anxiety attacks, fear of leaving their homes and fear of driving their cars. Many of them were undergoing treatment for depression. Most of the families reported that their children were unable to play outside due to verbal and physical harassment. Two victims reported miscarriages due to stress-related issues prompted by racist abuse. One victim, who was a minor, attempted suicide twice. Due to the abuse that they were experiencing, one family abandoned their house and went to live with relatives, another spent the nights at various friends' homes, only returning to the house during the day, and a third family sent their children to stay with friends in another county until they found different accommodation. These impacts are reflected in the range of contemporary NGO reports on experiences of victims of racist harassment in Ireland.[12]

The fact that immigrants were attacked at their homes, which should be the place where they feel safest, and the fact that the attacks had a racial element intensified the negative experience of the victims, as encapsulated in one participant's words:

> My kids are scared; they do not eat and are crying at night. They are afraid to go outside the house, my son cries and doesn't want to go to the school because he is afraid. This is a horror what is happening here. I'm afraid for my family, my partner is neurotic. I already cannot withstand mentally. I'm afraid that there will come the moment that I go to this group of minors and I start to fight with them, and I do not know how it will end. (Lukasz)

The impact of racism also affects the targeted group to which the victim belongs. As Iganski notes, the targeted individual merely constitutes the 'initial victim', with waves of harm generated spreading beyond the individual victim to others rendered fearful because of the incident.[13] There are repercussions at both the individual and community level. Taylor argues that race-hate crimes also function as 'message crimes', trying to transmit a message around a community, who belongs and who does not, which underlines the idea of immigrants as outsiders.[14]

Finally, among the Immigrant Council's cases studies there were some, albeit limited, examples of positive interactions between neighbours, where the victims received support and advice from their neighbours who referred them to the authorities or community organisations. Of the twenty-three cases of racism in social housing, four were referred to the Immigrant Council's service by concerned neighbours. In a final example of positive social interactions and solidarity, school children set up a Facebook page in support of the child who was suffering racist harassment and abuse in his estate. Recent research in Ireland shows that such interactions significantly reduce the impact on victims.[15]

The response of the local authority

The vast majority of clients (92 per cent) reporting racism and racially motivated anti-social behaviour in social housing came in contact with the Immigrant Council after unsuccessful interaction with the authorities, either their local authority or the Gardaí. They contacted the anti-racist helpline looking for advocacy services to expedite the progress of their case. Their cases show unjustified delays in official responses to their complaints. Zuzanna's family, whose house was burgled and vandalised with racist graffiti inside, complained that they had to stay in their flat for more than a week without touching anything, waiting for the council and insurance company to find the time to come. Other delays were as a result of staff changes within the local authority Housing Department. Zuzanna also reported that over a two-year period her case did not progress because the area manager overseeing her estate changed three times.

There are currently no legal responsibilities on local authorities to address the racist element of anti-social behaviour. Moreover, one solution offered by local authorities, namely a transfer on Exceptional Social Grounds, was also viewed as problematic. A concern raised was that rehousing only moves the victim and does not necessarily go towards addressing the problem. Zuzanna was offered new accommodation by a voluntary housing association and was willing to move but she felt that justice was not done as the perpetrators were not punished. Siobhán, whose son was a victim of racist abuse, was offered an immediate transfer which she declined saying 'Why should I move? I am standing up for my son! We haven't done anything wrong.'

A further complication is the unfeasibility of transfers on Exceptional Social Grounds given the well-documented shortage of social housing.[16] Housing can be viewed through the prism of resource competition theory, as people are in competition for scarce resources, namely an insufficient supply of local authority houses.[17] As interviewees from one local authority explained, someone seeking an Exceptional Social Grounds transfer placed in priority Band 1 on the Transfer List could be waiting more than five years to be rehoused.[18] This may go some way towards explaining why a 2011 study in Dublin found that some victims were 'waiting years for an offer of alternative accommodation from their local authority, all the while living in an environment of racist harassment'.[19]

Garda responses and investigation of complaints

In addition to inadequate responses from local authorities, clients reported a similarly poor response from the Gardaí. This involved delays and dissatisfaction with the investigation of repeated incidents. In the case of Hope's family, she reported four separate incidents over a two-month period, including a house burglary, slashed car tyres, a burned car and a threatening letter. A local Garda told Hope that their job was to confirm to the local authority that the reported incidents of a racist nature occurred. While anti-social behaviour is considered a civil matter and as a breach of a tenancy agreement, there can also be a criminal dimension as defined in the Criminal Justice Act 2006. In Hope's experience, incidents she reported to the Gardaí were not investigated any further, nor indeed were additional racist incidents she brought to the Garda's attention. Her experience was not isolated.

A family who stated that their house was being attacked on a regular basis by local groups of teenagers with stones, glass bottles, iron bars, fireworks and so on also experienced delays. When they reported an ongoing attack to their local Garda station, sometimes it took up to one hour for the patrol car to arrive, long after the perpetrators had fled (Lukasz). In the case of a third family, the everyday verbal harassment and intermittent pelting of their house with eggs, stones, empty cans and glass bottles was not investigated until a stone caused physical injury to one of the family members during an incident (Catalin).

It is important to note that there are examples where the intervention of the Gardaí was very effective in limiting or stopping the attacks. Lukasz and Imoudu both stated that increased patrols in their area significantly reduced the harassment they experienced. Dominika and Tadeusz reported that after the Gardaí cautioned the people responsible for the attacks, the harassment in their cases also decreased significantly. In one particularly successful case, Gardaí communicated regularly with the victims and people involved in the harassment, and a local family resource centre subsequently provided a platform for mediation. The range of interactions with Gardaí documented here are also reflected in the data recorded by ENAR Ireland, noting a particular absence of expertise to address repeat harassment.[20]

Barriers to complaints being taken seriously

A number of factors contribute to inadequate Garda responses to victims' complaints. In the first instance, the weaknesses in Ireland's current legislative structure to combat racial discrimination, which have been highlighted both nationally[21] and internationally, impinge on the Gardaí investigation process. In its concluding observations to Ireland in 2011, the Committee on the Elimination of Racial Discrimination (CERD) recommended that the state should advance current legislation in order to increase protection against racial discrimination.[22] Another shortcoming highlighted by CERD is the legal system's failure to consider race as 'an aggravating factor in a crime'.[23] This may consequently diminish the motivation to concentrate on racism that was experienced by the victims in the investigation by the Gardaí.[24]

Additional factors that compound what victims regard as a limited response on behalf of the authorities include issues around defining and recording racism. From their experiences, the Immigrant Council's clients provided evidence of a lack of knowledge among the Gardaí of what constitutes racism, resulting in inappropriate recording of racist incidents. This has been corroborated by other research.[25] Inappropriate recording leads to underreporting of racist harassment in social housing and therefore the issue is seen as of minimal impact or non-existant. An Eastern European family repeatedly reported instances of verbal harassment and property damage, including swastikas painted on their garden walls, to the local Garda station. While giving a statement after an incident, the family said they believed that they were victims of racism, but the officer said that 'it is not racism because they are not black' (Tadeusz). A similar story of refusal by the authorities to acknowledge the harassment and abuse as racially motivated was reported by a family of African origin. The family believed that they were being targeted because they were the only family in the estate of non-Irish background and they were also the only family experiencing the harassment. However, when they reported their case to the Gardaí, they were told that it is not racism 'just harassment' (Hope). Evident here is the failure of the Gardaí to apply the 2001 definition of a racist incident, which is defined as 'any incident which is perceived to be racist by the victim or any other person'.[26] This has also been identified in other research.[27] Finally, a lack of experience in dealing with racist incidents was also documented. In Siobhán's case, although local Gardaí's response to her complaints was positive, they admitted to her that this was the first time that they had come across something like that and they did not know how to deal with it.

Local authorities defining and recording racist incidents

A lack of understanding of racism was not just restricted to the Gardaí. A recurring feature in cases where victims made complaints of racially motivated harassment and abuse to local authorities was that they felt their complaints were not taken seriously during the investigation. One family suffered for five years from repeated verbal harassment and from physical abuse from children living in their estate; their children were unable to play outside; their toys were damaged or stolen, and the house was pelted with eggs on numerous occasions. The family recalled that when they talked to the area housing manager about their concerns her reaction was to laugh at some of the incidents. Dominika expressed her concerns that a failure to address the situation appropriately could allow it to escalate into something much more serious in the future, especially as the children who were engaging in the harassment got older. In her study on Afrophobia in Ireland, Michael warns of the risk that experiences of repeated harassment reported but not dealt with will become 'normalised in the neighbourhood and in police responses'.[28]

Lack of knowledge is also interconnected with the recording and investigation process. As a number of Immigrant Council clients found, some staff in the local authorities they dealt with did not have basic knowledge about what racism is, and therefore they did not record cases as racist even though the victims were reporting the harassment and abuse as such. A community volunteer stated that she accompanied one victim to an appointment with the community welfare officer. During the meeting it was discovered that out of seven reports that the victim had made to the Housing Department about racist harassment and abuse, only one was recorded in her files as being racist (Amaka).

A significant institutional barrier is that local authorities have adopted an administrative definition of anti-social behaviour that does not include or allow for considerations of racism. A project estate officer from one local authority explained how this impacted on how cases were administered and on how complaints were dealt with: 'If there are any sort of complaints it wouldn't be because it's a racist complaint, it's because it's an anti-social complaint.'[29] The current legal definition gives no incentive to focus on the racially motivated elements of anti-social behaviour complaints.

Furthermore, staff of local authorities are hindered by both a lack of understanding of the nature of racist incidents and the absence of special procedures to deal with incidents of such a nature. There are additionally no established procedures regarding the collection of data to be used as evidence in making a complaint. Different local authorities seemed to require different sets of evidence to prove the case. Amilah, whose family suffered from verbal harassment and property damage, was asked to provide letters from the Garda station confirming that the incidents happened. However, she was also asked to provide a letter from her doctor stating that the harassment was affecting her family's mental wellbeing, as well as providing a letter from her children's school stating that the racial harassment was impacting her children's ability to learn. Dominika, whose family based in the Midlands was harassed in a similar way, was asked to provide evidence without any particular guidelines as to how to collect it and what kind of evidence she should gather.

Conclusion

This chapter has shown that social housing is a site where immigrants experience a double exclusion because of racist harassment and violence. The first layer of social exclusion of members of ethnic minorities from the communities in which they live is the physical experience of racism and racially motivated anti-social behaviour. Victims of racist harassment and abuse in social housing suffer from persistent and prolonged patterns of abuse of a very serious nature. According to Immigrant Council statistics, racism in social housing is characterised by much higher levels of violence and property damage than any other social environment. Additionally, the fact that neighbours or people known to the victims perpetrate the vast majority of the incidents makes the attacks more personal and intensifies the experience of exclusion. Victims are seen as outsiders and targeted in the local authority housing estates where they are living. Victims suffer from mental distress, which influences their development of a sense of belonging to the particular community in which they live and to Irish society.

Ineffective responses by the state and local authorities to the issue of racism in social housing further perpetuate the exclusion which ethnic minorities experience. Currently the social housing sector has no system of policies or practices to effectively address the issue of racism. The lack of appropriate recording mechanisms results in the underreporting of racism and racially motivated anti-social behaviour in social housing, and therefore they are not seen as an issue in the sector. Lack of knowledge of what constitutes racism and a lack of understanding of the issue by local authority employees mean racism is not recognised as a problem. Additionally, the complaint mechanism that housing providers employ to deal with anti-social behaviour and the absence of racism within the legal definition add a further barrier to authorities effectively addressing the issue. The lack of understanding and the undermining of their experience intensify ethnic minorities' feelings of social exclusion and of being an outsider. On a broader societal level, a lack of appropriate response by the Gardaí and ineffective legislation to combat racism further compound the issue.

Local authorities are not merely housing providers. They also play a part in terms of 'sustaining communities',[30] which links into the broader agenda of inclusion, social cohesion and integration. Racism and racially motivated anti-social behaviour impact negatively on relations within communities and the development of 'sustaining communities'. Combating them is necessary due to the negative repercussions for the victims and their families, as has been outlined above. Moreover, both layers of exclusion need to be addressed simultaneously.

While social housing is not the only locus for racism 'at home', it is the type of tenure which is arguably most easily targeted for reduction through expert training, support and strategic partnerships between local authorities and An Garda Síochána, as well as being the responsibility of public sector institutions. The Irish Human Rights and Equality Commission Act 2014 introduced a positive duty on public sector bodies to promote equality and human rights and combat discrimination. Effective implementation of the public sector duty at local authority level is a necessary step in the process. Effort and investment in terms of policies and training are a priority, and initiatives on a local level need to be funded to ensure that people feel 'at home' in their homes and belong to communities without fear of racial harassment and violence.

Notes

1 Participants for the study came from within the Dublin area and outside of it. Pseudonyms are used throughout.
2 B. Ní Chonaill and T. Buczkowska, *Taking Racism Seriously: Experiences of Racism and Racially Motivated Anti-Social Behaviour in Social Housing* (Dublin: Immigrant Council of Ireland, 2016).
3 J. Pillinger, *Making a Home in Ireland: Housing Experiences of Chinese, Indian, Lithuanian and Nigerian Migrants in Blanchardstown* (Dublin: Focus Ireland and the Immigrant Council of Ireland, 2009), pp. 8–9.
4 S. Loyal, *Understanding Immigration in Ireland: State Capital and Labour in a Global Age* (Manchester: Manchester University Press, 2011), p. 254.
5 NASC, The Irish Immigrant Support Centre, *Stop the Silence: A Snapshot of Racism in Cork* (Cork: NASC, The Irish Immigrant Support Centre, 2012), p. 4.
6 CSO Census of Population 2016, 'Profile 1 housing in Ireland', www.cso.ie/en/releasesandpublications/ep/p-cp1hii/cp1hii/od/, accessed 3 February 2019.
7 National Consultative Committee on Racism and Interculturalism, *Building Integrated Neighbourhoods: Towards an Intercultural Approach to Housing Policy and Practice in Ireland* (Dublin: NCCRI, 2008), p. 15.
8 Immigrant Council of Ireland, *PSNI Recording 700% More Racist Incidents than Gardaí* (Dublin: ICI, 2014).
9 B. Fanning, B. Killoran and S. Ní Bhroin, *Taking Racism Seriously: Migrants' Experiences of Violence, Harassment and Anti-Social Behaviour in the Dublin Area* (Dublin: Immigrant Council of Ireland, 2011).
10 Immigrant Council of Ireland, *85% Increase in Racist Incidents* (Dublin: ICI, 2013); Immigrant Council of Ireland, *51% Rise in Reports of Racism during 2014* (Dublin: ICI, 2014).
11 L. Michael and S. O'Curry, *Reports of Racism in Ireland: 7th + 8th Quarterly Reports of iReport.ie, January – June 2015* (Dublin: ENAR Ireland, 2015); L. Michael and S. O'Curry, *Reports of Racism in Ireland: 8th + 9th Quarterly Reports of iReport.ie, July – December 2015* (Dublin: ENAR Ireland, 2016).
12 For example, L. Michael, *Reports of Racism in Ireland 17th + 18th Quarterly Reports of iReport.ie July–December 2017* (Dublin: ENAR Ireland, 2018).
13 P. Iganski, *'Hate Crime' and the City* (Bristol: The Policy Press, 2008), p. 94.

14 S. Taylor, *Responding to Racist Incidents and Racist Crimes in Ireland: An Issue Paper for the Equality Authority* (Dublin: Equality Authority, 2011), p. 41.
15 L. Michael, *Reports of Racism in Ireland: 15th + 16th Quarterly Reports of iReport.ie, January–June 2017* (Dublin: ENAR Ireland, 2018).
16 National Economic and Social Council, *Homeownership and Rental: What Road is Ireland On?* (Dublin: NESC, 2014), p. x.
17 P. Scheepers, M. Gijsberts and M. Coenders, 'Ethnic exclusionism in European countries: public opposition to civil rights for legal migrants as a response to perceived ethnic threat', *European Sociological Review*, 18:1 (2002), 17–34.
18 Ní Chonaill and Buczkowska, *Taking Racism Seriously*, p. 46.
19 Fanning, Killoran and Ní Bhroin, *Taking Racism Seriously*, p. 6.
20 Michael, *15th +16th Quarterly Reports*.
21 For example Taylor, *Responding to Racist Incidents and Racist Crimes in Ireland* and H. Clarke, *Recording Racism in Ireland* (Dublin: The Integration Centre, 2013).
22 Committee on the Elimination of Racial Discrimination (CERD), *Concluding Observation of the Committee on the Elimination of Racial Discrimination Ireland*, CERD/C/IRL/CO/3–4, paragraph no. 15.
23 Ibid. paragraph no. 20.
24 Fanning *et al.*, *Taking Racism Seriously*, p. 6.
25 Taylor *Responding to Racist Incidents*, p. 18 and H. Clarke, *Recording Racism in Ireland*, p. 14.
26 An Garda Síochána, *Your Police Service in Intercultural Ireland* (Dublin: Garda Racial and Intercultural Office, 2002 [PUBIE0196]).
27 J. Carr, *Experiences of Islamophobia: Living with Racism in the Neoliberal Era* (New York: Routledge, 2016), p. 58; Michael, *15th +16th Quarterly Reports*.
28 L. Michael, *Afrophobia in Ireland: Racism against People of African Descent* (Dublin: ENAR Ireland, 2015), p. 12.
29 Ní Chonaill and Buczkowska, *Taking Racism Seriously*, p. 45.
30 Department of the Environment, Heritage and Local Government, *Delivering Homes: Sustaining Communities Statement on Housing Policy* (Dublin: DEHLG, 2007).

Roma rights and racism

This chapter examines the extent to which Roma have their human rights realised in Ireland. It examines, from an intersectional perspective, how the operations, interactions and patterns of subordination, including racism and discrimination based on gender, ethnicity and migrant status, are embedded in institutions, legislation and policy, resulting in the exclusion and marginalisation of Roma. This research is based on interviews conducted by Roma with 108 Roma respondents, who provided information on a further 491 household members as part of a needs assessment.[1] The chapter discusses Roma experiences of discrimination and inequality when accessing public services and in public spaces with a particular focus on Roma women. It argues that 'neutral' policies combined with a legacy of institutional racism across Europe place many Roma in vulnerable situations. A narrow focus on formal equality and a narrative that 'equal treatment is synonymous with the same treatment' is used to legitimise policies that operate to exclude many Roma. Roma are pitched as the 'problem' and blamed for the exclusion they face, which is used to fuel further negative stereotypes about the community.

This research was conducted in response to recommendations set out in an Ombudsman for Children's report into the removal of Roma children from two families in October 2013 by Gardaí (Police).[2] The first removal was sparked by a Facebook message which was sent to a journalist and passed on to the Gardaí:

> Today was on the news the blond child found in Roma Camp in Greece. There is also little girl living in Roma house in Tallaght and she is blond and blue eyes … I am from [country in Eastern Europe] myself and it's a big problem there missing kids. The Romas robing [sic] them to get child benefit in Europe.[3]

Following this a seven-year-old blonde Roma child, who had been born in Ireland, was removed from her home by the Gardaí in Tallaght. She was placed in foster care and was returned to her family after two days when a DNA test disproved the claim that her family were child traffickers. A two-year-old boy in Athlone was also removed from his family following similar accusations and returned the following day after service providers working with the family confirmed his identity. The subsequent Inquiry, undertaken by the Ombudsman for Children, painted a damning picture of the treatment of both families by the state. It found that anti-Roma prejudice had resulted in mistreatment of both families. The actions of the state were found to undermine an already fragile trust with the Roma community.[4] These cases represented a very explicit and public example of the ways in which institutions can act upon ethnic stereotypes. Although the Minister of Justice and Equality at the time accepted all the recommendations of the Inquiry, the recommendations have yet to be implemented in full. However, the high profile of these cases was an impetus to take action in the broader policy sphere that had not been observed before in Ireland.

The historical development of organisations and institutions, and the way in which institutions enshrine dominant discourses around issues such as gender relations, ethnicity, class and conceptions of social justice, can work to produce and reproduce societal inequalities. In this context racism, patriarchy, class oppression and other discriminatory systems are embedded in our societal institutions, which have been developed with dominant groups as the reference point. Analyses of Irish social policy have noted longstanding experiences of differential rights and access to welfare goods and services in Ireland, which were derived from dominant constructions of family, gender roles, ethnicity and social class, and were underpinned by ideologies of nation-building.[5] This pushes those who do not fit with these dominant constructions to the outside. In this context feminist academics have used the concept of 'intersectionality' to analyse and challenge complex patterns of discrimination stemming from the convergence and indivisibility of different structures of oppression.[6] An intersectional analysis can be applied to the situation of Roma in Ireland, who experience racism on the basis of their ethnicity and exclusion based on their migrant status, and who also may experience class oppression and gender inequality, creating a unique experience at the intersections of these structures of oppression. It is important to apply this lens so that the most marginalised within groups are not ignored and so that we can start to unravel, deconstruct and challenge structural patterns of oppression, particularly where they are embedded in state policy.

The Council of Europe estimates that there are 10–12 million Roma in Europe. The term 'Roma' is used as an umbrella term by the Council of Europe to refer to people who identify as 'Roma, Sinti, Kale and related groups in Europe, including Travellers and the Eastern groups (Dom and Lom)'.[7] The Council of Europe notes that the origins of many Roma can be traced back to the Indian subcontinent, which their ancestors left around the tenth century. Today, the majority of Roma live in Central and Eastern Europe, with sizeable Roma minorities in Western Europe. Roma in Europe are a diverse group and vary widely in terms of religion, languages, occupations and ways of living.[8] Although nomadism has been central to Romani history and culture, a majority of Roma are now sedentary, especially in Central and Eastern Europe, where Romani communities were prevented from roaming and forced to be so.[9] Roma remain treated as outsiders in countries where they have had roots for centuries.[10]

A small number of Roma came to Ireland as seasonal workers in the 1990s and a number of Roma also sought asylum.[11] Following the Enlargement of the European Union in 2004, further Roma arrived in Ireland. By 2007 they had formally acquired the same rights and entitlements to work, mobility and to reciprocal accesses to social protection as migrants from other EU member states, although Ireland did not remove the requirement for work permits for Romanians until 2012.[12] The majority of the estimated 5,000 Roma in Ireland came from Romania but some had also previously lived in a number of other new EU member states including Slovakia, Czech Republic, Poland and Hungary.[13] The Roma in Ireland tend to live in multi-generational households.[14] The experience of Roma in Ireland is diverse. There are Roma living in extreme poverty, with some living in cars and in abandoned buildings; there are also Roma completing school, attending third-level education, working in a range of occupations and even, in one case, joining the Garda Síochána.[15]

The 2018 needs assessment conducted by the Pavee Point Traveller and Roma Centre mapped some 4,200 of those Roma living in the Republic of Ireland. It found that the majority of children (63 per cent) in Roma households were born in Ireland. Over half of all Roma children were Irish citizens.[16] Most came to Ireland to escape persecution, to improve their financial circumstances or to improve the lives of their children. As one respondent put it: 'we came from very bad financial situation ... and came here because we hoped that our children would be better off here.'[17] This echoed a focus group in another study: 'I came from Slovakia to escape from racism and discrimination and to stop living in poverty – to have a better life in Ireland.'[18] Another stated: 'We didn't have a nice life in Romania because we were persecuted by the Romanian government.'[19]

UN human rights bodies have raised serious concerns in relation to the human rights of Roma in Ireland. The UN Committee on the Rights of the Child expressed concern about the 'structural discrimination against Traveller and Roma children and their families' and disproportionate numbers of Roma living in poverty.[20] The UN Committee on the Elimination of Discrimination Against Women noted concern with the low level of participation of Roma in public and political life and the lack of access to child benefit payments for some Roma women.[21] If one considers the conclusions of such human rights bodies as indicative of outsider or insider status, then the Roma are outsiders in Irish society.

Legislative and policy contexts

Until recently Roma have been largely absent from national policy documents in Ireland and the most prevalent intervention by the state was 'voluntary repatriation', whereby Roma would be given a flight back to the country from which they came. Since 2007, most Roma have had the right to move freely and live within the European Union. However, this right is subject to conditions which are set out in the European Communities (Free Movement of Persons) Regulations 2015 which transpose the European Union Free Movement Directive into Irish law.[22] Under the Directive every EU citizen has a right of residence if they are a) workers or are self-employed; b) have sufficient resources not to become a 'burden' on the social assistance system and have comprehensive sickness insurance; or c) are enrolled in a private/public establishment for the purpose of study, have sickness insurance and have resources so that they or their family members will not become a 'burden' on the social assistance system. These criteria have been interpreted in a manner which has discriminated against Roma in Ireland by deeming them not to be entitled to social assistance.

More positively, there has been a drive by the European Commission to push all member states to develop National Roma Integration Strategies.[23] In response to such demands, and in response to activism by Irish-based non-governmental organisations, Roma have been included in the remit of national policies aimed at supporting children and young people,[24] and in the National Strategy for Women and Girls 2017–2020.[25] The most significant policy changehas been the development of the National Traveller and Roma Inclusion Strategy 2017–2021. This emerged in response tothe European Commission's 'EU Framework for National Roma Integration Strategies up to 2020' and the Council Recommendation on Effective Roma Integration Measures.[26] This represents the first national Strategy that has emphasised actions to promote Roma inclusion across government departments, with the exception of housing – an area of considerable need – where there are no Roma-focused actions. The Strategy has the potential to improve the situation of Travellers and Roma in Ireland, if implemented. However, to have a real impact in the Roma community, these actions will need commitment from government departments and to be backed by funding. The European Commission has pointed to the need for impact indicators, timeframes, budget and a rigorous monitoring and evaluation framework, in order to ensure effective implementation. None of this currently exists.[27] Also, the reality of the impact of the right to reside policy on many Roma means that state policies of inclusion will be hampered by another arm of the state, and this will need to be addressed.

Poverty and substandard housing

The 2018 Roma Needs Assessment revealed that around 20 per cent of respondents are completely marginalised from services and are experiencing extreme poverty. Over 10 per cent of respondents had no kitchen, no fridge or bathroom in their accommodation. There were reports of people living with no food, gas, electricity or water. One respondent reported living from discarded food from supermarkets and shops.[28] Overcrowding was identified as a major concern, with 44.8 per cent of respondents reporting that they did not have enough beds in their accommodation. Rat-infested housing was regularly reported throughout the research. 36.6 per cent of respondents reported that they had no tenancy agreement, leaving them vulnerable to eviction with no notice, and which means they have no documentation to prove where they have been living.[29] Time spent in the country did not automatically increase inclusion. For example, a forty-two-year-old woman who had lived in Ireland for nineteen years reported the following:

> My husband and I live with my son, his wife and five kids and my youngest child in a two bed apartment. We have been living here for six years, I sleep in the living room on the floor, in the same room is the kitchen, the dining room, sitting room and bedroom. It is very hard for me to get rent for myself.[30]

Roma respondents spoke regularly about feeling hopeless: 'hard life, very hard, but I don't know what to do, where to go, I am hopeless, please help me, help the Roma'.[31] For people in these situations there is little option but to engage in begging, for which many Roma are criminalised and imprisoned or receive fines. Seventeen per cent of adults across households said they begged to survive; a further 14 per cent said they had no income. Children from 25 per cent of households included in the research had gone to school hungry. Service providers have identified cases of Roma children who are malnourished.[32]

Such poverty itself acts as a major barrier to engaging with service providers. Public health nurses in particular report that they can find it difficult to access families with new-born babies. This is reflected in the following assertion by a Roma woman:

> We live at the moment in a house with no electricity, no gas and no facilities. I am afraid to go to authority. They can do bad things to my family. I have three children. I live from what we beg.[33]

A major fear among the Roma community in Ireland is that their children will be taken into care due to poor living conditions. This fear is rooted in

the experience of Roma children across Eastern Europe who are overrepresented in institutional care settings and who have in some cases been
removed from their families solely on the basis of economic or social conditions.[34] The cases described earlier of Roma children from Tallaght and
Athlone being forcibly removed from their families by the Gardaí have
exacerbated fear within the Roma community in Ireland of dealing with
the Gardaí, social workers and other service providers.

Employment and social protection

A key factor in this experience of poverty is a lack of access to employment.
Only 16.7 per cent of respondents in the Roma Needs Assessment reported
being in employment. 78.9 per cent of respondents reported feeling discriminated against in getting hired or getting a job. One man reported,
'When I was looking for a job, I asked for the boss and I was told that he
was not in and the staff was laughing at me.' Some respondents who were
in employment reported hiding their identity in order to secure and keep
employment. Women identified their own particular experiences with economic exclusion. Roma women in focus groups have reported that they are
often refused access to shops and stated, 'How can we get a job if we are
not even allowed in the shop?' Others said, 'When some people see us – they
just see our skirts and not us as women.'[35] The Big Issue was identified as
an important lifeline for some respondents. In some cases there were reports
of Big Issue sellers being victims of abuse and harassment, while in others
it led to positive relationships with service providers and the general public.
Some sellers were reported to have regular pitches and customers, and also
helped people with other tasks, such as helping to carry bags and return
shopping trollies.
      Many Roma have worked informally and so have not built up a formal
employment record. This is compounded for women who in the majority
of cases are taking on caring roles for children, which is not considered
formal work. Poorer women are more likely to work informally, or to beg
to survive, and they also are more likely than men to take on caring duties,
alongside this informal work. This lack of formal work record negatively
affects a person's ability to prove a connection with the Irish state, and to
claim basic support services such as child benefit. This lack of work record
also affects people who become homeless, as without employment or an
employment record they are unable to access social housing services. This
is outlined in a 2012 Department of Environment, Community and Local
Government circular setting out criteria for access to social housing for
non-Irish citizen migrants from EEA countries. These can only be considered for assessment if: '(1) they are in employment/self-employed in the
State; or (2) where they are not currently working/employed it is because

– they are temporarily unable to work because of illness/accident; they are recorded as involuntarily unemployed after having been employed for longer than a year, and they are registered as a job-seeker with the Department of Social Protection'.[36] This means the most vulnerable Roma who are homeless and do not have employment are left completely outside state supports. This policy pushes the most vulnerable Roma to the extreme margins of Irish society.

Along with meeting the right to reside, applicants for social protection benefits must also meet the criteria of the habitual residence condition, in order to access non-contributory benefits, including supplementary welfare allowance, child benefit, job seekers allowance and access to some employment and training supports, such as community employment. The habitual residence test is defined as 'meaning that a person has been here for some time, from a date in the past, and is intending to stay for a period into the foreseeable future. It implies a close association between the applicant and the country from which payment is claimed and relies heavily on fact.'[37] As with the right to reside, this has a particular impact on Roma. Failure to meet these requirements is a key reason for Roma living in extreme poverty in Ireland.

The first two aspects of the test consider the length of time you have been in the state and any absences. There are Roma who have lived in the state for years and cannot prove this. This lack of documentation is related to not having a tenancy agreement and in some cases fear of giving an address in case it results in eviction of all the tenants (in cases where people are living in overcrowded accommodation). Understanding documentation also emerged as an issue, as 71 per cent of respondents reported that they had difficulty reading English forms.

Given the low education levels reported, it is likely that a large number of respondents have poor literacy in their first language, along with challenges in English literacy. The other aspect to the habitual test is a formal work record, something that Roma often do not have. The deciding officers will also consider 'the person's main centre of interest', which could include whether close family is living with them, location of bank accounts, whether they have bought a house, and so on. The most marginalised Roma tend to have less administrative proof of living (and intention to remain) in the state. Pavee Point has come across cases where parents have applied for child benefit, their children have been attending school for several years and yet they have been told that they are not habitually resident. In this context the United Nations Committee on the Rights of the Child has recommended that the Irish state makes child benefit payments a universal payment that is not contingent on the fulfilment of the Habitual Residence Condition.[38]

The Roma Needs Assessment showed that 48.1 per cent of respondents were not successful in their social protection applications. Yet across households 47.3 per cent of respondents were reported as being habitually resident.[39] This suggests that approximately half of respondents could meet the criteria to access social protection payments. This ability to access some supports has been identified as extremely important to escape extreme poverty, to send children to school, to access training and to become increasingly included in Irish society.

Education

The experience of Roma in Irish state education is a key factor in shaping future employment opportunities. Systematic and structural discrimination against Roma in education across Europe is well documented, with Roma being placed into segregated and substandard schools or segregated within classrooms, and poverty acting as a barrier to school completion.[40] Therefore Roma adults who have migrated to Ireland may have had very limited or negative experiences in education. This was identified as a key concern by Roma in the Roma Needs Assessment. One respondent said, 'What I would like to change, lots of adults have no schooling, we need classes for people to learn, write and other skills.'[41] The lack of education was particularly exacerbated for Roma women; 41.1 per cent of Roma women had never been to school, in comparison to 22 per cent of Roma men.[42] The findings show gendered educational disadvantage, with Roma women facing a more widespread exclusion from education than Roma men. Given the links between poverty and a lack of education in Romania, it is most likely that these women have also come from situations of poverty. The ability of these Roma adults to immediately access formal employment when moving to another country is negatively affected by their experiences of education and varying literacy skills.

Despite their own poor experiences of education, many Roma adults felt that education offered great opportunities for their children, and service providers reported that families living in extreme poverty were still managing to send their children to school. However, there were reports of children going to school without adequate lunches (35 per cent of households) and in nearly 60 per cent of households respondents reported not having enough money for books and uniforms. Service providers did report issues with attendance and attainment levels of some Roma children, and the educational level and low literacy levels of parents were noted as a disadvantage in supporting their children in school.[43] The Roma Needs Assessment also reported that some children hide their Roma identity in school to protect against bullying and discrimination. One woman spoke about being taunted at school by being called 'gypsy'. Another respondent reported hearing a teacher refer to a Roma family 'as just here to get welfare'.[44] Nonetheless, in 6 per cent of households there was a person attending third-level education.[45] Education was posited as a place that offered opportunities for young

Roma. A deeper understanding is needed of Roma children's experiences in education. Ethnic data collection in primary and secondary schools and the use of such data for ethnic equality monitoring are crucial in this regard.

Discrimination

The 2015 Needs Assessment documented multiple experiences of racism, with over 80 per cent of respondents being discriminated against in the street or in public, including being shouted at and told to 'Go back to your own country'. Respondents reported feeling excluded because of this. 'Ireland is my home but I feel excluded, I don't know how to read or write very well. It is very hard to find work. People are looking down on us because we are Roma.' Women in particular spoke of being targeted due to their dress –, one woman said 'I would not dress in Roma [now] because we get treated badly, followed and discriminated against.'[46] It was also reported that those who had poor literacy and English experienced a higher level of discrimination, pointing to the intersection of ethnicity with other factors, such as socio-economic status and gender. One respondent said 'it's very bad because they do big discrimination for people who no reading and writing and about my clothes'.[47] Despite the layers of structural oppression that these Roma face, they are pitched as a 'problem' and blamed for the exclusion they face, which is used to fuel further negative stereotypes about the community at large.

The portrayal of Roma as outsiders has been prevalent in some Irish and international media outlets. The Logan Report noted that 'a number of media outlets report on Roma and Travellers only in the context of social problems and crime'.[48] These stereotypes are reflected in documented comments about Roma in Ireland on social media, such as '[it] makes me sick that people like that are living in Ireland on benefits and we had to leave the country to make a living' and 'the very reason we need to vote for a Brexit, thieving migrant scumbags'. Social media comments against Roma sometimes promote extreme racist actions, including 'petrol bomb them all' and 'Just resurrect Hitler for a few days he will get the job done...'.[49] Roma also report experiencing hate crime. In 2017 Pavee Point documented a complaint by a woman who was begging outside a shop and had a bucket of water thrown over her by a shop employee and in 2018 a Roma woman reported that she had been harassed by a group calling her 'gypsy' who later burnt her car out in her driveway. Reporting of hate crime by Roma is low, for many of the same reasons as other marginalised groups, including trust, access to reporting, trauma of reporting and lack of knowledge about reporting systems.[50]

Despite these experiences, interviews with Roma revealed resilience and strength. People in the community, often with very little resources, support each other.[51] This is also the experience observed in Pavee Point, whereby people who are surviving through begging and who are living in extreme poverty support each other. For some, the church is a source of community and a space where Roma can gather in a positive shared space. The Roma Needs Assessment suggested a complicated picture of negotiating identity and inclusion among Roma, with experiences of hiding identity in certain situations but also showing strong pride in their Roma identity in others. In a focus group in Pavee Point speaking about the difference between different generations of Roma, a young Roma man spoke about the common bond that Roma from all different countries have: 'we have a connection and there is a lot of pride in our community. I like the way we treat each other in the Roma community.' An older Roma woman concluded 'I see lots of change in our community – everybody is changing, but we are still Roma.'

Conclusion

As a community Roma have experienced intergenerational racism and are experiencing racism in Irish society, along with a failure of the state to adequately address their experiences as outsiders. The state reinforces their outsider status through the implementation of legislation and policies that exclude those who do not have the status of workers. The removal of Roma children into care, on the basis of their appearance, also demonstrates how stereotypes inform institutional behaviour. The experiences of Roma have strong parallels with the experiences of Irish Travellers, and so along with the status of migrants Roma experience a deep racism rooted in centuries of stereotypes of nomadic peoples. The section above shows how Roma face inequalities based on ethnicity and migrant status, but also along the lines of gender and socio-economic status.

The legislation and policy outlined above apply to all EU citizens, and in this way they are posited as neutral policies. However, the educational opportunities and secure living situations needed to access the formal work-force have not been available to many Roma, particularly those who have come from situations of poverty and particularly to Roma women, due to structural discrimination, and this operates alongside a pervasive anti-Roma racism in wider Irish society. It is within this context that some Roma live, caught perpetually outside the system. They cannot get the formal employment needed to enter it and cannot access the supports to gain employment. If living outside the system without documentation to prove residence, they can live in Ireland for many years without any change in their status. It is these Roma that are caught in the centre of intersecting structures of oppression.

This does not mean that all Roma are negatively affected by these policies. The Roma Needs Assessment documents positive experience of Roma in work, in training and in third-level education. An intersectional analysis allows us to demonstrate that while not all Roma are affected, nor are policies explicitly discriminatory on the basis of class or gender, their effect is not neutral because of their impact on those who are Roma and also have a particular gender identity and class position.[52]

Discrimination can be direct or indirect and is not always conscious. An understanding of this requires institutional attention to the impact of policies and practice. A narrow focus on formal equality and a narrative that 'equal treatment is synonymous with the same treatment' is used to legitimise policies that operate to exclude many Roma. It is clear that 'equal treatment' in the guise of formal equality is insufficient with regard to Roma who have experienced intersecting structural inequalities. The extent to which treating differentially situated people the same is inadequate is perhaps best captured by the UN Committee on the Elimination of Racial Discrimination when it states

> To treat in an equal manner persons or groups whose situations are objectively different will constitute discrimination in effect, as will the unequal treatment of persons whose situations are objectively the same.[53]

The impact of the exclusion faced by Roma in Ireland is starkly shown in the findings on poverty in the Roma Needs Assessment. This fuels negative stereotypes about Roma and can foster poor policy responses. As Matache notes, while Roma integration has become a comfortable topic to include in policy documents, anti-Roma racism has continued to be ignored. She asks us to consider the Romani child who is pushed to give up school:

> It is all too easy to read that child's situation as a result of the Roma placing less cultural value on education, and to disregard the possibility of exclusion. As a result, in several countries the primary focus is on targeting Romani culture and Romani families in efforts to ensure that Romani children enrol in school; little effort is made to change the unwelcoming school environment. It is apparently more convenient to focus efforts on integrating the oppressed than to work on dismantling discriminatory behaviours and actions by the oppressor.[54]

Despite the resultant exclusion from services and extreme poverty that Roma in Ireland can face, the policy response in Ireland has been very limited. New policy commitments that specifically aim towards Roma inclusion are welcome, although the potential for policies in different spheres to be working against each other exists. It is crucial to acknowledge systematic structural inequalities and to institutionalise substantive equality in order to progress Roma rights in Ireland. Existing state legislation and policy operate to exclude Roma, and ultimately following the guidance of UN Committee on the Elimination of Racial Discrimination and adopting special measures to promote Roma inclusion is vital.

Notes

1 Pavee Point Traveller and Roma Centre & Department of Justice and Equality, *Roma in Ireland – A National Needs Assessment* (Dublin: Pavee Point Traveller and Roma Centre & Department of Justice and Equality, 2018), p. 45.
2 Emily Logan, *Garda Sóchána Act 2015* (Section 42) *Special Inquiries relating to Garda Síochána Order 13* (Dublin: Ombudsman for Children, 2014).
3 Ibid., p. 65.
4 Ibid., para. 4.1.1.
5 B. Fanning, 'The construction of Irish social policy 1953–2003', in M. Peillon and M. P. Corcoran (eds), *Place and Non-Place – The Reconfiguration of Ireland* (Dublin: Institute for Public Administration, 2014).
6 L. McCall, 'The complexity of intersectionality', *Signs*, 30:3 (2005), 177–180.
7 Council of Europe, 'Descriptive glossary of terms relating to Roma issues', version dated 18 May 2012 (Strasbourg: Council of Europe Publishing, 2012), p. 4.
8 Commissioner for Human Rights of the Council of Europe, *Human Rights of Roma and Travellers in Europe* (Strasbourg: Council of Europe Publishing, 2012), p. 31.
9 OSCE High Commissioner on National Minorities, *Report on the Situation of Roma and Sinti in the OSCE Area* (The Hague: OSCE, 2000), p. 101.
10 Ibid., p. 20.
11 Roma Support Group and Pavee Point Traveller Centre, *Roma in Ireland: An Initial Needs Assessment* (Dublin: Pavee Point Traveller Centre, 2002), p. 11; A. Beesley, 'Government ends restrictions on hiring Romanians and Bulgarians', *Irish Times*, 21 July 2012.
12 B. Fanning, *Migration and the Making of Ireland* (Dublin: UCD Press, 2018), pp. 215–208.
13 R. Fay, *Irish Travellers and Roma: Shadow Report: A Response to Ireland's Third and Fourth Report on the International Convention on the Elimination of All Forms of Racism (CERD)* (Dublin: Pavee Point, 2011), pp. 36; Pavee Point Traveller and Roma Centre & Department of Justice and Equality, *Roma in Ireland*.
14 L. Lesovitch, *Roma Educational Needs in Ireland: Context and Challenges* (Dublin: City of Dublin Vocational Educational Committee, 2005), p. 23.
15 Fanning, *Migration and the Making of Ireland*, p. 208.
16 Pavee Point Traveller and Roma Centre & Department of Justice and Equality, *Roma in Ireland*, pp. 42–44.
17 Ibid., p. 44.
18 Quote from *Roma: One People – Many Lives* (Dublin: Equality Authority, Pavee Point Traveller and Roma Centre and NASC, 2014).
19 Ibid.
20 United Nations Committee on the Rights of the Child, 'Concluding observations on the combined third and fourth periodic reports of Ireland' (2016) CRC/C/IRL/CO/3–4.
21 Committee on the Elimination of Discrimination against Women, 'Concluding observations on the combined sixth and seventh periodic reports of Ireland' (2017) CEDAW/C/IRL/CO/6–7.

22 Directive 2004/38/EC of the European Parliament and of the Council of 29 April 2004 on the right of citizens of the Union and their family members to move and reside freely within the territory of the Member States (2004) OJ L158, 78.

23 European Commission, 'An EU framework for national Roma integration strategies up to 2020' (2011) COM(2011) 173 final.

24 Department of Children and Youth Affairs, *Better Outcomes, Brighter Futures – The National Policy Framework for Children & Young People 2014 – 2020* (2014).

25 Department of Justice and Equality, *National Strategy for Women and Girls 2017–2020: Creating a Better Society for All, 2017 – 2020* (2017).

26 Council of the European Union, 'Council recommendation of 9 December 2013 on effective Roma integration measures in the Member States' (2013) 2013/C 378/01.

27 European Commission, *Assessing the Implementation of the EU Framework for National Roma Integration Strategies and the Council Recommendation on Effective Roma Integration Measures in the Member States* (2016) COM (2016) 424, 64.

28 Pavee Point Traveller and Roma Centre & Department of Justice and Equality, *Roma in Ireland*, p. 62.

29 Ibid., p. 87.

30 Ibid., p. 88.

31 Ibid., p. 61.

32 Ibid., p. 61.

33 Ibid., p. 63.

34 Commissioner for Human Rights of the Council of Europe, *Human Rights of Roma and Travellers in Europe* (Strasbourg: Council of Europe Publishing, 2012), p. 16.

35 Roma focus group as part of the project 'Roma: One People – Many Lives' undertaken by the Equality Authority, Pavee Point Traveller and Roma Centre and NASC in 2013/2014.

36 Department of Environment, Community and Local Government, 'Access to social housing supports for non-Irish nationals – including clarification re Stamp 4 holders' (2012) Housing Circular 41/2012.

37 www.welfare.ie/en/Pages/Habitual-Residence-Condition–Guidelines-for-Deciding-Offic.aspx

38 United Nations Committee on the Rights of the Child, 'Concluding observations on the combined third and fourth periodic reports of Ireland'.

39 Ibid., p. 77.

40 L. Farkas, *Report on Discrimination of Roma Children in Education* (Belgium: European Commission, 2014).

41 Pavee Point Traveller and Roma Centre & Department of Justice and Equality, *Roma in Ireland*, p. 75.

42 Ibid., p. 70.

43 Ibid., pp. 110–115.

44 Ibid., p. 53.

45 Ibid., p. 110.

46 Ibid., p. 53.

47 Ibid., p. 51.

48 Logan, *Special Inquiries*, para. 4.2.8.
49 Documented comments on Facebook by Pavee Point Traveller and Roma Centre.
50 L. Michael, *Reports of Racism in Ireland: 15th+16th Quarterly Reports of iReport.ie, January–June 2017* (Dublin: ENAR Ireland, 2018).
51 Pavee Point Traveller and Roma Centre & Department of Justice and Equality, *Roma in Ireland*, p. 92.
52 K. Crenshaw, 'Demarginalizing the intersection of race and sex: a Black feminist critique of antidiscrimination doctrine, feminist theory and antiracist politics', *University of Chicago Legal Forum*, 139 (1989), 139.
53 United Nations Committee on the Elimination of Racial Discrimination, 'General Recommendation no. 32, the meaning and scope of special measures in the International Convention on the Elimination of All Forms [of] Racial Discrimination' (2009) CERD/C/GC/32, 3.
54 Pavee Point Traveller and Roma Centre & Department of Justice and Equality, *Roma in Ireland*, p. 3.

Normalising racism in the Irish media

The role of media in facilitating or hindering integration is often underestimated, or at best, narrowly imagined. Racist discourses produced in national and local news media indicate and often encourage hostility towards migrants. Moreover, their reading by migrants is part of the context for decision-making post-migration, of housing, education and employment, of safety and rights. For the children of migrants in particular, racist discourses which define them as 'outsiders' present a significant barrier to developing a strong sense of belonging. However, the role of media goes further still than that. Racism in the media speaks to the biases of the host society, but also to the ways in which racism gains currency or is combated in the public sphere. This chapter explores how Irish media outlets are facilitating and promoting the normalisation of racist discourses, and the implications of this for the construction of debates which take seriously the challenges of integration in practice and in the context of growing anti-immigrant racism.

A small and highly visible range of columnists in the largest Irish newspapers regularly vilify Muslims, Roma and Travellers, particularly drawing on ideas of barbarism, cultural genocide and population control, and defiantly testing the legal limits of incitement to hatred. However, changes in Irish media have been evident since 2008, with a growth (if slow) of ethnic minority and migrant representation in media, an increasing diversity of voices (although still predominantly in the community broadcasting sector) and even, since 2014, critical coverage of the Direct Provision system. Comparison with UK news media suggests milder and more nuanced forms of racist speech in Ireland.

Yet there are evident connections between racist discourses in Irish media and violence against migrants and ethnic minorities. In 2016, vigilante violence against Roma was preceded by regular publication of anti-Roma articles in the mainstream media. There is evidence of a documented rise in both racist speech and violence in Ireland after coverage of the racist election campaign of Donald Trump as President of the United States and the anti-immigration sentiment of the Brexit referendum in the UK. There are questions to be asked about the influence of far-right discourses on Irish media in this context. Not only do media discourses allow us to trace the emergence and reproduction of racist ideas in the public sphere, but they also operate to produce new and adapted forms of racist expression and, moreover, to offer the accounts of migrant integration most widely used in public debate. As such, they form an important part of the investigation undertaken in this book.

Regulation of racist publications

Racist publication is governed both through legislation and regulatory bodies. At an international level, this is contained within the governance of hate speech. The presently accepted definition of hate speech in European institutions is designed to protect minority groups from the damage which follows both direct incitement to hatred and indirect consequences of stereotyping and dehumanisation of such groups, and has been used by members to support the prosecution of media outlets which publish hate speech. Between 2014 and 2016 there were numerous rulings on media content across EU member states, including Bulgaria, the Czech Republic, Italy, the Netherlands, Poland and Romania, which recognised incitement against ethnic and national minorities.[1] The European Commission against Racism and Intolerance in the same period set out a definition for hate speech:

> Hate speech is the advocacy, promotion or incitement, in any form, of the denigration, hatred or vilification of a person or group of persons, as well as any harassment, insult, negative stereotyping, stigmatisation or threat in respect of such a person or group of persons and the justification of all these types of expression, on grounds, among others, of 'race', colour, national or ethnic origin, language, religion or belief, gender identity and sexual orientation.[2]

Ireland's only legislation against hate speech is the Prohibition of Incitement to Hatred Act 1989, introduced to prevent British far-right groups from using Ireland as a means of printing propaganda, and never seriously used to address racism in the media or other forms of hate speech in public. Despite calls for its wider use by academics and non-governmental organisations (NGOs), the Act operates primarily to defend the state from international pressure to legislate against hate crimes and hate speech, and to demonstrate that it takes racism seriously.

This chapter deals with racist incitement to hatred as well as the wider stereotyping of groups, and, further, the racist framing of contemporary issues which goes far beyond the remit of hate speech. In providing such an overview, the chapter demonstrates the continuing widespread tolerance for racist ideas which is produced and supported by the media in Ireland. These persistently cast immigrants as outsiders through criminalisation and dehumanisation, as well as through the legitimisation of political discourses which locate them outside the polity.

Monitoring racism in Irish media

Throughout the early 2000s, there was a slight upturn in both academic and NGO interest in recording and analysing the role of racism and citizenship discourses publications in Irish media. Irish media were described as 'inward-looking', failing to provide significant detailed information on new immigrant populations or the context of their emigration, and thus distorting the availability of relevant information for their readers.[3] The particular emphasis on the discourses of politicians evident during the 2004 Citizenship Referendum and the adoption in news coverage of racialising terms used by them led to the exclusion of alternative voices from the majority Irish population, including NGOs and experts on migration, not only through editorial prioritisation but also through the framing of immigration-related content.[4] Largely, however, the tabloid press in Ireland (containing much UK-based content) was ignored by such studies, and there has been no wider review of inflammatory language or unfair reporting.[5] News readership is highest for Irish-owned newspapers, but there are still significant sales of foreign-owned newspapers in Ireland. In the first half of 2017, Irish-owned newspapers accounted for just 53 per cent of the daily newspaper readership and 58 per cent of the Sunday newspaper readership.[6] Any analysis of the leading Irish newsprint publications is therefore incomplete without a similar analysis of the content of the Irish editions of UK newsprint media. All of these are members of the Press Council of Ireland and, as such, subject to its Code of Practice.[7]

Since 2011, there have been a small number of research publications which highlight the racist framings used in Irish media. A review of the 2013 incident in which Roma children in Ireland were illegally removed from their families drew on three broadsheets and two tabloids.[8] A study of representations of the 'new Irish' reviewed two broadsheets, the *Irish Times* and *Irish Independent*, and one free tabloid newspaper, the *Metro Herald*, along with two television news slots on RTE1 and TV3.[9] More generally, academic attention has turned to the participation of ethnic minorities in media publishing and broadcasting, and there are few specific regular reviews of racist language or ideas across Irish media, even by NGOs active in this area. Incidents of racism in the media and on social media are recorded by the European Network Against Racism (ENAR) Ireland through the iReport.ie racist incident reporting system, but extreme content on websites and social media commentary is reported much more frequently than newsprint or broadcast media, and it therefore does not provide a reliable picture of racism in this context.[10]

There have been few successes in attempts by NGOs to deter national media outlets from publishing racist statements, despite lengthy efforts particularly from Traveller representative groups to do so. Calls to deal with Traveller crime (the main theme of Traveller-related publications in Irish newsprint and broadcast media) have for decades blamed Traveller culture and implicitly or explicitly called for the forced assimilation of the community and erasure of their cultural heritage. When, in 1996, Pavee Point sought action against the author of a *Sunday Independent* opinion piece under the Prohibition of Incitement to Hatred Act 1989, which described Traveller culture directly in terms of a criminal life, compared Travellers to animals and described the non-criminal Traveller as the exception, the Director of Public Prosecutions and Gardai both said there was no evidence of any kind that she had broken any law.[11]

Since 2008, however, the content of Irish print and digital media has been subject to a system of independent regulation overseen by the Office of the Press Ombudsman. Member publications, including all national and regional newsprint media, sign up to the Code of Practice, and complaints can be made about individual articles or individual journalists. The Press Council examines appeals from the Ombudsman and provides oversight of the Code of Practice. Principle 8 of the Code of Practice on 'Prejudice' states that:

> The press shall not publish material intended or likely to cause grave offence or stir up hatred against an individual or group on the basis of their race, religion, nationality, colour, ethnic origin, membership of the travelling community, gender, sexual orientation, marital status, disability, illness or age.

Decisions of the Press Ombudsman give some indication of the latitude allowed to media outlets in publishing material which might be considered prejudiced, either in editorial materials or in the reproduction of such content as quotation. There are however a few examples from the Press Ombudsman of complaints about racism in the Irish media. All of them concern pieces published as 'opinion' in newsprint media.

Racism and legitimate opinion

By 2011, under this new system, there appeared to have been some progress achieved in addressing racism. The Irish Traveller Movement complained to the Ombudsman about language used in an *Evening Herald* article about Traveller criminality. The *Herald*, a popular Dublin tabloid paper, had published an article, headlined 'Traveller Gangs have become a mafia the law fears to tackle', which asked 'When did Travellers go from being crafts-people to establishing themselves as a pan-national crime gang?', and main-tained that 'many [Travellers have] turned to drugs and crime' and had become 'what appears to be Ireland's biggest crime gang'.[12] The newspaper defended the article on the grounds that it was an 'opinion' piece, rather than news, and stated that the purpose of the article 'was not to label the Traveller community as a whole, but to argue that there was a strong link between members of the Traveller community and illegal activity'. The Ombudsman ruled that:

> While the article is clearly an opinion piece, and as such is entitled to a rea-sonable amount of latitude, opinions reported as fact must observe basic standards of verifiability if they are not to give rise to potential issues in the context of the Code of Practice.[13]

In doing so, the decision established that opinion pieces in the press would not be exempt from the powers of the Ombudsman. When the newspaper subsequently appealed the decision, they submitted evidence of wrongdoing by some groups of Travellers, but the Council rejected the appeal, saying the evidence was insufficient to support the generalisations complained of, and proved only the press interest rather than the facts claimed.[14]

A further decision on opinion pieces in the Irish press followed in Sep-tember 2013 with a complaint against the *Irish Independent*. The complaint concerned a column by regular opinion writer Ian O'Doherty which con-tained racist statements and breached Principle 8 (Prejudice) of the Code of Practice for Newspapers and Magazines.[15] The complaint was brought by the ENAR Ireland on the grounds that the article advocated the expul-sion of all unemployed Roma people from Ireland. It stated that Roma beggars formed 'a parasitic, ethnic underclass who look on this country as a giant stupid cow to be milked whenever they see fit', and it asserted that many locals had 'found themselves surrounded by beggars – all of whom were Roma – and then had their belongings filched'. The Press Ombudsman upheld the complaint against the *Irish Independent*, despite the newspaper's claim that comment on aggressive begging was in the public interest, and that the singling out of Roma beggars was based on the author's personal experiences and not on their membership of the Roma community.[16] The Ombudsman found that the article contained 'a number of emphatic gen-eralisations about beggars of Roma origin that, in his opinion, were clearly capable of or intended to cause grave offence'.[17]

The decision has not, however, deterred O'Doherty and other opinion writers from using racist language and ideas in subsequent contributions to the press and broadcasting media. Indeed, significant latitude has been given in other decisions of the Ombudsman which would allow the press to believe that there are narrow circumstances in which a complaint of racism in opinion pieces might be upheld. For example, in the decision of 'Irish Refugee Council and the Irish Independent' (7 April 2016), the Ombudsman rejected complaints that an article entitled 'When drunk, they get angry and want to show women who's in charge' about sexual assaults in Cologne breached the principle of prejudice and was xenophobic against Germany's Arab population. The criteria on which the decision was made centred on whether the piece included 'material that was intended to or likely to cause grave offence or stir up hatred against any ethnic group'.[18] In June 2016, a complaint about another *Irish Independent* article on Travellers was rejected by the Press Ombudsman after the complainants refused a right to reply. The Irish *Daily Mail* on 8 April 2014 had published a commentary piece under the heading 'If Travellers want ethnic status, they ought to get rid of those slash hooks and settle'.[19]

Opinion columns allow the most controversial racist statements, although previous research has shown that the framing of issues in news coverage can be much more powerful in directing public opinion. But there are reasons to believe that they are not subjected to the same standards of fact-checking or evidence as 'news' articles, and more explicit statements are permitted because Editors know that these drive readership to their publications, and increasingly to their websites. This lower standard was most obviously demonstrated by the *Irish Times* in explanation of its 2017publication of an article, 'The alt-right movement: everything you need to know,[20] which contained both racist language and ideas, and downplayed the extremist racist views within "alt-right"' identified discourses. Opinions Editor Paddy Smyth wrote: 'the purpose of the Opinion and Analysis section is to inform readers about the issues of the day, offer insights and give them something to think about'. He went on, 'Ultimately we trust in the ability of our readers to make their own minds up.' The implication is that the same standards of research which are expected in other parts of the paper are not expected in the opinion column. The same point was relied on in the Opinion Editor's later explanation in a radio debate on Newstalk Drive: 'we should not be concerned about protecting our readers'.[21]

What is omitted from the discussion is the obligation of the press to protect those groups who are subject to prejudice and are protected by the Code of Standards. In publishing Pell's article, the *Irish Times* clearly disappointed a segment of its readership. The ENAR Ireland iReport.ie website received the largest number of reports about a single media outlet in four years. The most common reasons for reporting the article were concerns about normalisation of racist language in the press, followed by concerns about giving credibility to supporters of the 'alt-right' and glamorisation of far-right ideologies and their proponents.[22] There were careful distinctions made by respondents in describing the piece as being racist. The inclusion of racist and inflammatory language in the piece was, for most respondents, sufficient. Nine further described the lack of context and fact-checking as influencing their judgement of the piece to be racist speech (rather than simply about racist speech). In addition, six respondents explicitly recognised that the article itself caused distress and fears for safety of ethnic minorities in Ireland. The publication of the Pell article suggests that the 2011 Press Council decision on opinion pieces has had little impact in the competition among media outlets for readership and web traffic.

Explicitly racist commentary is not however the preserve of 'professional controversialists', and it is no surprise that it is again predominantly aimed at Travellers and Roma. On the recognition of Traveller ethnicity in Ireland, the *Irish Independent* featured a column by a leading Irish political scientist which questioned whether this might give Travellers an excuse not to participate fully in society, engaging neither in education nor health. It sought to lay the blame for decades of exclusion at the feet of the Travelling community as a whole, and ignored the reason that the call for equality was precisely because Travellers wanted equal access to education and health. Moreover it went further, suggesting that celebrating Traveller culture meant celebrating sexualisation of children, forced marriage and negative lifestyles.[23] Another column in the same paper on ethnic recognition of Travellers also focused on criminality.[24]

An *Irish Examiner* editorial in late 2017 rebuked Traveller representative organisations for not having 'expressly condemned' violence in the Traveller community.[25] In particular, Pavee Point, who already run a high-profile conflict resolution programme, were called upon to be more vocal. 'Such a valuable support group would do themselves, and the community they seek to help, a great service by acknowledging that violence among certain sections of Travellers is a problem.' However, such calls were previously the subject of a debate in 2015 in which both Pádraig Mac Lochlainn TD and Pavee Point raised the issue of the double standard, in which Travellers were expected to police each other, which they expressly rejected.[26] That double standard is one which is frequently applied to ethnic minority groups, and implies that those who do not report crime, for whatever reason, are themselves part of a criminal culture. The reality is that Irish Travellers experience significant abuse by police and have little access to protection or justice.

Depictions of Roma in Irish print and broadcast media offer an insight into the most vocal forms of racist stereotyping and criminalisation of any group. Further, it is possible to see how broadcast media increasingly use nuanced discussion points which invite comment which could reasonably be anticipated to include racist stereotyping and incitement to hatred. Prejudice against Roma in the Irish media was well established when, in 2012, the Broadcasting Authority of Ireland Public Consultation on a Draft Code of Fairness, Objectivity and Impartiality in News and Current Affairs in the Broadcast Media invited submissions. The Irish Traveller Movement's submission drew attention to a specific General Comment by the Committee on the Elimination of All Forms of Racial Discrimination which specifically sought to 'encourage awareness among professionals of all media of the particular responsibility to not disseminate prejudices and to avoid reporting incidents involving individual members of Roma communities in a way which blames such communities as a whole', and 'to encourage and facilitate access by the Roma to the media'.[27] A review of representations of Roma in the Irish mainstream media demonstrates that there continues to be significant need for both.

Coverage of the removal of Roma children from a family in Dublin in 2013 raised questions about the use of racist stereotypes in identifying and even creating news stories in Ireland. In the aftermath of coverage of the 'Maria' case in Greece, in which a Roma child was removed from its biological parents under suspicion of human trafficking,[28] Gardai and the Health Service Executive removed a child and provided access and information to the media at the time of her removal. A senior Garda was arrested in 2015 over the provision of information about the case to the journalist who first published the story. Coverage of the story later included the publication of images of the children on national television and in the print media. Pavee Point submitted a complaint to the United Kingdom Press Complaints Commission relating to the *Daily Mail*'s coverage of the story, arguing a breach of Clause 1 (accuracy) and Clause 12 (Discrimination) of the Editors' Code of Practice (applicable in the UK). On Clause 12, the Commission refused to find the story discriminatory in the absence of any complaint from the family concerned.[29] The *Daily Mail*'s story included references to the age of the parents and children ('they were young teenagers when their first child was born'), the size of the family and their financial situation ('The family, who survive on benefits, live with their six children') and allegations about illegal weapons, drugs and stolen credit cards, as well as the removal of phones and laptops by police for investigation.[30] Presented intertwined with the story of 'Maria', the coverage implied that the child was stolen as part of wider criminal activity among the Roma community.

The image of the Roma beggar is well established in Ireland, but most often reproduced as a naturally criminal figure. From the 2011 TV3 documentary, *Bogus Beggars*, which was portrayed as an exposé of fraudulent panhandlers,[31] to opinion columns asserting their criminality, there is no shortage of examples of the stereotype being reproduced.

Media representations of Roma in Ireland clearly mirror and expand on the discourse alive in British media in which they are regularly associated with 'crime and anti-social behaviour (benefits-claiming, stealing, abduction and arrests) and settlement (camping, shanty towns, homelessness)'.[32] The newsworthiness of such stories is reflected in the fact that the

2013 child removal case became 'the most tweeted about topic in Ireland that year'.[33] An effort at balance in the *Sunday Independent* the following month, in which a journalist posed as a 'Roma beggar', demonstrates the failure of Irish media to connect with the Roma experience. Despite containing factual historical information about the Roma in Europe, the piece contained no accounts from Roma people and reproduced non-Roma assertions about them.

The growing representation of Roma criminality in the Irish media as the most hated of immigrant groups has been complemented by online vigilantism, prompting vigilante activity on at least one occasion and sustained violence against Roma families. A number of Roma families had to be evacuated from their homes in Waterford in October 2014 after a mob of 200, organised on Facebook, attacked their homes. In January 2017, the FM104 Phoneshow asked 'Should Roma Gypsies be banned from begging? Would such a drastic measure help those actually in need or is it wrong to target an ethnic minority simply because some are seen as "scammers"'? The framing of the discussion, which appeared to legitimise the targeting of a particular ethnic group, presented a rhetorical question (such targeting would be illegal) for the purpose of producing discussion which could be reasonably anticipated to include racist comments.[34] Media coverage of the Pavee Point Roma Needs Assessment released in January 2018 was more nuanced. FM104 this time appeared to take a more sympathetic approach, with a Phoneshow entitled 'The Roma community is living in severe poverty in Ireland', but a significant proportion of the calls broadcast on the show utilised stereotypes and racist ideas to depict the Roma community – 'They're robbing bastards, they're filthy dirty'. The host Keith Ward drew the audience's attention to the show's Facebook page which he said contained racist and even genocidal comments. In *The Sun*, an opinion column by the same radio host sympathised with Roma exclusion, and noted the extreme language used about them by callers on his own show: 'Terms "scum" and "parasite" were repeated on air and online countless of times, reminiscent of the slurs against Jews in 1930s Germany'. He nevertheless went on to hold the whole Roma population in Ireland responsible for the actions of some: 'I think the Roma community need to meet us halfway. They can't expect respect from some Dubliners when the criminal elements in their group exist. The blame in this case should be shouldered 50/50.'[35]

Denials of racism, or the extent of racism, are common in relation to the Roma, as other groups. Even after the failure of the 2013 child removal case, the *Irish Times* published a piece by columnist John Waters entitled 'Racism isn't the most ominous aspect of these child snatchings', which focused on other institutional failures with the effect of downplaying the racist 'child-snatching' stereotype underpinning the case. While there were critical responses to the case and the role of the media that followed, and even reference to the experiences of the family, these evidently did not lead to a wider reflexivity in the Irish media about Roma or its racist framing of news coverage.

No debate on immigration?

Along with the fact that Ireland refuses asylum to 90 per cent of applicants,[36] there is prominent coverage of refused asylum seekers. There is an assumption that refused asylum seekers are 'bogus'. This theme is a long-running one, dating back to the peak of inward migration, and highlights the racial framings which are applied to the subject of asylum and asylum seekers. In 2000, for example, the chairman of the Irish Refugee Council wrote to the *Irish Times* complaining that a spokesman for the Department of Justice had explained a backlog of asylum seekers by 'the strong economy [and] attractive social welfare rates', and left out the situations from which people sought asylum.[37] This context of departure, which the present book seeks to situate alongside the conditions of the arrival and integration of various immigrant groups, is a recognisable silence in much of the coverage of the asylum issue.

The framing of asylum as a security issue is evident in its coverage within the broadsheet newspapers. In 2008, the *Irish Independent*'s Security Editor claimed 'Bogus asylum seekers escaping deportation', using the term 'illegals' and 'asylum shoppers', implying that 'last-minute judicial reviews' to prevent deportation were used to support fraudulent asylum claims.[38] In 2012, the same author claimed 'Two-thirds of failed asylum seekers had used false identities', proposing that Somalis 'used the UK as a back door to Ireland while others were involved in asylum shopping'.[39] The refugee crisis in the Mediterranean has raised other questions about security, and increasingly migrants are portrayed as dangerous in the context of Calais or refugee camps across Europe and their determination to cross borders. In the Irish context, there has been only a small public turnaround on the use of Direct Provision to house asylum seekers (where they are available for easy deportation), despite growing evidence of abuse, trauma and malnutrition in the system, and that is related to the continuing explicit depictions of 'bogus asylum seekers'.

The subject of asylum abuse, like other subjects which attract racial stereotyping, appears consistently alongside allegations of silencing against the left, and unjust accusations of racism. For example, in 2005 the then Minister for Justice, Equality and Law Reform, Michael McDowell TD, responded to what he called 'a grossly inaccurate picture of developments', claiming that:

A small but well placed minority of commentators have sought to create the impression that Ireland's treatment of asylum seekers is harsh and unfair. They have consistently concealed the real facts from the Irish people. Moreover, they have sought to create the impression that anyone who points out the true situation is engaging in political racism. They hint at international comparisons which do not exist. They refuse to address the very large abuse of asylum protection in Ireland. They claim to believe that it is wrong to point out what is happening lest it create prejudice against genuine asylum seekers. They are engaging in a form of verbal intimidation of those who would tell the truth.[40]

Opinion writer Kevin Myers, who in 2017 was the subject of debate over anti-Semitic comments which cost him his job,[41] was among the most prolific anti-immigration columnists in the early 2000s, publishing articles with brazen headlines such as 'The problem isn't racism, it's the tidal wave of immigrants', and more particularly with a common theme that his comments should be 'taken as a warning shot at the left liberal agenda which makes it "racist" to discuss any of the practicalities with immigration'.[42]

From the early 2000s, there were repeated 'warnings' in the Irish media about the failures of multiculturalism in the UK and Europe, and the necessity to avoid similar policies here. It is well noted that similar 'warnings' were being sounded across Europe, even recognising that there was no shared definition or mode of multiculturalist policymaking.[43] The notion of the writer voicing 'hard truths' has been robustly countered in academic research,[44] but it is no surprise to find that these warnings continue, bolstered by suppositions about Muslims in Ireland, and increasingly connected to state failures (criticised by left and right) to seriously address integration policy. Carr has noted two main themes common to coverage of international events as they related to Islam in 2016, including the notion of a cultural clash between Islam and the West with religion at the heart of the problem, and the notion of Muslims as an 'enemy within'.[45]

Similar fearmongering is offered (if based on rather older 'race science' thinking, now revived) by Professor William Reville in the *Irish Times* in his regular columns in the Science section. In a January 2017 piece entitled 'Let's talk about the link between immigration and low reproduction rates', we are offered an opportunity to 'think' about fertility rates in Europe, in what amounts to a low dog-whistle to ideas of overbreeding migrants that reflects popular white supremacist ideas of the impending near-extinction of the 'white race'.[46] Fearmongering of cultural loss and immigration here draws on long-disproven ideas of racial and cultural purity, echoing the scientific racism of Europe's darker past.

Repeated condemnations of the 'absence' of a debate on immigration and calls for 'honesty' on immigration suggest that there is a sleight of hand on the part of government as well as an inevitable cost to immigration in the pressures on housing and services which is not balanced by its benefits.[47] Burroughs notes in a review of media coverage of illegal immigration:

[N]egative representations of illegal immigrants are juxtaposed with denials of racist remarks among elites and justifications for racist and xenophobic sentiments. ...texts that refer to illegal immigration allow for legitimised expressions of racism. Indeed, 'negative' and exclusionary texts about illegal immigration are convenient outlets for expressions of racism.[48]

Fear of upsetting minority groups, or of giving information about migration to the public, are common accusations among those columnists driven to write again and again about the issue. David Quinn connects voter fraud in Tower Hamlets and sexual abuse in Rotherham with terrorism in attacking the 'political correctness' around Islam in Ireland.[49] Not content to suggest that there is dishonesty in government on the issue, he goes further and suggests that this in itself is currency for emerging far-right movements.[50] The election of Donald Trump and result of the EU referendum in Britain have provoked much observation about the nature of populist politics. The connections being made between concerns about the need for a 'debate', and the presentation of selected events and statistics which feed racialising stereotypes of Muslims and 'non-nationals', suggest that the debates which are taking place are not adequately cognisant of this particular framing of 'Irish first'. At the time of writing, the most prolific racism against those born outside Ireland is in discussions of housing, demonstrated by this *Irish Independent* opinion:

> Only 10pc of the non-European citizens on the waiting list are refugees, so the vast majority are economic migrants. Surely an economic migrant, by definition, should be allowed into a country only when they can contribute to the economy. Otherwise, you are disadvantaging Irish citizens, such as those on the housing lists. ... We need to look at those aspects of our immigration policy that we have control over, which is to say immigration from outside the EU. And we need to look more closely at how the social housing system is being abused by some people and do something about that as well.[51]

Moreover, the housing crisis offers a convenient cover for racism – an 'us' versus 'them' which masks the contributions made to the Irish economy by many migrants – that reflects Burroughs's argument that such issues are a convenient outlet for racism.

Fertile ground for the proliferation of us-versus-them narratives in Ireland is provided by public radio. Since the 2004 Citizenship Referendum, the role of radio phone-in shows has been considered intermittently as the site of racist discourse, but the nature of the archival data makes it difficult to undertake reviews of this content.[52] Nonetheless, they warrant a brief exploration, not least because they are the location for many of the current debates about the limits of racist speech in Irish media. Kevin Myers and others continue to offer dire warnings around multiculturalism, increasingly oriented towards white supremacist tropes of 'white genocide', as evidenced by the trailer for an appearance by Myers on George Hook's 'Newstalk' FM programme: 'Kevin Myers fears for future generations of Irish as a minority in their own country'.[53]

In such narratives, Myers and others reproduce the discourses which are increasingly shared on Irish social media and which have evident roots in international far-right movements.[54] Facebook has been a particular producer of collective racist statements as people respond to negative news stories or posts about ethnic groups and share them with their networks. It has also been home to new Irish white supremacist groups, anti-immigration groups and Islamophobic groups emerging online with links to (and mostly dominated by members of) international far-right groups, and these have produced much content on the social media accounts of media outlets.[55] There are regular opportunities for the reproduction of those racist statements through phone-in chat shows, as well as social media.

The Niall Boylan 4FM 'Ireland Talks' phone show hosted a series of programmes which debate the issue of racism, which attract high numbers of listeners and which persistently feature racist stereotyping as part of the discussions. These have included, 'Would you call someone a racist if they would only use a taxi with a white driver?',[56] and 'Is it racist to want housing to go to Irish people first?'[57] 4FM were previously the subject of an unfavourable Broadcasting Authority of Ireland judgment in 2013, when a complaint against the David Harvey show was upheld for allowing racist and prejudicial comments to be aired by callers to the programme. These comments included statements that 'blacks' are 'very lazy', 'black Africans' always 'get up on their high horse' if challenged, 'blacks' have a certain DNA related to their work ethic and practices, and Filipinos in Ireland are 'scammers'. Further, callers to the programme of African ethnicity were treated differently from other callers, and asked by the presenter or another caller about their legal status as a resident in Ireland.[58] Like the later Boylan shows, the issue of racism itself was part of the discussion, with callers claiming 'You will be "locked up straightaway" and "not get away with it" if you make racist comments in Ireland.'[59] The debate on racism itself and its place in publishing and broadcasting in Ireland is a persistent subject of interest at the time of writing for those in the media.

Giving airtime to racism

When British celebrity commentator Katie Hopkins was invited to appear on the *Late Late Show* in 2016, RTE received more than 1,600 complaints prior to her appearance.[60] Hopkins has been repeatedly invited by the state broadcaster, appearing on the *Late Late* in 2014, 2015 and 2016, as well as various radio programmes, even after public censure for a 2015 column which advocated gunships to deal with migrants in the Mediterranean, whom she likened to cockroaches. The article in question, the most extreme in a wide range of published pieces relying on racist tropes, attracted criticism even from the United Nations (although no censure from the Independent Press Standards Organisation, since migrants are not a protected group).[61] The Broadcasting Authority rejected a complaint about her comments on migrants when she appeared on Today FM show 'The Last Word' in 2017 to discuss that same article, on the basis that her comments and defence of the article were editorially justified in the context of a discussion on free speech versus hate speech and suitably challenged throughout.[62] The public response against Hopkins in Ireland led to online news website Joe.ie announcing that they would no longer publish stories about Katie Hopkins.[63] No other media outlet followed suit.

When the *Irish Times* ran an 'opinion' piece on the American 'alt-right' which contained both racist language and ideas and downplayed the extremist racist views within 'alt-right'-identified discourses, broadcast media programmes on TV and radio were quick to spot the potential for lively debate about the limits of racist speech. The *Claire Byrne* show on RTE was just one of the programmes which invited Pell on after the publication of the article. The panellist debate regularly features 'controversial' opinion columnists and has been broadly criticised for failing to challenge false and racist claims made by panellists in the course of the programme.[64] The intention of the production team in establishing this debate appeared to be to cause controversy without properly considering that the debate centres extremist speech, giving undue exposure to commentators who put hate speech into the media. Hate speech, of the kind published by both Nicholas Pell and Brenda Power, who were panellists, has been well documented as producing direct and indirect harms to ethnic minorities, women and other less powerful groups. RTE, in inviting both Pell and Power to represent the defence of freedom of speech, arguably failed to hold extremists to account for the impact of their incitement to hatred. Both Pell and Power argue for an unlimited right which permits the expression of white supremacist, racist and genocidal views. It also, by means of the structuring of the debate, improperly positioned Colm O'Gorman of Amnesty International and Rosemary McCabe of the *Irish Times*, both defenders of free speech, in opposition to it, and prevented them from presenting a nuanced understanding of the issue.

Broadcast media is at the forefront of arguments in Ireland about freedom of speech, suited as that medium is to discussion and debate in real time. The Broadcasting Authority decision on Katie Hopkins as well as the earlier decisions on 4FM demonstrate that there is a place in Irish broadcasting for racist language and commentary, so long as it is robustly challenged. The repeated invitation of opinion columnists known for crossing the line into hate speech, however, suggests that there is a high editorial tolerance for prejudice. While this is frequently explained as being in the public interest, there is no doubt that the ratings which follow are a significant factor in such programming decisions.

Coverage of an attempt by Identity Ireland and PEGIDA to hold a rally against the growth of Islam in Ireland demonstrates the neutrality of Irish media towards far-right movements, with many news articles simply reproducing statements by the nascent political party about the event and the counter-protest without contextual information about the relevant groups involved. The *Irish Times* article 'Anti-Islamic group Pegida Ireland to be launched at Dublin rally' gave statements only from supporters of the group made at their press conference, where they were 'delighted to have an opportunity to warn people in Ireland about the dangers of radical Islam' and 'said Ireland should look to Britain to see the mistakes made by allowing in large numbers of Muslims who fail to integrate'. It also included statements from Tommy Robinson of the English Defence League, who advised the Irish public, 'you have to close your borders as does the rest of Europe'.[65] The *Irish Times* however offered equal coverage elsewhere of the opposition to the PEGIDA rally.[66] Only The Journal.ie carried a significant amount of information about PEGIDA's activities in other countries, as well as the policies of Identity Ireland.[67]

In the *Irish Times*, Courts Correspondent Mary Carolan called PEGIDA's arrival 'a wake-up call for migration policy' and advocated strongly for a national debate on migration and the 'urgently needed' development of multicultural policies.[68] The *Sunday Independent* offered little balance, in contrast, and ran an opinion piece entitled 'Remind me ... who the fascists are again here?' which derided the 'current incarnation of modern liberalism [that] seems to be more concerned with banning things they don't like and shutting down any debate they find "offensive"', and suggested that the public are not wrong 'to be concerned about the impact of mass Muslim immigration'.[69]

Recent coverage of a very small protest led by a Kerry councillor against the opening of a Direct Provision centre to house asylum seekers demonstrates the fascination of the media with racist ideas, and the prominence of their coverage.[70] The event received coverage from the *Irish Times*, *Irish Examiner* and the *Irish Independent*-owned paper *The Kerryman* in December 2017.[71]

Each of these stories emphasised, in the headlines and content, the narrative of conflict between Irish homeless and the state obligations to receive asylum seekers, and minimised the experience of asylum seekers. Each quoted the Councillor: 'I'm not saying that these people haven't gone through bad times. Of course, I'm sure they have. But you should see what some of our people are going through.' The *Irish Times* and *Irish Examiner* both also included claims from protestors that suggested the asylum seekers were to be treated with suspicion, because they carried iPhone 6s, smoked and had 'brilliant English', and the Councillor's claim that 'We have no knowledge of the vetting procedures these people have been through'. *The Kerryman* added further comments from the Councillor: 'They're out of their minds drinking coffee since they arrived' and 'I fear for Killarney and what might happen. I want them away from Killarney and away from the nearby school'.[72] Only local newspaper the *Killarney Advertiser* covered opposition to the protest from local residents, who had launched a petition against the protest, and an organisation representing minority groups.[73]

Conclusion

The above review of recent debates and rulings on racist speech in Ireland's news media demonstrates a number of important shifts. It is clear that there is now a place firmly established for racism in the Irish public sphere. Comparisons with foreign-owned media companies misrepresent the vitality of racist ideas in Irish debate, while overlooking the level of consumption of foreign-owned outlets in Ireland, in print, digital and broadcast media, but particularly including those outlets of the British press published here which are so well known for anti-immigrant sentiment. There have been, since 2016, far fewer examples of explicitly racist speech in Irish media, although many more examples of racism being used as a means of audience engagement. However, the caution of the press and broadcasting regulatory bodies in responding to explicitly racist language has expanded the scope of what may be said in the 'public interest'. Academics and NGOs concur that there is little efficacy in, or political will to use, existing legislation on incitement to hatred. Broadcasters and editors are well aware that racist speech, or even debates about racism, produce significantly more racist speech into the public sphere. Responsibility for this is primarily resisted through diversion of public engagement away from proprietary websites and through social media platforms where there is no accountability on their part for monitoring racist speech. Yet outrage at racist speech in Irish news media is limited and appears to emerge directly in relation to the standing of the publication or broadcaster which publishes it. While there are often rebuttals of racist speech, more frequently there is no effective response to far-right racism. The failure of Irish news media to seriously address the effects of the racist ideas that have gained currency has resulted in an increasingly central place for racism in public debate.

Notes

1 Fundamental Rights Agency, *Incitement in Media Content and Political Discourse in EU Member States*. Contribution to the second Annual Colloquium on Fundamental Rights – November 2016 (European Union Agency for Fundamental Rights, 2016).

2 European Commission against Racism and Intolerance, *ECRI General Policy Recommendation No. 15 on Combating Hate Speech*, adopted on 8 December 2015' (Strasbourg: Council of Europe, 21 March 2016), p. 16.

3 A. Haynes, E. Devereux and M. J. Breen, 'In the know? Media, migration and public beliefs', *Translocations*, 5:1 (2009), 2.

4 M. Breen, A. Haynes and E. Devereux, 'Citizens, loopholes and maternity tourists: Irish print media coverage of the 2004 citizenship referendum', in M. Corcoran and M. Peillon (eds), *Uncertain Ireland* (Dublin: IPA, 2006), pp. 55–71.

5 C. Kenny, 'Finding a voice or fitting in? Migrants and media in the new Ireland', *Media, Culture & Society*, 3:2 (2010), 311–322.

6 'Irish newspaper circulation January–June 2017' (n.d.), ilevel.ie/media-blog/print/102950-irish-newspaper-circulation-january-june-2017-island-of-ireland-report, accessed 8 February 2019.

7 Press Council of Ireland, 'Member publications' (n.d.), presscouncil.ie/member-publications, accessed 8 February 2019.

8 A. Marron, A. Joyce, J. Carr, E. Devereux, M. Breen, M. Power and A. Haynes, 'Print media framings of those blonde Roma children', in A. Haynes, M. Power, E. Devereux, A. Dillane, and J. Carr (eds), *Public and Political Discourses of Migration: International Perspectives* (London: Rowman and Littlefield International, 2016), pp. 117–134.

9 N. O'Boyle, J. Rogers, P. Preston and F. Fehr, '"New Irish" in the news', *Irish Communication Review*, 14:1 (2014), 3–16.

10 L. Michael, *Reports of Racism in Ireland: 15th–16th Report of iReport.ie: January–June 2017* (Dublin: ENAR Ireland, 2018).

11 M. E. Synon, 'Time to get tough on tinker terror "culture"', *Sunday Independent*, (28 January 1996.

12 'Traveller gangs have become a mafia the law fears to tackle', *Evening Herald*, 14 September 2011.

13 Press Ombudsman, 'Irish Traveller Movement and the Evening Herald' (Dublin: Press Council of Ireland, 16 February 2012), presscouncil.ie/irish-traveller-movement-and-the-evening-herald-2273, accessed 8 February 2019.

14 Ibid.

15 I. O'Doherty, 'Begging – but I thought it was freedom of expression?', *Irish Independent*, 30 September 2013.

16 Press Ombudsman of Ireland, 'European Network Against Racism Ireland and the Irish Independent' (Dublin: Press Council of Ireland, 20 December 2013), presscouncil.ie/european-network-against-racism-ireland-and-the-irish-independent, accessed 8 February 2019.

17 Press Ombudsman of Ireland, 'European Network against Racism Ireland and the Irish Independent'.

18 Press Ombudsman of Ireland, 'Irish Refugee Council and the Irish Independent' (Dublin: Press Council of Ireland, 7 April 2016), presscouncil.ie/about-us/recent-decisions-and-news/irish-refugee-council-and-the-irish-independent, accessed 8 February 2019.

19 Press Ombudsman of Ireland, 'Irish Council for Civil Liberties, Pavee Point Traveller and Roma Centre and the Irish Daily Mail' (Dublin: Press Council of Ireland, 23 June 2016), presscouncil.ie/about-us/recent-decisions-and-news/irish-council-for-civil-liberties-pavee-point-traveller-and-roma-centre-and-the-irish-daily-mail, accessed 8 February 2019.

20 N. Pell, 'The alt-right movement: everything you need to know', *Irish Times*, 4 January 2017.

21 Newstalk, *Newstalk Drive*, 5 January 2017, 12:00.

22 Michael, *15th–16th Report of iReport.ie: January – June 2017*.

23 E. O'Malley, 'We can celebrate Traveller culture but old worries are still there', *Irish Independent*, 5 March 2017.

24 A. Fitzgerald, 'Opinion: poverty is at the root of Travellers' crime problem', *Irish Independent*, 19 March 2017.

25 'Our view: violence among Travellers: we must admit that it is a problem', *Irish Examiner*, 14 December 2017.

26 C. Gleeson, '"Extremely naïve" to say no criminal elements within Travelling community', *Irish Times*, 5 November 2015.

27 General Comment XXVII (Fifty-seventh Session, 2000) Discrimination Against Roma2, A/55/18 (2000) 154.

28 H. Smith, '"Maria" case reveals Greek bureaucracy close to collapse', *Irish Times*, 26 October 2013.

29 Pavee Point, 'UK Press Complaints Commission finds against Pavee Point' (Dublin: Pavee Point, 27 January 2014), paveepoint.ie/uk-press-complaints-commission-finds-against-pavee-point/, accessed 8 February 2019.

30 L. Eccles and D. Martin, 'Now blonde girl found at a Roma home in Ireland: blue-eyed child of seven is led away by police and social workers', *Daily Mail*, 22 October 2013.

31 S. Joyce, M. Kennedy and A. Haynes, 'Travellers and Roma in Ireland: understanding hate crime data through the lens of structural inequality', in A. Haynes, J. Schweppe and S. Taylor (eds), *Critical Perspectives on Hate Crime Contributions from the Island of Ireland* (London: Palgrave, 2017), pp. 325–354.

32 Z. Cihan Koca-Helvaci, 'Social misfits or victims of exclusion? Contradictory representations of Irish Travellers in the Irish press', *Irish Journal of Applied Social Studies* 16:1 (2016), Article 3, arrow.dit.ie/ijass/vol16/iss1/3, accessed 8 February 2019.

33 Marron et al., 'Print media framings of those blonde Roma children', p. 119.

34 FM104 Phoneshow, 'Should Roma gypsies be banned from begging?', 17 March 2017, fm104.ie/on-air/shows/fm104-phoneshow/podcasts/march/should-roma-gypsies-be-banned-from-begging/, accessed 8 February 2019.

35 K. Ward, 'Many Roma in Ireland are living in terrible conditions but they need to meet us halfway to solve the issues', *The Sun*, 22 January 2018.

36 J. Cusack, 'Ireland refuses asylum to 90pc of applicants', *Irish Independent*, 20 November 2016.

37 P.O'Morain, 'Horror of situations refugees flee from overlooked', *Irish Times*, 13 January 2000.

38 T. Brady, 'Bogus asylum seekers escaping deportation', *Irish Independent*, 5 January 2008.

39 T. Brady, 'Two-thirds of failed asylum seekers had used false identities', *Irish Independent*, 21 May 2012.

40 Minister for Justice, Equality and Law Reform, *Statement by the Minister regarding the Real Facts about the Asylum and Deportation Systems* (Dublin: Department of Justice and Equality, 7 June 2005).

41 *Irish Examiner*, 'Kevin Myers apologises for column but insists not anti-semitic or misogynistic', 1 August 2017.

42 K. Myers, 'The problem isn't racism, it's the tidal wave of immigrants', *Irish Independent*, 5 September 2007.

43 A. Lentin and G. Titley, *The Crises of Multiculturalism: Racism in a Neoliberal Age* (London: Zed Books, 2011), pp. 27–28.

44 G. Titley, 'Backlash! Just in case: 'political correctness', immigration and the rise of preactionary discourse in Irish public debate', *Irish Review*, 38 (Spring 2008), 94–110.

45 J. Carr, 'Islamophobia in Ireland National Report 2016', in E. Bayrakli and F. Hafez (eds), *European Islamophobia Report 2016* (Istanbul: SETA, 2016), pp. 273–292, p. 285.

46 W. Reville, 'Let's talk about the link between immigration and low reproduction rates', *Irish Times*, 19 January 2017.

47 D. Quinn, 'Scale of immigration piling huge pressure on essential services', *Irish Independent*, 3 March 2017.

48 E. Burroughs, *Irish Institutional Discourses of Illegal Immigration: A Critical Discourse Analysis Approach*, Unpublished PhD Thesis (National University of Ireland, Maynooth, 2012), 255.

49 D. Quinn, 'It's telling that we excuse Islam's "aberrations", but not the Church's', *Irish Independent*, 9 June 2017.

50 D. Quinn, 'Ignoring crimes by immigrants just plays into the hands of the far right', *Irish Independent*, 24 February 2017.

51 D. Quinn, 'We need to talk about housing … and those "playing the system" must be part of the conversation', *Irish Independent*, 15 September 2017.

52 Breen, Haynes and Devereux, 'Citizens, loopholes and maternity tourists'.

53 G. Hook, 'Kevin Myers fears for future generations of Irish as a minority in their own country', https://twitter.com/ghook/status/837286880156794880, 2 March 2017.

54 L. Michael, *Reports of Racism in Ireland. 13th–14th Report of iReport.ie: July–December 2016* (Dublin: ENAR Ireland, 2017).

55 Ibid.

56 Classic Hits 4FM, 'Ireland talks: 'Would you call someone a racist if they would only use a taxi with a white driver?', 3 July 2017.

57 Classic Hits 4FM, 'Ireland talks: 'Is it racist to want housing to go to Irish people first?', 20 December 2017.

58 Broadcasting Authority of Ireland, 'Complaint made by: Ms. Sharon Murphy on behalf of Galway One World Centre – Ref. No. 26/13', *Broadcasting Complaint Decisions October 2013* (BAI, 2013).

59 Ibid.

60 Journal.ie, 'Despite pre-show deluge, only 20 "formal" complaints to RTÉ about Katie Hopkins', *thejournal.ie*, 16 November 2016, thejournal.ie/hopkins-rte-complaints-3083242-Nov2016/, accessed 8 February 2019.

61 'Katie Hopkins' migrant "cockroaches" column resembles pro-genocide propaganda, says the United Nations', *Belfast Telegraph*, (24 April 2015; J. Plunkett, 'Katie Hopkins' migrants column was in bad taste – but Ipso doesn't cover that', *The Guardian*, 28 July 2016.

62 Broadcasting Authority of Ireland, 'Complaint made by: Mrs. Ravnita Joyce – Ref. No. 114/16', *Broadcasting Complaint Decisions April 2017* (BAI, 2017).

63 Joe.ie, 'You spoke, we listened: no more Katie Hopkins stories on JOE' (n. d.),
    joe.ie/life-style/you-spoke-we-listened-no-more-katie-hopkins-stories-on-
    joe-513863, accessed 8 February 2019.
64 Rabble.ie, 'Unchallenged racism on national TV', 8 September 2015,
    rabble.ie/2015/09/08/unchallenged-racism-on-national-tv/, accessed 8 February
    2019.
65 B. Roche, 'Anti-Islamic group Pegida Ireland to be launched at Dublin rally',
    Irish Times, 30 January 2016.
66 B. Roche, 'Anti-racism protest to counter Pegida Ireland launch', *Irish Times*, 3
    February 2016.
67 J. Mercille, 'Anti-Islamic group Pegida are coming to town. We can't afford to
    laugh and dismiss them', The Journal.ie, 5 February 2016, www.thejournal.ie/
    readme/pegida-ireland-2585259-Feb2016/, accessed 8 February 2019.
68 M. Carolan, 'Pegida's arrival a wake-up call for migration policy; national
    debate on migration and development of multicultural policies urgently needed',
    Irish Times, 12 February 2016.
69 I. O'Doherty, 'Remind me ... who the fascists are again here?', *Sunday Indepen-
    dent*, 13 February 2016.
70 Independent.ie Newsdesk, 'We should see after our own first' – Councillor pro-
    tests against accommodation centre for asylum seekers', *Irish Independent*, 16
    December 2017.
71 A. Lucey, 'Dozens protest outside centre for asylum seekers in Killarney', *Irish
    Times*, 16 December 2017; A. Lucey, 'Protesters raise concerns over newly
    opened asylum centre in Killarney', *Irish Examiner*, 16 December 2017; S.
    Fernane, 'Grady: "Asylum seeker protest will continue"' *The Kerryman*, 23
    December 2017.
72 Fernane, 'Grady: "Asylum seeker protest will continue"'.
73 *Killarney Advertiser*, 'Protest planned as community lashes out at lack of con-
    sultation on asylum seeker plan', 15 December 2017.

Children and young people on the margins

In the Republic of Ireland, children have long been ancillary to immigration policy and decisions, with their specific needs and rights frequently overlooked. This chapter will explore the impact of the absence of clear law and policy on children's lives. It will consider the barriers to children obtaining immigration status and applying for citizenship. It will focus on the problems created by uncertainty around children's immigration status that extend into adulthood and place ceilings on opportunities, including restricting access to third-level education. The chapter draws on research undertaken by the Immigrant Council of Ireland in 2016.

According to the 2016 Census there were 535,475 'non-Irish' representing over two hundred different nationalities and a further 104,784 people who described themselves as dual nationality with Irish being part of that dual identity. Of those who described themselves as having dual nationality, 34,761 (33 per cent) were aged 0–14 and 14,384 (13.7 per cent) were aged 15–24. 12.3 per cent of non-Irish nationals were aged 0–14 years.[1] In 2016, there were approximately 157,318 foreign national/dual nationality children in Ireland, accounting for approximately 12.1 per cent of the total population of Ireland aged 0–19 years.

Despite the significant numbers of migrant children and young people now living in Ireland, until relatively recently the contemporary phenomenon of child migration in Ireland was relatively unexplored. Traditionally, migration discourse has focused on adult migrants, with children considered as secondary subjects of concern and dependent on their parents, families or others.[2] Much of the available research that has focused on inward migration and migrant experiences of living in Ireland to date has also predominantly focused on adults. A notable exception in this regard is the body of research that has been undertaken in relation to separated children seeking asylum.[3] There is also a growing body of literature and research regarding migrant children and issues related to Direct Provision, poverty, identity, racism and integration.[4] Existing research concerning adults has identified, directly or indirectly, some key issues for children such as difficulties accessing third-level education or separation from a parent arising from restrictive family reunification policies.[5] But beyond the figures published by the Central Statistics Office, very little is known about migrant children in Ireland, especially within the immigration system itself and any consequences arising for them relating to migration status.

In 2015, having observed an increase in the number and breadth of queries relating to the immigration status of children and young people, the Immigrant Council of Ireland decided to conduct research with young migrants, to document their migration experiences, identify what their needs might be and make recommendations regarding the legal framework required to address those needs comprehensively.

The *Child Migration Matters* research, including thirty-two case studies, documented the experiences of young migrants who had travelled to Ireland as children, recording their experiences of arriving in and growing up in Ireland, engaging with the immigration system and, where relevant, living in the care of the state.[6] These young migrants came from a broad range of backgrounds in terms of their age, immigration status, nationality and gender. Of the young people featured in the case studies, nineteen were female and thirteen were male. Of those interviewed, twenty had spent time in the care of the state as children. One had been the subject of a supervision order. The participants included young people with many different immigration permissions, as well as young people who had naturalised as Irish citizens. The research also documented the experiences of professionals, in particular social workers, guardians *ad litem* and youth advocates, who represent and support migrant children, in trying to support these young people to navigate the immigration system and/or access other services, especially third-level education.

Broadly, the research found that children, like adults, migrate for diverse and complex reasons; political, social and family life, economic, educational and environmental. For most, their move to a new country is precipitated by multiple factors, including political instability, social and economic factors such as poverty and environmental reasons including food and/or water shortages. Because of the multiple reasons for migration, many travel within groups that reflect these various factors; some travel as refugees and asylum seekers seeking protection from harm and others as economic migrants seeking a better life, while others seek to reunite with family or friends who have already moved.

Residence status in Ireland

Current Irish immigration law imposes an obligation on all non-European Economic Area (EEA) foreign nationals born outside of Ireland to apply for immigration permission and to register with the Garda National Immigration Bureau (GNIB) from the age of sixteen. Failure to do so is an offence punishable on conviction by a maximum fine of €3,000 and/or up to twelve months' imprisonment.[7]

In accordance with Irish immigration law, the Minister for Justice and Equality has discretion to grant residence permission, as well as to attach conditions regarding length of stay and other entitlements, such as access to employment and family reunification. The residence permission granted may also be deemed reckonable for the purposes of assessing future eligibility to apply for Irish citizenship by naturalisation. As a matter of administrative policy and practice, children are deemed to derive their residence status from their parent/s or legal guardian/s and, as such, children are not regarded as individual rights holders entitled to access residence status in their own right. This is especially problematic for children who are living with parents who may be without formal residence status (a situation which applied to some of the children in the study) and for separated children who are living in the care of the state, either having arrived unaccompanied or following child protection interventions.

Although no quantitative data were available, the research identified a number of key issues. First, despite the statutory obligation imposed on minors to apply for immigration permission and to register, there is no guidance published by the Irish Naturalisation and Immigration Service (INIS) or the GNIB regarding the application process itself, the residence permission that may be issued to a child in any particular situation, or the residence status of a foreign national child born in Ireland but who is not entitled to Irish citizenship at birth. Furthermore, it appears that no internal guidance is even provided to immigration officers tasked with determining individual applications for residence permission. This means that an immigration officer who deals with an application by a young person for immigration permission has no guidelines to help the decision on whether to grant that permission, or what type of permission should be granted. This has led to significant inconsistency in practice, with young people in almost identical situations being dealt with in various different ways. Related to, or perhaps directly as a result of, the lack of guidance provided in relation to the duty on young people to register once they turn sixteen, there was evidence that some children, including those living in the care of the state, did not comply with the obligation to register because they were not aware they were required to do so, nor were their primary carers including foster carers and social workers.

As noted above, for those young people who did make application for immigration permission, there was also evidence of a lack of consistency regarding the type of permission that was granted. In some instances, a young person was granted Stamp 4 residence permission, which allows for full access to social protection and employment. However, some young people with similar immigration history and family circumstances were granted Stamp 3 permission to reside as a dependent family member only, which means they had no access to social protection or employment; others were granted Stamp 2, which is sometimes referred to as a 'student permission', providing that the person is allowed to live in Ireland only for study purposes with no right to access social protection and only limited permission to work. The research also demonstrated an apparent lack of awareness on the part of social workers and other professionals working with young people about the differences between the various types of immigration permission, which is crucial to understanding whether the permission granted in a particular case is appropriate. For example, Stamp 2 student permission does not permit access to social protections, can restrict access to the labour market and is not deemed reckonable for the purposes of applying for citizenship. Stamp 2 is also subject to a maximum seven-year period, after which the person either has to secure different immigration permission, which can be very difficult to do unless the person qualifies for residence permission under a specific residence scheme, or leave the state. It is arguable therefore that it is inappropriate to issue such residence permission to a child in care who intends to stay in the state long term and especially if their primary reason for coming to Ireland was not to access education.

Significantly, the research documented that in some instances children were discharged from state care without any steps having been taken to obtain appropriate or any residence permission on their behalf while in care. In these circumstances, the case studies highlighted very stark situations of young persons who have ended up in poverty, sometimes homeless or in prostitution. These issues directly affect the individuals concerned, by undermining their future development and wellbeing, and also affect wider society.

Finally, however, despite the above findings, the research also demonstrated some evidence of positive practice, particularly in respect of young people in care who had allocated social workers or appointed guardians *ad litem* who made interventions to ensure that residence- and citizenship-related matters were addressed at the appropriate time and, where necessary, were planned and budgeted for during the aftercare planning process. There was also evidence that in some cases where a young person had failed to apply on time for immigration permission, or had been given an inappropriate permission, it was possible to engage with INIS to regularise the situation in the best interests of the child by providing the appropriate permission.

Access to third-level education

The issue of access to third-level education emerged as the top priority for the young people and support workers consulted for the *Child Migration*

Matters report and mirrors the findings of earlier research on migrant experiences of integration and motivation for applying for Irish citizenship.[8]

Under the provisions of the Student Support Act 2011 and Student Support Regulations 2017, certain categories of migrant children are not eligible for financial support for third-level education.[9] This is despite the fact that they may have been lawfully resident and settled in Ireland for a number of years and have completed their secondary and, in many instances, primary education in Ireland. Several of the young people interviewed for the 2016 research could not afford to attend third-level education because their immigration status restricted their access to financial support. Under the terms of the Free Fees Initiative, only Irish, EEA and Swiss citizens and their family members, those with refugee status and their family members, and those with subsidiary protection or leave to remain following a decision not to issue a deportation order are eligible for free fees. They must also meet other criteria such as fulfilling a required period of residency in the state.[10] This means that young people from outside of the EEA who fall outside the eligibility criteria must pay international student tuition fees unless an individual college waives these fees on a discretionary basis. For many courses, these can be up to and in excess of €20,000 per year.

Students who meet the criteria for a grant from Student Universal Support Ireland (SUSI) receive at a minimum a fee grant that covers the annual student contribution charge or registration fee. Students who are not eligible for a SUSI fee grant must themselves pay this fee (currently €3,000 per year) to their higher education institutions. Eligible students who fall below specified income thresholds also receive a maintenance grant to subsidise other costs of education such as accommodation, travel and textbooks.

A number of Irish universities have been designated as 'Universities of Sanctuary', awarded by the City of Sanctuary, which includes schemes for either scholarships or waiving of non-EU and standard fees and arranging supports for students who are in the Direct Provision system and those with refugee status.[11] While these schemes are to be welcomed for allowing for access to third-level education by some members of these marginalised groups, it does not detract from the substantive point that this is 'grace and favour' on an individual basis rather than providing a general right of access to third-level education.

The Student Support Act 2011 and Student Support Regulations 2017 stipulate that only certain categories of non-EEA citizen are eligible for a student grant from SUSI. The Student Support Act 2011 defines 'student' as a person who is ordinarily resident in the state, meaning resident for three out of the previous five years, among other conditions.[12] Additionally, a person must fit within prescribed nationality or residence categories. They must be family members of an EEA citizen, have refugee status or have been granted subsidiary protection. Furthermore, persons prescribed by the Minister for Justice and Equality in the regulations, and with the consent of the Minister for Finance, also qualify for financial support.

When prescribing a class of person, the Minister must have regard to matters including: (a) the period for which they have been ordinarily resident in the state; the basis on which they were granted permission to reside within the state; (c) the conditions attached to their permission to reside within the state; (d) the degree of connection they are likely to have to the state; (e) their entitlement to benefits or services provided by a Minister of the Government, a local authority, the Health Service Executive or the holder of any office or a body; and (g) resources available for the provision of student support. The Student Support Regulations 2017 are the most recent regulations that set out the types of eligible permission. They limit the types of permission allowed to: (a) a person who has been granted humanitarian leave to remain in the state prior to the coming into operation of the Immigration Act 1999; (b) a person in respect of whom the Minister for Justice and Equality has granted permission to remain following a determination not to make a deportation order; and (c) a person granted subsidiary protection. The regulations also include family members of a person exercising their EU right to free movement and dependent children of people who are married to, or in civil partnerships with, Irish nationals residing in the state.

The restrictive use of these residence categories does not appear to be based on a rational or justified aim, or driven by or linked to immigration policy of the Department of Justice. The current regulations exclude young people who were granted permission to reside on an exceptional basis or based on discretionary grounds, as well as young people who were granted permission to reside with their Irish-citizen siblings. Many of the young people in the care of the state are granted permission to reside on exceptional grounds without a deportation order proposal first being issued against them. They are unable to access financial support for further education. However, if action had been taken to secure their immigration status at a later, more precarious time, after the issuing of a deportation order proposal, they would be eligible for free fees and to apply for a grant. It is arguable that this arbitrary policy restricts access to education on the basis of immigration status and is in breach of Ireland's commitment to respect the right to education without discrimination, including discrimination on the grounds of immigration status.[13] The inability of migrant youth, especially those who have lived in Ireland for significant lengths of time, to access third-level education on equal terms also gives rise to concerns regarding risks of social exclusion and marginalisation, including within the labour market.

Access to citizenship

At an international level, it is recognised that the enjoyment of citizenship is a key element in promoting social cohesion. In addition to security of residence status, access to citizenship is regarded as an essential precondition to achieving integration.[14] To facilitate integration into society, migrant children should be given access to citizenship so they can enjoy the same economic and social benefits as other children. Citizenship can often be the key to accessing fundamental rights such as education, particularly higher education. It is also essential for migrant children to enjoy equal access to civil and political rights. Therefore, Irish citizenship allows migrant children to contribute to, and participate more fully in, Irish society. As well as practical benefits, citizenship can also have psychological benefits for children. It can contribute to a sense of belonging, stability and certainty, and allows them to feel equal to their peers.

Irish citizenship is regulated by the Irish Nationality and Citizenship Act 1956, as amended by the Irish Nationality and Citizenship Act 2004. Irish citizenship can be acquired through birth, descent or naturalisation. Since a Referendum in 2004, Article 9 of the Irish Constitution limits Irish citizenship by birth to persons with at least one parent who 'is an Irish citizen or entitled to be an Irish citizen' and to those in respect of whom citizenship is provided for 'by law'. The implementing legislation introduced a residence requirement. A child born on the island of Ireland to non-Irish nationals will not be entitled to Irish citizenship on birth unless one of their parents has been legally resident on the island of Ireland for at least three of the previous four years.[15] Time spent living in Ireland as an asylum seeker, undocumented migrant or resident with international student permission does not qualify as 'reckonable residence'. This means that in some cases a child may have been born in Ireland and lived his or her entire life in Ireland without being entitled to Irish citizenship, simply because the immigration status of his or her parents does not qualify.

A child born abroad who had a grandparent born on the island of Ireland or a parent who had claimed their Irish citizenship before the child's birth is automatically entitled to claim Irish citizenship by applying for a foreign birth registration.[16] However, issues can arise where a child's birth was never registered in the Foreign Birth Registry despite the entitlement to become an Irish citizen in that way. This can result in a young person in this situation continuing to be subject to Irish immigration control and treated as a non-EEA national for all state purposes.[17]

Individuals can also apply for Irish citizenship through naturalisation when they have completed a specified period of lawful residence in Ireland, in line with certain conditions.[18] Naturalisation is granted at the absolute discretion of the Minister for Justice and Equality. Applicants must be 'of full age' or 'a minor born in the State'.[19] For a certificate of naturalisation for a child, the 'applicant' means the 'parent or guardian of, or person who is in loco parentis to, the minor'.[20] This means that children cannot apply for naturalisation independently. They are reliant on the application being made by their parent or guardian. This fails to recognise the evolving capacity and growing autonomy of children, despite international obligations under the UN Convention on the Rights of the Child that Ireland has ratified. It can also prevent access to citizenship where the parent or guardian is not available or willing to submit an application in respect of a child, or where there is disagreement about who can act as the child's guardian for the purpose of the application.

Several other barriers to citizenship were identified in the *Child Migration Matters* report. The INIS website states: 'An application on behalf of a child cannot be made until one of their parents is naturalised first, unless they were born in the State or are of Irish associations.'[21] This policy is reflected in the application forms that are available on the Irish Naturalisation and Immigration Service website. This position is the opposite of reduced residence requirements which exist for children in some jurisdictions. For example, in Slovakia applicants over eighteen years must have eight years of residence to apply for citizenship, but children can apply if they have three years' uninterrupted permanent residence.

The Irish Nationality and Citizenship Act 2004 does allow the Minister to grant an application for naturalisation even if the conditions are not met, provided that the applicant is of 'Irish associations', which is defined as 'related by blood, affinity or adoption to a person who is an Irish citizen'.[22] However, the situations in which successful applications are made on the basis of Irish associations are unclear. Some applications on the basis of Irish siblings have been refused on the grounds that the Minister does not consider this to be a sufficiently strong association, a position which is arguably irrational, while other applications on the same grounds by promising sports stars have been successful.[23]

These provisions, together with the accompanying application forms, restrict the naturalisation eligibility of children whose parents have not yet naturalised. The requirement for a parent to naturalise first delays the child's access to citizenship – it is not possible for the applications to be submitted and considered concurrently.[24] This policy does not appear to have a rational basis. Parents, as well as children, have a right to choose whether they seek Irish nationality. Considerations might include whether their country of origin permits dual nationality, personal loyalties and the high cost of a certificate of naturalisation, if granted. Where a parent's application for naturalisation is refused (e.g. on grounds of a conviction), their children are penalised because of crimes they did not commit. The impact can be particularly severe where a child was taken into state care because of parental abuse which also resulted in a criminal record and the refusal of the parent's application for naturalisation.

In Ireland, there is a significant lack of clarity and an absence of consistency in the processing of applications for naturalisation in respect of children. This is the experience of the Immigrant Council and of child welfare practitioners, solicitors and barristers consulted during the 2016 research. Social workers and guardians *at litem* expressed their frustration at the lack of clarity and certainty around the processes and requirements for naturalisation, particularly in respect of children in the care of the state.[25] One social worker spoke of making applications for naturalisation on behalf of two children who were both subject to full care orders in almost identical circumstances. One application was granted while the other was refused, with no apparent justification.[26] Attention to the position of migrant children in care is particularly warranted given that migrant families in Ireland are up to ten times more likely to find themselves subject to child protection interventions.[27]

The *Child Migration Matters* report made a series of recommendations aimed at resolving these issues in a manner that met the needs of migrant children and young people and promoted their capacity, autonomy and integration.[28] For example, it was recommended that the Minister for Justice and Equality amend the Irish Nationality and Citizenship legislation to clarify that children can make applications for naturalisation independently on meeting specified criteria and on the completion of prescribed lengths of residence, and that a fee waiver should be granted in cases of hardship. It was further recommended that social workers should be accepted as having the authority to sign applications for the naturalisation of children in the care of the state; that time spent in the care of the state is counted as 'reckonable residence' for citizenship regardless of whether a parent held a legal residence permission during that time; and that sworn affidavits of birth be accepted in respect of children who cannot acquire identity documentation from the authorities in their countries of origin despite making reasonable efforts to do so, where it is not reasonable to expect that they return to their country of origin to obtain documentation and where their identity is accepted by other state authorities. To date, none of these recommendations has been adopted.

Relationship between residence status, citizenship and integration

Several previous research reports have highlighted the relationship between immigration status, integration, access to citizenship and the potential for social exclusion. For example, research published in 2008 and 2011 highlighted the fundamental extent to which temporary immigration status affects a person's ability to make long-term plans, participate fully in society and, ultimately, that person's successful integration or marginalisation arising from the restrictions that temporary residence imposes on decision-making, self-sufficiency and capacity to benefit from basic economic, political, social and cultural opportunities, as well as access to critical services and social benefits/protections.[29]

Delays in addressing a child's immigration status in a timely manner can restrict or prevent their access to further education, employment, social welfare and housing as access is dependent on secure immigration status. The policies of many departments outside the Department of Justice and Equality have a profound impact on the lives of young migrants. This is particularly true of policies that determine access to education, employment, housing and social welfare. It appears that, in drafting policies around eligibility for assistance in accessing those services, adequate consideration is not given to the wide range of situations in which immigration permission is granted to individuals. Instead, policies are drawn narrowly, listing very specific permission scenarios. This failure to consider the rights of children in different situations restricts their access to education, employment, housing and social welfare in a manner that is ultimately detrimental to the rights of the children and young people concerned.

Conclusion

Migrant children are not a homogeneous group and their individual lived experiences may be very different. However, although varied, the case studies in the *Child Migration Matters* report provide a compelling narrative of young lives, full of challenge and complexity. Similar to the findings of earlier research, the relationship between a child's residence status and access to other rights was highlighted.

Immigration law and practice in Ireland operates in a way that marginalises some migrant children. There are a number of barriers to children obtaining immigration status, including a lack of transparent guidelines around the registration of children with the immigration authorities and a general lack of awareness about the duty for such children to register. Irish law excludes many children from eligibility for naturalisation even if they have resided in the state since birth, by linking the child's entitlement to naturalisation with the immigration status of that child's parents. These limitations can result in ceilings on opportunities such as the child's ability to access education, to access appropriate social welfare supports and accommodation, the right to earn a living and the right to respect of family relationships.

Although not explicitly explored in the report, the case studies (and the experience of service providers) suggest that children and young people are keen to be granted residence status so they are able to access education and employment just like their Irish peers. Similarly, this can be the motivation for applying for Irish citizenship, and this can also be an expression of identity by young people who have been born in or who have grown up in Ireland. Young people do not choose to remain outsiders but, arguably, this is the outcome of state-imposed policy and bureaucracy.

In 2016, the UN Committee on the Rights of the Child (UNCRC) examined Ireland's compliance with the UN Convention on the Rights of the Child and expressed concern at the current inadequacy of Ireland's migration law framework to address the needs of migrant children, pointing, in particular, to the lack of timely information and advice provided to them to address their residence status. Emphasising the requirement that all children are entitled to the full protection and implementation of their rights under the UN Convention on the Rights of the Child regardless of their migration status or that of their parents, the UNCRC then made specific recommendations for Ireland to adopt a comprehensive legal framework and to ensure that the framework included clear and accessible procedures for conferring immigration status on children.[30] However, it was not prescriptive regarding the specific measures that should be taken. The need for these recommendations to be implemented, in the interests of migrant children and young people in Ireland, remains pressing and clear.

Greater transparency in the operation of the immigration system, and recognition of the autonomy and evolving capacity of children in relation to naturalisation, could make a real difference to the realisation of young people's rights, and ultimately their lives. When accurate and timely advice and supports are provided, there can be a real difference to the realisation of a young person's rights and, ultimately, their life. The current 'othering' and exclusions imposed on young people by and within the immigration system is entirely avoidable.

Notes

1 All figures from the Central Statistics Office unless otherwise stated: www.cso.ie.
2 J. Bhabha, J. Kanics, D. Senovilla Hernandez and K. Touzenis (eds), *Migrating Alone: Unaccompanied and Separated Children's Migration to Europe* (Geneva: UNESCO, 2010), p. 92.
3 See, for example, E. Quinn, C. Joyce and E. Gusciute, *Policies and Practices on Unaccompanied Minors in Ireland* (Dublin: ESRI, 2014); M. Ní Raghallaigh, *Foster Care and Supported Lodging for Separated Asylum-Seeking Young People in Ireland: The Views of Young People, Carers and Stakeholders* (Dublin: Barnardos and HSE, 2013); S. Arnold and L. Sarsfield Collins, *Closing a Protection Gap* (Dublin: Irish Refugee Council, 2012).
4 P. Szlovak and J. Szewczyk, *Voices of Young Migrant Men* (Dublin: Immigrant Council of Ireland, 2015).
5 H. Becker, C. Cosgrave and M. Labor, *Family Reunification – A Barrier or Facilitator of Integration? Country Report Ireland* (Dublin: Immigrant Council of Ireland, 2013).
6 K. Mannion, *Child Migration Matters: Children and Young People's Experiences of Migration* (Dublin: Immigrant Council of Ireland, 2016).
7 Section 13, Immigration Act 2004.
8 A. Feldman, M. Gilmartin, S. Loyal and B Migge, *Getting On: From Migration to Integration: Chinese, Lithuanina and Nigerian Migrants' Experiences in Ireland* (Dublin: Immigrant Council of Ireland, 2008).

9 Student Support Regulations 2017 (SI No. 126 of 2017).
10 Higher Education Authority, Student Finance Course Fees (2018).
11 See further http://universities.cityofsanctuary.org, accessed 28 January 2019.
12 Section 14 of the Student Support Act 2011.
13 Article 13 of the European Convention on Human Rights, together with Protocol 1, Article 2. See further *Bah v the United Kingdom* [2011] ECHR 1448, *Belgian Linguistics case (No.2)* (1968) 1 EHRR 252, *Ponomaryov v Bulgaria* (2011) 59 EHRR 799 and *R (Tigere) v Secretary of State for Business, Innovation and Skills* [2015] UKSC 57.
14 Mannion, *Child Migration Matters*, p. 226.
15 Irish Nationality and Citizenship Act 2004, Section 6, 6A and 6B.
16 See generally M. Stanley, *Immigration and Citizenship Law* (Dublin: Round Hall, 2017), pp. 854–855.
17 'African girl wins her long fight to prove Irish citizenship', *Irish Independent*, 14 April 2013.
18 Irish Nationality and Citizenship Act 1956 as amended by the Irish Nationality and Citizenship Acts 2001 and 2004, part III Conditions: '15 (a)(i) is of full age or (ii) is a minor born in the State; (b) is of good character; has had a period of one year's continuous residence in the State immediately before the date of the application and, during the eight years immediately preceding that period, has had a total residence in the State amounting to four years; (d) intends in good faith to continue to reside in the State after naturalisation; and (e) has (i) … made a declaration of fidelity to the nation and loyalty to the State, and (ii) undertaken to faithfully observe the laws of the State and to respect its democratic values'.
19 Section 15 of the Irish Nationality and Citizenship Act 1956 (as amended).
20 Section 16 of the Irish Nationality and Citizenship Act 1956 (as amended). The Minister may, in his absolute discretion, grant an application for a certificate of naturalisation in the following cases, although the conditions for naturalisation (or any of them) are not complied with: (a) where the applicant is of Irish descent or Irish associations; (b) where the applicant is a parent or guardian acting on behalf of a minor of Irish descent or Irish associations; (c) where the applicant is a naturalised Irish citizen acting on behalf of the minor child of the applicant.
21 Section 16 of the Irish Nationality and Citizenship Act 1956 (as amended).
22 Section 16(2) of the Irish Nationality and Citizenship Act 1956 (as amended) provides that a person is of Irish associations if (a) he or she is related by blood, affinity or adoption to, or is the civil partner of, a person who is an Irish citizen or entitled to be an Irish citizen, or (b) he or she was related by blood, affinity or adoption to, or was the civil partner of, a person who is deceased and who, at the time of his or her death, was an Irish citizen or entitled to be an Irish citizen.
23 Mannion, *Child Migration Matters*, p. 229. See also 'U-turn over refusal to hear young athlete's naturalisation claim', *Sunday Times*, 22 February 2015.
24 C. Cosgrave, *Living in Limbo: Migrants' Experiences of Applying for Naturalisation in Ireland* (Dublin: Immigrant Council of Ireland, 2011), pp. 27 and 53.
25 Mannion, *Child Migration Matters*, p. 231.
26 Ibid., p. 231.

27 C. Coulter, *Childcare Law Reporting Project: Final Report* (Dublin: Child Care Law Project, November 2015), www.childproject.ie, accessed 28 January 2019.
28 Mannion, *Child Migration Matters*, p. 241.
29 Feldman et al., *Getting On*; Cosgrave, *Living in Limbo*.
30 See paras 67 and 68, UN Committee on the Rights of the Child, Concluding Observations on the combined third and fourth periodic reports of Ireland, 1 March 2016, CRC/C/IRL/CO.

Immigrant-origin children and the education system

The position of immigrants – individuals who move permanently to a foreign country – in society is influenced by the structures and policies of the receiving society, as well as the characteristics of immigrant families themselves. International research has highlighted the crucial role of schools in helping immigrant-origin children and young people to settle into the new society.[1] Like all other children, immigrant-origin children spend a large part of their day at the school, where they encounter students and teachers from the majority culture and learn to adjust to a new institutional environment, its rules and regulations. Quite often these may differ markedly from that of their countries of background. For decades, the Irish educational system has been based on relative national homogeneity. This explains the ad-hoc character of policy responses to cultural diversity in schools.

Because immigration to Ireland has been a relatively recent phenomenon, the children and young people being discussed in this chapter are almost always the children of first-generation immigrants – even if they are not first-generation immigrants themselves. Typically, immigrant-origin children are defined as those whose parents – either one or both – are born abroad, though sometimes the focus is on the parents' country of origin or nationality, and sometimes the focus is on home language, ethnicity, religion or legal status.

Immigrant-origin students in Ireland often find themselves in a situation whereby, on the one hand, they are 'outsiders' with little familiarity of the nature of the Irish school system. On the other hand, the highly educated profile of immigrant families means that they often possess the kinds of social and cultural capital valued by the school system. However, the ease with which immigrant-origin students settle in a school may vary across nationalities, linguistic or religious groups, and social class depending on various types of capital at their disposal. In other words, the extent to which immigrant-origin students are 'insiders' or 'outsiders' may vary across a number of characteristics. Some groups of young people can be particularly marginalised and experience exclusion in the Irish education system and beyond. Other groups may be marginalised in some settings, or life domains, but not necessarily in others. This chapter explores the experiences of immigrant-origin children in the academic and social spheres – both equally important for laying necessary groundwork for the future lives of these young people.

A distinctive feature of the immigrant population in Ireland is its diversity in terms of country of origin, legal status, religious affiliation, ethnicity and language proficiency. Census 2016 results show that the immigrant body is drawn from 180 countries, with the largest national groups now originating from Poland, the UK and Lithuania.[2] This diversity, as well as dispersal across the country, may hinder the development of some ethnic enclaves in the Irish context; however, there is evidence of significant numbers of immigrants from some countries, such as Poland, that are well settled and some of which have even established formal networks and Sunday schools. Two-thirds of immigrants to Ireland are from other EU countries and one-third are from non-EU countries. EU nationals are free to live and work in Ireland, but non-EU groups must enter the country on the basis of an employment or student visa or as an asylum seeker or programme refugee. Most people come to Ireland to work, though there is an increasing proportion of students among the non-EU population and some asylum seekers and refugees.

Census 2016 data show that the non-Irish population is (at 66 per cent) predominantly white. Of all non-Irish citizens 9 per cent were black and 14 per cent were Asian, with 10 per cent classified as other or mixed ethnicity. The Republic of Ireland's immigrant population is linguistically very diverse, speaking 182 native languages.[3] Over two-thirds (68 per cent) speak a language other than English (or Irish) at home. Over half (55 per cent) of those who speak a language other than English report that they speak English 'very well', though English-language proficiency varies significantly by length of time living in Ireland and national origin. Census 2016 data show that whereas over 80 per cent of the Irish population are Catholic, just under half of the non-Irish population are Catholic. This is relevant given the dominance of the Catholic Church in the education system in Ireland, particularly at primary level.[4]

Compared with the Irish population, the Economic and Social Research Institute's Integration Monitor shows that immigrants to Ireland are highly educated. In 2015 almost half working age non-Irish adults had third-level qualifications, compared with just over one-third of Irish working age adults.[5] This may have implications for their children's attainment. However, existing research finds that immigrants to Ireland fare less well than Irish nationals in the labour market across a range of dimensions, including (see Chapter 5) access to higher-paid and higher-status jobs, experience of discrimination at work, and levels of unemployment.[6] Such differential earnings and opportunities may impact on educational opportunities, especially when it comes to accessing extra-curricular activities, like music and drama, many of which need to be paid for. While income levels of UK-origin families were similar to those of Irish families, Western European families tended to have higher incomes. Eastern European and Asian families tended to have lower incomes than Irish families but the lowest incomes were found among African families.

Large-scale studies of children, like the *Growing Up in Ireland* study, allow researchers to compare the outcomes of immigrant-origin children with the host population.[7] Much of the literature in this review draws on these data, or other nationally representative data like the Programme for International Student Assessment (PISA), a global educational study, which aims to evaluate education systems worldwide by testing the skills and knowledge of fifteen-year-old students. The longitudinal nature of the *Growing Up in Ireland* study has also allowed researchers to follow children over time, facilitating investigation of the role of duration in immigrant outcomes. There are, as well as these quantitative studies, a range of qualitative studies which give a richer understanding of the experiences of immigrant-origin children.

The academic sphere

Educational achievement is important for upward mobility for all groups in a society. Academic progress is particularly important for immigrant-origin children as many immigrant families, despite their high levels of educational attainment, experience downward mobility – working in occupations below their skill level.[8] Coming from a different education system and speaking a different language is likely to render immigrant children as outsiders.

As in many other countries, immigrants in Ireland – most of whom are first-generation immigrants – have high expectations for their children. Using *Growing Up in Ireland* data at the age of nine years, our research shows that more than 90 per cent of African and Asian mothers expect their children to go to third-level education, compared with around 70 per cent of Irish mothers. Immigrant-origin children also tend to have more positive attitudes towards school and their teachers than Irish children. For example, just under half of children of Eastern European, African or Asian origin report that they always look forward to school, compared with just under one-quarter of Irish children.[9] This is in line with the first comprehensive study on immigrant-origin children, published in 2009, which found that they are perceived by school teachers and principals as highly motivated, in some instances as 'model children'.[10]

The *Growing Up in Ireland* survey followed the nine-year-olds as they made the transition to secondary school. Some immigrant-origin children were found to underperform academically compared with their native-born counterparts. At age nine, distinguishing by country of origin, English reading test scores are significantly lower among those from Eastern Europe, Asia and Africa, with the largest gap found for Eastern Europeans.[11] Family background and school attended explain part of this gap, but a greater role is played by native language: a gap in English reading scores remains for children of Eastern Europeans even after controlling for language difficulty. For mathematics, no gap was found for the children of Eastern European, Western European and Asian mothers. The data indicate modest difference in mathematics scores between the children of African mothers and those with white Irish mothers but this disappears once background characteristics, including financial hardship, are taken into account. As one might expect, linguistic capabilities (how well students speak English) affect educational achievement for nine-year-olds, particularly in the case of English reading scores.[12] Standardised tests in mathematics, reading and spelling in 2nd and 6th classes of primary school, which test different age groups, indicate lower scores for children from non-English-speaking backgrounds compared with their Irish peers.[13] The findings of these largely echo the *Growing Up in Ireland* data.

Growing Up in Ireland survey tests administered to thirteen-year-olds assessed in verbal and numerical reasoning produced evidence of lower verbal reasoning scores among immigrant students at thirteen, although no significant differences in numerical reasoning scores.[14] Students from an English-language background performed significantly better than students from other language backgrounds.[15] For numerical reasoning, the authors actually find slightly higher scores among non-English-speakers. Similar patterns are found using the 2015 PISA survey, which tested 'literacy' in reading, mathematics and particularly science at the age of fifteen. There is no difference, on average, between immigrant-origin students and Irish students in science scores. However, immigrant-origin students from non-English-speaking backgrounds have both lower scores in English reading and slightly lower scores in mathematics.[16]

While overall differences are relatively modest, immigrant-origin students may struggle academically in a curriculum that requires high levels of language skills, particularly at second level. This is especially the case for those with English-language difficulties. Recognising the need to bring immigrant-origin students 'up to speed', the main targeted support in Irish schools is language support.[17] It has been argued that language proficiency acquires particular importance in academic assessment because particularly low proficiency can mask students' actual knowledge.[18] While there is a need to assist immigrant-origin students in acquiring proficiency in the language of instruction, it is also important to ensure that appropriate assessment approaches are used.

What about progression through school? A small-scale study suggests that in some schools, immigrant-origin students were significantly less likely to take higher-level subjects in their Junior Certificate examinations compared with Irish students – even if they had the same language fluency, gender and socio-economic background.[19] In the same vein, a large-scale qualitative study from 2008 showed that migrant students in Ireland faced multiple barriers in terms of access to schools, placement in classes, year groups and types of secondary school programme, where they tend to be steered into less academic tracks and lower-ability classes.[20]

While the above studies provide some insight into how immigrant-origin children are faring in the Irish educational system, to date there are no data on performance in state-level exams (Junior Certificate, Leaving Certificate) that distinguish immigrant-origin and Irish students sufficiently to allow ongoing monitoring of their comparative academic progress. It is also not possible to follow the post-school pathways of immigrant children, including their progress (or not) into higher and further education and subsequent entry into the Irish labour market.

The social sphere

While academic achievement and attitudes to school are important for both school experience and later life chances, the social sphere is equally relevant to considering whether children are 'insiders' or 'outsiders' in Irish society. Social interaction provides a variety of protective functions – a sense of belonging, emotional support, and a source of information. While this is important for all individuals in society, the protective functions provided by social interaction are of particular importance for newly arrived immigrant families and their children. But the migration process itself can interrupt access to these, where migrants' stay is transient and they need repeatedly to adapt to new systems and networks and make new friends.

International research suggests that the positive effects of diversity seem to be linear: students attending more (ethnically) mixed schools tended to report more favourable attitudes towards migrants.[21] Elsewhere it has been found that cross-group friendships are particularly important in promoting positive views.[22] However, in Ireland research has found that the proportion of migrant students in a school does not necessarily have a notable effect on the attitudes of other children. Rather, getting to know immigrant-origin children by means of shared interests and activities seems to be more important in terms of encouraging positive attitudes.[23]

Friendships are important to all children but offer additionally a protective social function to those new to a country and school. In Ireland, data show that immigrant-origin children have at least some close friends, but the number of close friends differs significantly by national group – Eastern Europeans are more likely than other groups to report that they have few friends. Asian children also tend to have fewer friends than their Irish counterparts.[24] While previous research has indicated that smaller friendship networks may be explained by the lack of English-language proficiency among some immigrants, additional analyses indicate that differences in the number of friends by national group is not explained by having limited English. This indicates that the reasons for smaller friendship networks, at least as measured here, may lie elsewhere. However, another study examining friendship groups in Irish schools found that proficiency in speaking English was central to forming friendships.[25]

Immigrant-origin children also experience incidences of racially motivated bullying in Ireland. A study of Irish primary schools has shown that name-calling, particularly racist name-calling, has been used by some children to assert a superior status to black immigrant-origin children.[26] Another study found that Eastern European and African children report higher incidences of bullying than Irish children.[27]

Children's wellbeing and self-perception vary by national groups. A 2016 study found that at age nine, children from immigrant families[28] are less confident across all domains than children from Irish families; in other words, they see themselves as less popular, are less happy and more anxious, report poorer behaviour, and are more self-critical of their academic abilities and their body image. However, by thirteen, when all the children were at second-level schools, children from an immigrant background were found not to differ from their Irish peers, on average.[29] This finding suggests an improvement in wellbeing for the group over time, but further research is necessary to distinguish between different groups of immigrant children and investigate which children see an improvement in their wellbeing.

Engagement in sport and cultural activities enables students to meet others and make friends. In Ireland, participation in sport and fitness activities is popular across all groups. However, there are significant variations in participation levels between groups, with Asian and Eastern European primary and secondary students less likely to engage in these activities. Differences can also be observed in participation in cultural activities, with Asian and Eastern Europeans again less likely to take part. The fact that the majority of organised cultural and sports activities among this group require payment could also explain lower participation among lower-income migrant groups.[30] However, there is some evidence that immigrant-origin young people become relatively more involved in sports and cultural activities over time.[31] This most likely reflects improved English-language proficiency, greater adjustment to life in a new country and greater familiarity with the kinds of out-of-school activity available. However, some national origin differences persist, with Asian teenagers less likely to take part in these structured activities even when they have moved to secondary schools. In addition, language also matters – those from a family whose first language is not English continue to have lower rates of participation at the age of thirteen. Because earlier involvement in sporting and cultural activities is predictive of later participation in these pursuits during secondary education, it is important to focus on encouraging such involvement within primary schools.

While all immigrant-origin children face certain challenges when moving into a new country, some groups can be considered particularly vulnerable: refugee and asylum-seeking children, unaccompanied minors and children of Roma origin. Programme Refugee children often travel in the company of their parents because family units are prioritised for resettlement by the Irish government.[32] Programme Refugee children have access to free primary and post-primary education. In addition, refugee children may access free third-level education if they have lived in Ireland for three years or more. While asylum-seeking children await a decision on their claim, they may access free primary and post-primary education. However, they are not eligible for free third-level education, even though some universities operate limited scholarship schemes (see Chapter 12). Unaccompanied minors (children who travel on their own to seek protection in a country other than their own) have often experienced significant trauma during their migration experience, and this presents additional challenges for accessing education.[33] Finally, Roma children face extreme poverty in Ireland.[34] Poverty and poor living conditions are repeatedly identified by both education stakeholders and the Roma community as a formidable barrier to accessing education. If parents cannot access social welfare payments or suitable housing, school attendance and participation become secondary to providing more basic needs like food and shelter.

The role of schools and the education system

The following discussion focuses on how the insider–outsider situation plays out in the education system for immigrant-origin children and young people. Here we consider first some features of the education system that tend to exclude children from an immigrant background, though often not explicitly designed to do so, and then we examine the emergence of policies to support these children and young people in Ireland.

Past research has found that schools' admission criteria tended to favour Irish-born populations with strong historic links to the area and schools. This resulted in a situation whereby many new arrivals to the country attended schools that were not oversubscribed, such as schools catering for more deprived populations in urban areas.[35] More recent research has shown that little has changed. Immigrant-origin children at the age of nine are still more likely to attend disadvantaged schools

(DEIS), particularly children of Eastern European and African origin. A 2015 ESRI study found that while just 9 per cent of Irish children attended Urban DEIS Band 1 schools, 17 per cent of Eastern European children and 25 per cent of African children did so.[36] This is likely to be due to school admission practices and because immigrant families tend to settle in more deprived areas because housing is cheaper.[37] The presence of immigrant-origin children in DEIS schools has, in some instances, resulted in a boost in the academic achievement of such schools, with many immigrant-origin children seen as 'model students' with high motivation and aspirations. At the same time, previous research has shown that children attending DEIS schools do not perform academically as well as those in non-DEIS schools for a variety of reasons including resources and less experienced teachers.[38] Therefore this is likely to be the case for immigrant-origin children as well. The Education (Admission to Schools) Bill 2016 aims to address school enrolment policies that previously tended to disadvantage families new to an area. It also seeks to end waiting lists and allows for an introduction of annual enrolment structures, thus promoting transparency and fairness in admissions for pupils and their parents. While this is a welcome development, it remains to be seen if the new legislation changes the situation for immigrant families in real terms.

Another area where potential insider–outsider positioning occurs is school patronage and the provision of religious education in Irish schools. Ireland is an interesting case study as its educational system (particularly at primary school level) is largely denominational despite increasing religious diversity among its population. A forum on school patronage was set up in 2011, with its advisory group establishing the potential for divestment of patronage.[39] There have been some changes, though progress has been slow, with only a small number of schools divested from religious patronage. While parents may opt their child out of religious education, doing so may emphasise difference between children, something that parents may wish to avoid. Children removed from religious education classes may feel self-conscious and different from other children.[40]

Another issue is that most primary and secondary school teachers are still white, Irish and middle class.[41] So far there has been little focus on promoting diversity in teacher education programmes.[42] Insufficient understanding of the cultural backgrounds of immigrant-origin students may result in teachers seeing them in 'deficit' terms, 'lacking' something.[43]

Targeted support measures, capable of meeting the needs of students from a number of different cultural and linguistic backgrounds, are needed to ensure that immigrant-origin children have the same opportunities as others. A key policy initiative to date has been the Intercultural Education Strategy, 2010–2015, launched in September 2010. This combined an emphasis on intercultural guidelines with English-language tuition, which accounted for a large part of the financial resources devoted to the strategy.

While the strategy aims that 'all education providers are assisted with ensuring that inclusion and integration within an intercultural learning environment become the norm',[44] the extent to which (the mostly white Irish) school principals and teachers are committed to implementing these guidelines is not known.

The resource allocation model for children for whom English is an additional language (EAL) has changed over time. Since the 2012/2013 academic year EAL funding has been merged with special needs funding, with funding for schools dependent on the total number of students requiring either learning support or language support. Schools have autonomy to switch teaching hours between special needs support and English-language support. This model makes it difficult to assess the actual amount of resources allocated to children from an immigrant background, and thus monitor the implementation of the intercultural education strategy, given that spending on EAL represents such a large proportion of spending on this. Immigrant-origin students in Ireland can also avail of other supports put in place in schools for all children, including the pastoral care support and additional resources provided through the DEIS programme.

Conclusion

Many studies of immigrant-origin children in Ireland focus on academic achievement and attainment as well as social interaction. Early educational advantage is often seen as a cornerstone for improved life chances. A higher level of education is understood to predict higher earnings, better health and a longer life, and vice versa. Research in Ireland has shown that immigrant-origin young people are more at risk of poor educational outcomes than 'native' young people, but that there is considerable variation among as well as within groups. Additional risks of poor educational outcomes arise when students' families are undocumented, are refugees from war zones, are living in poverty, have little formal education and have little understanding of the social structures of the new adopted country. Immigrant-origin young people will vary in the type and number of supports they need to enable a successful transition and adjustment to school and neighbourhood.

Many immigrant-origin children have an 'outsider' status in terms of previous experience in a different education system or interrupted schooling. In particular, poor proficiency in the language of instruction is likely to make it difficult for some immigrant-origin children to perform at the same level as 'native'-born children, particularly in English reading. We have noted that differences in mathematics are typically much smaller, with some studies finding that immigrant children do not on average differ from Irish children. Overall, the achievement gap is largest in English reading for children of Eastern European background while it is greatest for children of African background in mathematics. This may be because there tends to be a correlation between low income and low levels of mathematics achievement for the general population, and children of African backgrounds in Ireland are more likely to live in low-income households.

In general, immigrant-origin children are found to have very positive attitudes to school, and their parents to have high educational aspirations for them. Whether this translates into later achievement remains to be seen. Some educational policies seem to encourage 'othering' of immigrants in terms of access to schools and pathways within schools, which can contribute to these young people not reaching their potential and having poorer subsequent labour market outcomes. Understanding the diverse nature of immigrant groups and monitoring their outcomes are essential in developing appropriate school policies and practices.

While social relations are important for all the individuals in a society, the protective functions provided by social interaction are of particular importance for newly arrived immigrant families and their children. Immigrant families may need to renegotiate their position in the receiving countries several times and many are likely to experience a sense of dislocation. Irish studies have indicated that while all children may find social relations with peers and teachers strained at times, in some cases cultural distance contributes towards the 'outsider' status of immigrant-origin children. Eastern European and Asian children tend to have fewer friends than Irish peers at age nine, though this is not the case for African children. Eastern European, Asian and African children are also less likely to play team sports than Irish children, though the gap is smaller for African children. All three groups (Eastern European, Asian and African children) are less likely to do cultural activities like music and drama at age nine than Irish children, which may be related to both lack of parental knowledge about these opportunities and income differences. Differences in sport and cultural activities are much smaller at thirteen, though Asian teenagers are still less likely to take part in these activities by thirteen than Irish teenagers. In terms of wellbeing, immigrant-origin children overall have lower levels of wellbeing at age nine but not by age thirteen. This is encouraging, suggesting that time in the country plays an important role and that immigrant children's social integration may be improving, at least for this cohort of children.

While the insider–outsider dichotomy has been contested, the approach is useful in understanding barriers that immigrant-origin young people may face in the schools of the receiving country, despite the apparently deterministic undercurrent of the dichotomy. This chapter has shown that while the concept is useful, it is far from clear-cut. While some immigrant-origin children may be 'insiders' in terms of shared language, they can be 'outsiders' in other areas such as religion. Or, having high educational aspirations may reflect the same values as held by the majority of the Irish population, while various other criteria may render highly educated immigrant parents with high aspirations still as 'outsiders'. Even though immigrant-origin students may often find themselves in an 'out-group' when entering the country, many are likely to develop various strategies to negotiate fields such as religious background, ethnic group and class in different institutional contexts. Focusing on structural barriers that limit the effectiveness of strategies adopted by immigrants and highlighting their considerable agency is vital in devising policies and practices of intercultural education that support all children in reaching their potential.

Notes

1 A. Gitlin, E. Bunedia, K. Crosland and D. Foumbia, 'The production of margin and center: welcoming–unwelcoming of immigrant students', *American Educational Research Journal*, 40:1 (2013), 91–122.
2 Central Statistics Office 2017, Census 2016 summary results. Available online at www.cso.ie, accessed 30 January 2019.
3 2016 Census data, Irish Travellers, Ethnicity and Religion. See www.cso.ie.
4 Ibid.
5 A. Barrett, F. McGinnity and E. Quinn (eds), *Monitoring Report on Integration 2016* (Dublin: ESRI, 2017).
6 Ibid.
7 *Growing Up in Ireland* is the national longitudinal study of children and youth in Ireland. The child cohort started in 2008 with 8,500 children aged nine years and followed them up at age thirteen. Detailed information was collected from parents, teachers and the children themselves. See www.esri.ie/growing-up-in-ireland/, accessed 30 January 2019.
8 P. O'Connell and F. McGinnity, *Immigrants at Work: Ethnicity and Nationality in the Irish Labour Market* (Dublin: Equality Authority and ESRI, 2008).
9 F. McGinnity, E. Quinn, G. Kingston, and P. J. O'Connell, *Annual Monitoring Report on Integration 2011* (Dublin: ESRI/The Integration Centre, 2012).
10 E. Smyth, M. Darmody, F. McGinnity and D. Byrne, *Adapting to Diversity: Irish Schools and Newcomer Students* (Dublin: ESRI, 2009).
11 M. Darmody, F. McGinnity and G. Kingston, *The Experiences of Migrant Children in Ireland* (Dublin: ESRI, 2016).
12 M. Darmody and E. Smyth, 'Immigrant student achievement and educational policy in Ireland', in L. Volante, D. Klinger and O. Bilgili (eds), *Immigrant Student Achievement and Education Policy: Cross-Cultural Approaches* (Cham: Springer, 2018), pp. 119–135.
13 L. Kavanagh, G. Sheil, L. Gilleece and J. Kiniry, *The 2014 National Assessments of English Reading and Mathematics. Volume II: Context Report* (Dublin: Educational Research Centre, 2016).
14 Compared with a non-immigrant mean score of 99.98, immigrant students scored 97.71 in verbal reasoning. Mean scores for numerical reasoning were 99.78 (non-immigrant) and 99.60 (immigrant). See Darmody and Smyth, 'Immigrant student achievement'.

15 Students from an English-language background scored 98.51 on average in verbal reasoning, compared with 93.51 for those from a non-English-speaking background. Ibid.

16 Ibid.

17 D. Faas, B. Sokolowska and M. Darmody, '"Everybody is available to them": support measures for migrant students in Irish secondary schools', *British Journal of Educational Studies*, 63:4 (2015), 447–466; M. Taguma, M. Kim, G. Wurzburg and F. Kelly, *OECD Reviews of Migrant Education: Ireland* (Paris: OECD, 2009).

18 A. Keogh and J. Whyte, *Getting On? The Experiences and Aspirations of Immigrant Students in Second Level Schools Linked to the Trinity Access Programmes* (Dublin: The Children's Research Centre, Trinity College, 2003).

19 V. Ledwith and K. Reilly, 'Two tiers emerging? School choice and educational achievement disparities among young migrants and non-migrants in Galway City and urban fringe', *Population, Space and Place*, 19:1 (2013), 46–59.

20 M. Darmody, D. Byrne and F. McGinnity, 'Cumulative disadvantage? Educational careers of migrant students in Irish secondary schools', *Race Ethnicity Education*, 17:1 (2012), 129–151.

21 J. Hughes, A. Campbell, S. Lolliot, M. Hewstone and T. Gallagher, 'Inter group contact at school and social attitudes: evidence from Northern Ireland', *Oxford Review of Education*, 39:6 (2013), 761–779.

22 K. Davies, L. R. Tropp, A. Aron, T. F. Pettigrew and S. C. Wright, 'Cross group friendships and intergroup attitudes: a meta-analytic review', *Personality and Social Psychology Review*, 15 (2011), 332–351.

23 M. Darmody and E. Smyth, '"When you actually talk to them …" Recognising and respecting cultural and religious diversity in Irish schools', in I. Honohan and N. Rougier (eds), *Tolerance in Ireland, North and South* (Manchester: Manchester University Press, 2015), pp. 17–34.

24 Darmody, McGinnity and Kingston, *Experiences of Migrant Children*.

25 S. McDonnell, 'Speaking distance: language, friendship and spaces of belonging in Irish primary schools', in M. Theobald (ed.), *Friendship and Peer Culture in Multilingual Settings: Sociological Studies of Children and Youth*, 21 (Bingley: Emerald, 2016), pp. 33–53.

26 D. Devine, M. Kenny and E. Macneela, 'Naming the "other": children's construction and experience of racisms in Irish primary schools', *Race, Ethnicity and Education*, 11:4 (2008), 369–385.

27 McGinnity, Quinn, Kingston and O'Connell, *Annual Monitoring Report*.

28 A family was defined as being an immigrant family if both parents had been born outside Ireland, and a non-immigrant family if at least one parent had been born in Ireland.

29 E. Smyth, *Well-being and School Experiences among 9 and 13 Year Olds: Insights from the Growing Up in Ireland Study* (Dublin: ESRI, 2016).

30 M. Darmody and E. Smyth, 'Out-of-school social activities among immigrant-origin children living in Ireland', *Economic and Social Review*, 48:4 (2017), 419–439.

31 Ibid.

32 Programme Refugees are persons with an international protection need who are resettled to Ireland upon request from the United Nations High Commissioner for Refugees.

33 M. Darmody and S. Arnold, 'Refugee children and young people in Ireland: policies and practices', in J. L. McBrien (ed.), *Educational Policies and Practices of English-Speaking Refugee Resettlement Countries* (Rotterdam: Sense Publishers, forthcoming).

34 Pavee Point Traveller and Roma Centre & Department of Justice and Equality, *Roma in Ireland – A National Needs Assessment* (Dublin: Pavee Point Traveller and Roma Centre & Department of Justice and Equality, 2018).

35 D. Byrne, F. McGinnity, E. Smyth and M. Darmody, 'Immigration and school composition in Ireland', *Irish Educational Studies*, 29:3 (2010), 271–288.

36 F. McGinnity, M. Darmody and A. Murray, *Academic Achievement among Immigrant Children in Irish Primary Schools*, ESRI Working Paper No. 512 (Dublin: ESRI, 2015), aei.pitt.edu/88123/, accessed 31 January 2019.

37 Research using Census data for Dublin found immigrants more likely to be living in disadvantaged areas, see T. Fahey and B. Fanning, 'Immigration and socio-spatial segregation in Dublin, 1996–2006', *Urban Studies*, 47:8 (2010), 1625–1642.

38 S. McCoy, A. Quail and E. Smyth, 'The effects of school social mix: unpacking the differences', *Irish Educational Studies*, 33:3 (2014), 307–330.

39 J. Coolahan, C. Hussey and F. Kilfeather, *Report of the Forum's Advisory Group* (Dublin: Forum on Patronage and Pluralism in the Primary Sector, 2012).

40 E. Smyth and M. Darmody, 'Religious diversity and schooling in Ireland', in M. Darmody (ed.), *The Changing Faces of Ireland: Exploring the Lives of Immigrant and Ethnic Minority Children* (Rotterdam: Sense Publishers, 2011), 125–144.

41 E. Keane and M. Heinz, 'Excavating an injustice? Nationality/ies, ethnicity/ies and experiences with diversity of initial teacher education applicants and entrants in Ireland in 2014', *European Journal of Teacher Education*, 39:4 (2016), 507–527.

42 C. Ní Laoire, N. Bushin, N. Carpena-Méndez and A. White, *Tell Me About Yourself: Migrant Children's Experiences of Moving to and Living in Ireland* (Cork: University College Cork, 2009).

43 D. Devine, 'Value'ing children differently? Migrant children in education', *Children & Society*, 27:4 (2013), 282–294.

44 Department of Education and Skills, and Office of the Minister for Integration, *Intercultural Education Strategy, 2010–2015* (Dublin: Department of Education and Skills and the Office of the Minister for Integration, 2010), 2, www.into.ie/ROI/Publications/OtherPublications/OtherPublicationsDownloads/Intercultural_education_strategy.pdf, accessed 30 January 2019.

13 Orla McGarry

Young Muslims as insiders and outsiders

Against the backdrop of the hyper-politicisation of migration in Europe and increased levels of Islamophobia in Western society more generally, Muslims are frequently accused of rejecting inclusion in mainstream society choosing instead to socialise within co-religious communities characterised by distinct cultural and religious practices.[1] These perceptions of Muslims as 'outsiders' living within European society are extremely problematic for Muslim youth negotiating inclusion and 'insider status' in contemporary Ireland. Young Muslims often find themselves torn between two differing, and often conflicting, cultural and social templates; the norms of Irish society and the religious, cultural and social values of Islam. Daily life frequently necessitates a complex series of balancing acts, findings ways to uphold religious and migrant identities while engaging with, and negotiating inclusion within, mainstream society.[2] Expectations that they conform to the norms of mainstream society, attending school and engaging in other social activities, while simultaneously upholding the cultural distinctiveness and religious practices of their migrant and religious communities, can pose a significant challenge to young Muslims. This challenge has been exacerbated by the increased visibility of Muslim communities across Europe since 2007, as a result of violence perpetrated by a small minority of adherents to an extreme interpretation of Islam.[3]

This chapter examines the experiences of teenaged members of a rurally based Muslim community in County Mayo in the Republic of Ireland. Drawing on qualitative research conducted with thirty-three teenagers, it explores factors mediating exclusion and inclusion, examining the strategic and innovative approaches of Muslim youth to negotiating their inclusion in Irish society. Age at the time of immigration is underlined as a major factor affecting the experiences of young migrants which is frequently overlooked in policies and initiatives aimed at fostering inclusion. The chapter engages with wider debates regarding expressions of ethnic and religious identity by young Muslims in Europe. It critiques essentialist views of contemporary pluralist society which problematise expressions of religious and cultural difference as assertions of 'outsider-ness' or withdrawal from wider society. It instead posits public expressions of religious identity as assertions of social membership and symbols of active participation in contemporary Irish society. The discussion highlights the maintenance and valorisation of cultural distinctiveness as an intrinsic element of the negotiation of inclusion and belonging in wider Irish society for Muslim youth.

Migrant youth in contemporary Ireland

Both the Republic of Ireland and Northern Ireland are relative newcomers to the superdiversity associated with the contemporary age of mass migration.[4] As a result, the discourse of social inclusion is relatively underdeveloped. In particular, there is a lack of understanding of the processes through which younger members of ethnic and religious minorities negotiate their positions in contemporary Irish society. For young migrants and members of ethnic minority communities, negotiation of inclusion in contemporary Ireland can be a challenging process. Young migrants in Ireland often have to overcome prejudice and racism, with some experiencing isolation and exclusion on a daily basis as a consequence.[5] These challenges are especially relevant to younger members of Irish-based Muslim communities who are faced with the challenge of reconciling the values and behaviours associated with their Islamic beliefs with the secular norms of Western society.

Studies conducted with young Muslims highlight the difficulties of fitting in and feeling included in wider society while adhering to, and maintaining, important aspects of their religious and ethnic backgrounds. Some aspects of Western culture are seen as incompatible with the tenets of Islam for young Muslims. For example, Valentine et al. detail the difficulties arising for male Muslims in negotiating 'insider' status within the context of a British society where much social interaction involves the consumption of alcohol. For these males, the central place of alcohol in many social contexts necessitates a politicised and conscious choice between the accepted mainstream norms of social behaviour and their religious and ethno-cultural affiliations. Participants in the study described feeling torn between their religious beliefs and social pressures to consume alcohol, with these pressures impacting negatively on their sense of inclusion in British society.[6]

Other studies have highlighted the ingenuity of young Muslims in using religious practices, such as dress and prayer, to assert their position within European society. Young Muslim females in the UK have been shown to embrace religious and ethnic markers to appropriate their membership of British society. These everyday practices can be seen as politicised actions and expressions of a social and cultural identity that is at once compatible with Islam and membership of wider society. Rather than creating barriers between their religious identities and ethnic affiliations and their identities as British citizens, practices such as wearing a *hijab* or veil and public prayer are conveyed as a means of actively asserting their position in, and participating within, British society.[7] Similarly, previous work on the strategies of young female Muslims in the West of Ireland has highlighted discourses of difference as a key strategy in assertion of social inclusion.[8]

These studies underline the complex and nuanced dynamics of inclusion and exclusion for young Muslims in Western society; distinctions between 'insider status' and 'outsider status' are shown to be tenuous and permeable. Crucially, young Muslims are shown as individuals to be the primary architects of their personal biographies, continuously reconciling conflicting norms and expectations of their religious and cultural backgrounds with the secular norms of Western society.[9] However, the negotiation of inclusion and the journey to becoming an 'insider' is a complex process which can be complicated by a number of factors. Successive studies have examined the effect of race, socio-economic background and gender on the negotiation of inclusion among young Muslims in Western society.[10] To date, however, age at the time of immigration is a factor which has been largely overlooked in empirical studies of the experiences of young Muslims in European society.

Work carried out with young migrants of diverse backgrounds in the US has shown age at the time of immigration to be a major differential affecting experiences in the destination society.[11] The category of youth is too broad to allow for an in-depth understanding of the experiences of young migrants. The experiences of second-generation migrants and migrants arriving in the host country as young children differ significantly from those of migrants who arrive during late childhood and adolescence. Arrival at a younger age affords a longer period to adapt to cultural differences and to negotiate inclusion in the destination country. In contrast, migrant youth who arrive during the formative teenage years are more likely to have internalised the cultural and social norms of the country of origin before migration. They are consequently faced with a greater challenge in adjusting to life in the destination country which is compounded by the complex process of identity formation associated with adolescence.[12] In addition, the greater academic pressure experienced during this life stage can cause many young people to experience distress.

In order to allow for an insightful understanding of the difference in experience of immigrants depending on their age of arrival, Rumbaut's typology of generational cohorts differentiates between the experiences of migrants born in the destination country (2.0 generation) and those who arrived in the destination country between the ages of zero and five years (1.75 generation). Migrants arriving between the ages of six and twelve years are seen as the 1.5 generation cohort, while migrants arriving between the ages of thirteen and seventeen years are theorised as belonging to the 1.25 generation cohort. The different experiences of these cohorts exert a significant effect on their educational success and social inclusion:

- *1.25 generation cohort*: Arriving between thirteen and seventeen years, they may either attend secondary school in the destination country or may enter the workforce directly.
- *1.5 generation cohort*: Arriving between six and twelve years as primary school-aged children, they have typically begun to read and to write in the country of origin but continue their education in the destination country.
- *1.75 generation cohort*: Arriving between zero and five years, education takes place in the destination country.
- *2.0 generation cohort*: Being born in the country of their parents' migration, 2.0 generation members complete all education in the country of migration.[13]

The effect of generational cohort differences on Muslim youth has not received extensive investigation in the academic canon to date. This represents a significant lacuna as the challenges affecting later-arriving generational cohorts are exacerbated and intensified in the case of Muslim youth, given their increased visibility and the need to reconcile very different sets of religious and social-cultural norms in their daily lives.

Background of the research project

This chapter is based on research on the experience of growing up as a member of a Muslim population, and was carried out with a group of thirty-three teenagers living in Ballyhaunis, a small rural town in the Republic of Ireland.[14] Ballyhaunis presents a unique context for research on the dynamics of inclusion and exclusion for young members of an ethnic and religious minority community in contemporary Ireland. Ballyhaunis has proportionally the highest immigrant population on the island of Ireland, with 39.5 per cent of the inhabitants of the town registered as non-Irish national in the Census of 2016.[15] In addition, the Muslim population of Ballyhaunis is one of the longest-established migrant populations in Ireland, dating from the early 1970s when a local meat plant was established to export meat slaughtered in the *halal* (traditional Islamic) manner to the newly accessible European market. Initially the Muslim population grew slowly; it consisted in the 1970s of an insular network of six families; but had increased to thirty families of Pakistani and Middle Eastern origin by the 1990s. The Muslim presence was further augmented by the foundation of a Direct Provision centre in the town in 2001, which is the residence of

Muslims from a variety of countries. At the time of writing the Ballyhaunis Muslim population consists of approximately 350 people from a variety of ethnic and cultural backgrounds.[16]

This unique demographic profile provides an opportunity to explore the experiences of Muslim youth negotiating their inclusion in Irish society. As a long-established migrant population, it features a high proportion of 2.0- (Irish-born) and 1.75-generation migrants (arriving before the age of six years) whose families arrived during the earlier phase of the community. In addition, continued expansion during the boom years and the foundation of a Direct Provision centre in the town have ensured the presence of 1.5- (arriving between six and twelve years) and 1.25- (arriving between thirteen and seventeen years) generation Muslims from a variety of socio-economic and ethnic backgrounds. This heterogeneity was reflected in the research sample: of the thirty-three teenaged Muslims who participated, the majority (twenty-five participants) was of Pakistani origin, with six participants coming from Middle Eastern or African backgrounds. There was also some diversity in legal and socio-economic status; six participants were in Ireland as asylum seekers, while the families of all other participants had migrated as economic migrants.

The research design consisted of focus groups and individual interviews, as well as the youth-oriented methods of photographic contribution and the creation of an interactive research blog site.[17] This complex and in-depth research approach elucidated the complex dynamics of inclusion and exclusion which characterise the daily lives of Muslim teens.

Inclusion and negotiating insider status

The inclusions and exclusions that punctuate the daily lives of participants and the sense of being an 'insider' or 'outsider' emerged as important themes cross-cutting all aspects of the research. All participants related inclusion and belonging as vital issues in their day-to-day lives; however, there were marked differences in the experiences of participants from the different generational cohorts. Second-generation migrants (born in Ireland) and 1.75-generation cohort participants (who had arrived in Ireland before the age of six years) felt significantly more comfortable with, and confident of, their place in Irish society. These participants portrayed themselves as 'insiders' in the school setting and within wider society. This was attributed to having had the opportunity to become involved in sporting and other recreational activities at a younger age as well as to simply 'knowing how to get along'. Issues of exclusion and marginalisation were, in contrast, discussed by more recently arrived participants from the 1.5- (arrived between six and twelve years) generational and 1.25- (arrived between thirteen and seventeen years) generational cohorts.

Participants from the 1.75 and 2.0 cohorts, who had spent their child-hoods in Ballyhaunis, generally enjoyed positive relationships with their indigenous Irish peers and portrayed themselves as feeling included in Irish society. Female participants from these cohorts stated that they felt equally comfortable socialising with Muslim and non-Muslim peers in school:

> Haleema (female, aged seventeen): I have my Irish best friends and then I have these ones [indicating fellow participants].
> I: Right and how do you decide who to sit with at lunchtime?
> Haleema: It depends on the mood really, I might decide to sit with one set of friends one break, and then to sit with this lot the other break.

Male participants spoke more frequently than female participants of conflicts and even racialised bullying taking place at school. However, males from the 2.0 and 1.75 cohorts suggested that these negative experiences mainly affected recently arrived participants rather than 'established' migrants:

> Adeel (male, aged fifteen): Some Muslims are kind of famous like, then no one will say anything to them, and then some of them aren't. Some people get slagged [teased/bullied] and some people don't.
> Hadi (male, aged fifteen): Yeah.
> Ghaffar (male, aged fifteen): I don't get slagged.
> I: What makes the difference?
> Adeel: I'd say him, him and him and me, [indicates Hadi, Ghaffar and Maaz] us don't get slagged, then the rest of the lads do.
> Maaz (male, aged fifteen): ''Cos like we've grown up with them since, like we've went to school with them and all that, since Scoil Íosa [the local primary school].

The experience of attending the local primary school was seen as having given these participants an opportunity to establish strong relationships with other young people living in the town and afforded an 'insider' status that is a source of respect in the wider community.

More recently arrived participants reported experiencing high levels of social exclusion and isolation. Participants from the 1.25-generation cohort, who had migrated during their teenage years, in particular, were more likely to report feeling frustrated and lonely in the school setting:

> Saad (male, aged sixteen): Not so much here. I don't like much Ballyhaunis, I'm sorry ... Some [people] they say hi and then some people they think they are too cool like. They don't want to talk like ... the people here is too involved. Too taken up with themselves.

Paila, a 1.5-generation migrant, described how difficult it was to form friendships with other students in the secondary school:

> Paila (female, aged thirteen): Yeah, I have about five [friends] here, but in the last place I lived I had loads, twenty, twenty-two. In primary school you can

make loads of friends, meet loads of people ... But when you come to a higher
level, you can't really make any. 'Cos they make their own group and they
stay with them. They won't let you come in. That's the thing I hate about the
high [secondary] school.

Paila had previously attended primary school in a different part of Ireland
before moving to Ballyhaunis at the age of twelve where she enrolled in the
local secondary school. She highlighted the augmented difficulties in negotiating inclusion in secondary school, when peer groups are seen as having
already been established. It is of note that Paila was living within the Direct
Provision system and, at the time of interview, had been relocated three
times during her stay in Ireland. On her most recent move she had left the
school where she had successfully attained 'insider status', and established
a strong friend network, to begin again in a new town and school. This
exemplifies the manner in which the Direct Provision system, and the fre-
quent relocation of asylum seekers in particular, exacerbates the challenges
already facing young migrants in Irish society.[18]

Recreational activities and becoming an insider

Recreational and extra-curricular activities are widely acknowledged as
providing a vital outlet for social and personal development for migrant
youth.[19] Recreational activities have been shown to be a crucial forum for
identity formation during adolescence, providing important opportunities
for social positioning as well as skill development.[20] The extra-curricular
activities which take place in the Ballyhaunis Community School and
through the local branch of the Gaelic Athletic Association (GAA) provide
important opportunities for interaction between members of the different
ethnic and socio-demographic groups in Ballyhaunis.[21]

The majority of male 1.75 and 2.0 cohort participants played hurling on
the local GAA team and on the school team, attending training sessions
after school up to five times a week.[22] This was seen as pivotal in establishing identity as an 'insider':

> Hadi (male, aged fifteen): We play a lot of sport and just say we play all the
> people who play Gaelic, and we play hurling, and we know all the people
> who play hurling and they're all our friends. And they stick up for you. And
> then when the other fellows bully ya, they're probably good friends with the
> other ones, and they might say commere [come here], and they're like, 'leave
> him alone, he's my friend'. They'll just shut up and go away. 'Cos then they'll
> know we're friends with them.

The level of acceptance by, and intimacy with, the indigenous Irish population which was gained by 2.0- and 1.75-generation members of the

established group was illustrated by the fact that they had been given joking nicknames on the hurling pitch:

> Hadi (male, aged 15): They're really sound [nice] like. They have all kind of nicknames for us when we're playing. Like you know Haider, they call him Setanta.

Setanta, also called Cuchulainn, is a legendary figure from Irish folklore renowned for his supernatural hurling skills. This nickname is highly complimentary and prestigious and it is not surprising that it was a source of pride for participants. For these young males, taking part in GAA events and on sports teams through school was an important gateway to inclusion in Irish society.

In contrast, no members of the 1.25- and 1.5-generation cohorts participated in GAA activities or other school-based sporting activities. A high level of skill in Gaelic football and hurling is required to engage in training sessions and to represent the local school and GAA club at teenage level. Young migrants who have not been afforded an opportunity to learn these skills from a young age are thus precluded from participation. Participants from the 1.25 and 1.5 cohorts reported not understanding how the games worked or lacking the basic skills necessary to play football and hurling. As Ballyhaunis, like many rural towns, lacks many other public facilities and outlets for young people, these young migrants found themselves experiencing social isolation.

Discussions of sports and participation in extra-curricular activities also featured less frequently in females' contributions, primarily as they were precluded by parents from attending mixed-gender social activities. Female participants from the more established 2.0 and 1.75 cohorts emphasised that the provision of recreational facilities suitable for Muslim females, such as female-only sporting events or supervised recreational activities, were necessary:

> Parasa (female, aged eighteen) well i think this [a newly opened sports facility in the town] is very fancy ... but i would love to see some other things developed for girls as well ... its always has been bout boys ... its time they need to do something for girls'

> Ujula (female, aged sixteen): they should seriously consider doing something for girls and ONLY for girls ... I think they should have like a centre where there are different activities goin' on or a club but only for girls ... [sic.]

Through their posts to the research blog site, these female participants emphasised the importance of being afforded opportunities to negotiate and appropriate their inclusion in Irish society in a similar manner to that afforded to their male counterparts. It is of note that females from the 1.25 and 1.5 cohorts did not express such views, suggesting perhaps that these females were not sufficiently confident of their position in Irish society to assert their rights in this manner.[23]

The success of the GAA in facilitating interaction and engagement between males from the 2.0 and 1.75 cohorts and members of the indigenous Irish population highlights the immense potential of recreational and sporting organisations to promote intercultural engagement and social inclusion in contemporary Ireland. However, the isolation experienced by members of the 1.25 and 1.5 cohorts underlines the need for the development of initiatives specifically targeting later-arriving migrant youth. The GAA *Inclusion and Integration Strategy 2009–2015* includes many positive steps for the promotion of inclusive practices. As a new strategy is currently due for development, it is to be hoped that this will include further steps to specifically benefit members of the 1.25 and 1.5 generational cohorts.[24]

'Insider status' and cultural identity

The dynamics of inclusion and exclusion are complex and nuanced for young members of ethnic and religious minority groups. Successive studies have shown that, while a certain amount of adaptation is necessary to attain a sense of inclusion in the mainstream society, feelings of true belonging are linked to maintenance of core or vital aspects of ethnic identity.[25] For the participants in this study, the distinctions between 'insider' identity and 'outsider' identity were blurred. The maintenance of key elements of their identities as 'outsiders' was conveyed as a central element of discourses of social inclusion. For participants, inclusion and acceptance in mainstream Irish society were more complex than simply 'blending in' with Irish peers; being an 'insider' necessitated being accepted as different. Rather than seeing assertion of their distinct ethnic and religious identities as a means of remaining 'outsiders' and setting themselves apart from mainstream society, participants framed their public appropriations of difference as a means of negotiating inclusion and acceptance.

There were marked differences in the manners in which participants from the various generational cohorts chose to assert their difference. Participants from the 2.0 and 1.75 cohorts (Irish-born or having arrived in Ireland before twelve years old) were confident in claiming unique identities which balanced their positions as members of the wider Ballyhaunis community with their cultural and religious identities. Indeed, this was conveyed as a part of daily life rather than an explicit strategy. The confidence of growing up in Ballyhaunis and knowing 'how to go on' enabled these participants to incorporate elements of their ethnic and cultural identities unconsciously into their social repertoires.[26] In contrast, participants from the 1.25 and 1.5 cohorts (who arrived in Ireland between the ages of six and seventeen years) were conscious of their need to assert their positions within the school environment and Irish society more generally. Perhaps reflecting their greater sense of being 'outsiders', these participants explicitly detailed their strategies for the negotiation of a more inclusive position.

The unconscious merging of their ethnic identities and their identities as 'insiders' in Irish society was exemplified by male participants from the 2.0 and 1.75 cohorts. These participants, having spent their childhoods in Ballyhaunis, frequently participated in GAA events. In situations where Pakistani members of the Muslim population played together, they communicated in Punjabi, their language of origin:

> Haider (male, aged seventeen): He's in goals and Ghaffar is the other defender, and I'm a defender, so we just talk in our own language [Punjabi] [...] and we just tell each other like to go in to the other position and like to pass the ball and all that.

This use of Punjabi as a *lingua franca* on the hurling pitch was colourfully conveyed as a useful strategy in preventing the opposition from understanding their tactics. More significantly however, this transposition of the community language of Punjabi to the mainstream playing fields is evidence of the confidence of these participants in their unique position in Irish society. For these participants, being an 'insider' means more than blending in; it means being able to express their unique cultural identity while fully participating in Irish society. Decisions by the local GAA club to include foods appropriate to their religious requirements affirmed the sense of belonging that these participants enjoyed:

> Hadi (male, aged fifteen): I really like it when the managers and all that remember that we're from a different country so instead of getting chicken and all that they get us fish cos we tell them fish is good. So we're really thankful to them as well.

Female participants similarly asserted their religious and cultural biographies in the local school setting through their choice of dress. Significantly, females from the 2.0 and 1.75 cohorts (Irish-born and arriving before the age of six years respectively) were more likely to practise *hijab*, covering their hair when attending school. Dress codes have elsewhere been shown to provide female Muslims a means of appropriating their unique position in Western society, asserting their social membership while appropriating their religious and ethnic identities.[27] The *hijab* was seen by these females as an extension of the school uniform:

> I: And do you always wear the same one [*hijab*] or do you have different colours?
> Ommata (female, aged fourteen): Different colours, I have pink, I've got beige, I've got white, I've got green and I've got em, red and purple.

I: Do you always wear navy or black to school?
Ommata: Yeah, I think it goes best.

This simple choice of a colour that was complementary to the school uniform highlights how natural and unconscious the reconciliation of religious and ethnic identities with the norms of Irish society are for 2.0 and 1.75 cohorts, who have internalised these types of adaptation from an early age.

For members of the more recently arrived 1.25 and 1.5 cohorts, negotiating their position as Muslims in Ireland was a more conscious project. These participants were more likely to explicitly mention equality and recognition in their interviews. The perceived need for a special prayer room for Muslims on the school premises was a recurring theme during interviews. This was seen as a necessary step that would cement their inclusion in the school. As demonstrated in Ryan's study of Muslim identity in the UK, appropriation of public spaces for the visible and audible practise of religion is an essential element of a discourse which merges religious identity and British citizenship.[28] Similarly, in this study participants from the 1.5 and 1.25 cohorts believed that the provision of prayer facilities on the school premises would enable them to convey and assert their position within contemporary Irish society:

> Sabaha (female, aged seventeen): Em … I'd create a place where I could like, pray. 'Cos like every time the priest comes and does like masses and stuff. Well here, we'd get to pray as well so we'd be equal, both sides.

Sabaha's view that the provision of prayer facilities would afford equal status to Muslim students is indicative of a conscious desire to have their inclusion acknowledged and recognised. This highlights the centrality of the recognition and acceptance of religious difference to young Muslims' sense of inclusion in Irish society.

In light of its importance as a mechanism for the negotiation of a balance between distinctive cultural identity and participation within Irish society, there is a need for a more adequate recognition of the role of religion in the lives of migrants in educational and public settings. In particular, there is a need for clear directives regarding the wearing of religious garments and religious worship in educational institutions. A 2008 report by the Department of Education and Skills recommends, but does not insist, that school principals and boards of management accommodate religious symbols to a reasonable extent. The decision of the Department of Education and Skills to abnegate responsibility for this issue to school principals has been criticised by the Irish Council for Civil Liberties as 'a policy not to have a policy'.[29] The lack of certainty on this issue has the potential to cause severe disruption to young members of religious minorities as they negotiate their inclusion in Irish society.

Conclusion

The increasing suspicion around Muslim communities in contemporary Western society is an issue that is problematic for Muslim youth who seek to negotiate their acceptance and inclusion in the environments where their daily lives are situated. Sensationalist and Islamophobic popular and alternative right media coverage frequently frames Muslim communities as socially bounded groups choosing to remain apart from mainstream society. Muslim youth in particular are regarded with suspicion, as 'outsiders' living within European society. Indeed, expressions of religious identity have come to be frequently conflated with the issue of radicalisation. In response to these dangerous and essentialist perceptions, this chapter has attempted to shed light on the complex dynamics of inclusion and exclusion among Muslim teenagers living in the rural West of Ireland.

This chapter has highlighted that young Muslims are faced with the difficult task of negotiating a social identity that reconciles the norms and expectations of secular Irish society with the religious and ethnic practices of their ethno-cultural and religious background. It has broken new ground by analysing the impact of the age at which participants immigrate to Ireland on their success in negotiating inclusion in Irish society. Migrants from the 2.0 and 1.75 cohorts generally enjoy 'insider status' and socialise freely with people of diverse ethnic backgrounds, while migrants from the 1.25 and 1.5 cohorts, who arrived during their late childhood or teenage years, are more likely to experience social isolation and exclusion in their daily lives. While it is perhaps not surprising that age at the time of immigration has an effect on the experiences of young migrants in Ireland, the extent to which this factor impacts on the everyday experiences of inclusion and exclusion is a finding that merits consideration and action at a policy level.

The manner, and extent, of young Muslims' appropriation and invocation of their distinct religious and cultural identities in the construction of their biographies as Irish Muslims highlight the complex dynamics of social engagement and belonging in contemporary Ireland. Dichotomous distinctions between 'insider' and 'outsider' identity are not adequate to afford an understanding of the importance of cultural independence in negotiations of social inclusion. Far from indicating a wish to remain apart from mainstream Irish society, assertion of cultural distinctiveness and religious difference can be a key component in the negotiation of inclusion and belonging. This is indicative of the need for further academic and political engagement with the nuanced processes through which the positions of 'insider' and 'outsider' are negotiated and redefined. This recognition, acceptance and celebration of difference is vital to the future development of a cohesive and open society in Ireland in which young members of ethnic and religious minorities can freely negotiate the terms of their social and cultural inclusion.

Notes

1 S. Ahmed and J. Matthes, 'Media representation of Muslims and Islam from 2000 to 2015: a meta-analysis', *International Communication Gazette*, 79:3 (2016), 219–244.

2 J. Stuart and C. Ward, 'A question of balance: exploring the acculturation, integration and adaptation of Muslim immigrant youth', *Psychosocial Intervention*, 20:3 (2011), 255–267.

3 J. Carr, 'From suspect to suspecting: Muslim communities in Ireland and the Irish gaze', in Seyed-Abdolhamid Mirhosseini and Hossein Roubez (eds), *Instances of Islamophobia: Demonising the Muslim 'Other'* (London: Lexington, 2015), pp. 53–66.

4 S. Vertovec, 'Super-diversity and its implications', *Ethnic and Racial Studies*, 30:6 (2007), 1024–1054.

5 R. Gilligan, P. Curry, J. McGrath, D. Murphy, M. Ní Raghallaigh, M. Rogers, J. Scholtz and A. Quinn, *In the Front Line of Integration: Young People Managing Migration to Ireland* (Dublin: Children's Research Centre, Trinity College in association with the Trinity Immigration Initiative Children, Youth and Community Relations Project [Online], 2010), pp. 10–11, 30, 40–42, www.tara.tcd.ie/handle/2262/36886, accessed 3 February 2019.

6 G. Valentine, S. L. Holloway and M. Jayne, 'Contemporary cultures of abstinence and the night-time economy: Muslim attitudes towards alcohol and the implications for social cohesion', *Environment and Planning A*, 42 (2010), 8–22.

7 R. Mohammad, 'Making gender, ma(r)king place: youthful british Pakistani Muslim women's narratives of urban space', *Environment and Planning A*, 45 (2013), 1802–1822.

8 B. McGrath and O. McGarry, 'The religio-cultural dimensions of life for young Muslim women in a small Irish town', *Journal of Youth Studies*, 17:7 (2014), 948–964.

9 O. McGarry, 'Knowing "how to go on": structuration theory as an analytical prism in studies of intercultural engagement', *Journal of Ethnic and Migration Studies*, 42:12 (2016), 2078–2083.

10 O. Scharbrodt, 'Shaping the public image of Islam: the Shiis of Ireland as "moderate" Muslims', *Journal of Muslim Minority Affairs*, 31:4 (2011), 518–533; T. Abbas, 'The impact of religio-cultural norms and values on the education of young South Asian women', *British Journal of Sociology of Education*, 24:4 (2003), 411–428.

11 A. Portes and R. Rumbaut, *Immigrant America: A Portrait* (Berkeley, CA: University of California Press, 2nd edn, 1996), pp. 313–314.

12 J. W. Berry, J. S. Phinney, D. L. Sam and P. Vedder, 'Immigrant youth: acculturation, identity, and adaptation', *Applied Psychology*, 55 (2006), 303–332, pp. 303–305.

13 R. Rumbaut, 'Ages, life stages, and generational cohorts: decomposing the immigrant first and second generations in the United States', in A. Portes and J. DeWind (eds), *Rethinking Migration: New Theoretical and Empirical Perspectives* (New York: Berghahn Books, 2008), pp. 342–387.

14 In line with ethical requirements, pseudonyms are used to protect the anonymity of individual participants. However, the name of the town where the research took place has not been altered in publications.

15 Central Statistics Office Ireland, 'Census of population 2016 – profile 7 migration and diversity', cso.ie/en/releasesandpublications/ep/p-cp7md/p7md/p7anii/, accessed 3 February 2019; The Migration Observatory, 'Northern Ireland: Census profile', migrationobservatory.ox.ac.uk/resources/briefings/northern-ireland-census-profile/, accessed 3 February 2019.

16 Exact numbers of the Muslim population are difficult to obtain due primarily to the frequency with which asylum seekers living in Direct Provision are relocated.

17 O. McGarry, 'Repositioning the research encounter: exploring power dynamics and positionality in youth research', *International Journal of Social Research Methodology*, 19:3 (2016), 339–354.

18 B. Fanning and A. Veale, 'Child poverty as public policy: Direct Provision and asylum seeker children in the Republic of Ireland', *Child Care in Practice*, 10:3 (2004), 241–251.

19 A. Walsh, *Make Minority a Priority* (Dublin: National Youth Council of Ireland, 2017), pp. 44–48.

20 E. H. Sharp and J. D. Coatsworth, 'Adolescent future orientation: the role of identity discovery in self-defining activities and context in two rural samples', *Identity*, 12:2 (2012), 130–134; O. McGarry, 'Narratives of recreation and community belonging among migrant youth', in L. Moran, K. Reilly and B. Brady (eds), *Narrating Childhoods Across Contexts: Knowledge, Environment, and Relationships* (Basingstoke: Palgrave Macmillan, 2018).

21 The Gaelic Athletic Association was founded in 1884 to promote traditional Gaelic sports throughout Ireland. Most parishes in Ireland have a local GAA club which organises competitive and social sporting events for all age groups.

22 Hurling is an indigenous Irish field sport contested by teams of fifteen players, using wooden sticks called hurls and a small leather ball known as a *slíothar*. Contests on a local, national and international level are organised by the GAA.

23 O. McGarry and B. McGrath, '"A virtual canvas" – designing a blog site to research young Muslims' friendships and identities', *Forum: Qualitative Research*, 14:1 (2013), 1–21, p. 13.

24 O. McGarry, 'Identity formation among teenaged members of the Muslim population of Ballyhaunis, Co. Mayo' (unpublished PhD thesis, NUI Galway, 2012), p. 265.

25 Stuart and Ward, 'A question of balance', pp. 255–256.

26 McGarry, 'Knowing "how to go on"', pp. 2082–2083.

27 McGrath and O. McGarry, 'The religio-cultural dimensions of life', pp. 958–960.

28 L. Ryan, '"Islam does not change": young people narrating negotiations of religion and identity', *Journal of Youth Studies*, 17:4 (2014), 447–450.

29 Ruadhán Mac Cormaic, 'No Directive on hijabs in classroom to be issued', *Irish Times*, September 24, 2008, cited in C. Hogan, 'Accommodating Islam in the denominational Irish education system: religious freedom and education in the Republic of Ireland', *Journal of Muslim Minority Affairs*, 31:4 (2011), 554–573, p. 557.

Brexit, borders and belonging

The focus of this chapter is on the emerging implications of the decision of the United Kingdom to leave the European Union (Brexit) for the lives of migrants on both sides of the border between the Republic of Ireland and Northern Ireland. Brexit is likely to reduce the rights and entitlements of future prospective immigrants to Northern Ireland but it is becoming increasingly likely that the impact on many migrants from European Union countries, and in particular those from countries that joined the EU after 2004, may be mostly experienced as an ominous mood music that inculcates feelings of insecurity and a sense of being an outsider to a greater extent than before. This chapter examines how Brexit may lead to a growing divergence between the experiences and perceptions of migrants from the new EU member states living in Northern Ireland and in the Republic of Ireland, and whether feelings of being a greater outsider in one jurisdiction than the other might affect decisions where to settle.

Not all migrants have the same rights and entitlements. Those from EU member states living in other EU countries enjoy some rights and entitlements on a reciprocal basis that have not been extended to migrants from non-EU countries. Migration is policed through complex regulatory systems that can be enforced internally as well as at border crossings. These regulatory systems are stratified and position some (non-EU migrants) as outsiders to a greater extent than others (those from EU member states). Pre-Brexit systems of stratification have been broadly similar in both Northern Ireland and in the Republic. In the case of Northern Ireland, reduced rights of residency and access to employment may directly affect future EU migrants and reposition them as outsiders to a greater extent within existing stratified systems of regulation. Post-Brexit restrictions affecting new migrants from EU countries in Northern Ireland are likely to restrict these in similar ways to how migration from non-EU countries is currently regulated. The impact of Brexit on immigrants who have settled in Northern Ireland may mostly be upon perceptions which affect how and to what extent people think of themselves as welcome or as outsiders. A post-Brexit divergence in the experiences and perceptions of migrants from the same EU countries who have settled on different sides of the border between the Republic and Northern Ireland is likely. Much of the focus of this chapter is on Poles as a case study, not just because these constitute the largest group in Ireland likely to be affected by Brexit; but also because some research has been undertaken on the perceptions of Polish migrants in the United Kingdom to Brexit while none has been undertaken on those of Lithuanians, Latvians and others who have also settled in both Irelands.

Borders and the common travel area

Policy and political responses to immigration in the Republic of Ireland have long been influenced by open borders with the United Kingdom of Great Britain and Northern Ireland. As Brexit looms, along with restrictions on the free movement of future migrants from European Union countries (other than the Republic), it is salutary to recall both how Irish independence from the United Kingdom triggered the large-scale emigration of Irish Protestants and how the United Kingdom imposed controls on migration from the Irish Free State during the Second World War.

After independence the free movement of people between the Irish Free State and the UK continued as before. However, the imposition of migration restrictions was proposed on a number of occasions. In July 1927 the Conservative Party government established an interdepartmental committee which considered representations from the Scottish Board of Health seeking to limit Irish immigration on the grounds of employment shortages. In 1928 a delegation of Scottish Presbyterian Church leaders met with the Home Secretary requesting immigration controls. An (internal civil service) intergovernmental conference held in July 1928 considered introducing restrictions on economic migrants from both the Irish Free State and from Northern Ireland. The advice of the Dominions Office (which was responsible for Irish affairs), in response to these and other such demands, was that 'persons of Irish Free State nationality were British subjects by birth in one of his Majesty's dominions and as such could neither be excluded or deported'.[1] In 1928 the Irish Free State was asked to consider reciprocal arrangements which would allow for the deportation of those who became a charge on the poor rate in Britain and vice versa. An eventual (1932) response to this request stated that the Free State government would be willing to consider individual cases but that it would not support a more general scheme. In 1932 the new Fianna Fáil government led by Eamon de Valera set about removing the oath of allegiance to the British monarch. As Anglo-Irish relationships deteriorated, new consideration was given by the Home Office to restricting migration from Ireland along the lines proposed in 1928.[2]

In June 1940 free movement from Ireland was suspended for the duration of the Second World War. Irish migrant workers were required to
obtain visas and the expectation was that they would leave Britain after
their contracts of employment had come to an end. A permit office was
established in Dublin aimed at directing migrants towards agricultural and
industrial work in Britain. In February 1941 the Irish Department of Agriculture was asked by its Scottish equivalent to interview Irish applicants to
the Women's Land Army in order to assess their suitability. Irish officials
conducted interviews in Dublin and forwarded their reports to officials in
Scotland and Northern Ireland.[3] Similarly, the recruitment of industrial
workers and the allocation of visas for those who were selected also became
highly organised. Between 1940 and 1945 a total of 198,538 permit cards
were issued to migrants from Ireland.[4] Most were unskilled labourers with
backgrounds in building or farm work. In Britain many of these worked in
construction and in factories. Those assigned to work in English factories
or building airfields and military bases were accommodated in segregated
barracks for the duration of their contracts. Almost half the men who were
recruited were under twenty-five years old.[5] Migrants from the twenty-six
counties also worked as farm labourers in Northern Ireland.

After the war visa requirements were removed and, when the Irish Free
State declared itself a Republic, free movement became enshrined in new
UK legislation. The Ireland Act 1949 stated that 'the Republic of Ireland is
not a foreign country for the purposes of any law in force in any part of
the United Kingdom'.[6] When in 1962 the United Kingdom imposed restrictions on migration from its former colonies (under the Commonwealth
Immigration Act) these restrictions did not apply to migrants from the
Republic of Ireland. Irish citizens retained distinctive rights to settle in and
work in the UK. Furthermore, the British Nationality Act 1981 did not
include Irish citizens in the legal definition of an 'alien'. Under this Act an
'alien' was somebody who is not a Commonwealth citizen, a British protected person or not a citizen of the Republic of Ireland.[7]

The Irish state, for its part, offered reciprocal rights to citizens of the
UK. Further, it extended an all-island entitlement to Irish citizenship. The
partition of Ireland in 1920 split Irish nationalists fighting for independence
and triggered the Irish Civil War (1922–1923), but the principle of a united
Ireland remained a nationalist political aspiration. Article 2 of the 1937
Constitution of the Irish state, *Bunreacht na hÉireann*, asserted that the
national territory consisted of the whole island of Ireland, its islands and
the six counties that, after partition, remained part of the UK. *Bunreacht
na hÉireann* had left open the question of how citizenship was to be allocated, providing (in Article 9) only that citizenship status would be determined in accordance with law. It was presumed that the *jus soli* principle
of citizenship by birth would continue to apply as part of the inherited body
of common law. Simply put, those born within the jurisdiction of the Irish

state were entitled to Irish citizenship. The children of Irish citizens were also deemed to be entitled to citizenship. The Irish Nationality and Citizenship Act 1956 provided for citizenship by place of birth as well as on the basis of descent. In the context of a constitutional claim of all-island sovereignty, Irish law permitted those born in Northern Ireland to become Irish citizens.

In 1999, following the 1998 Belfast Agreement, a subsequent referendum in the Republic and legislative change (the Nineteenth Amendment to the Constitution Act 1998), Article 2 was revised to explicitly assert the right of anyone born in the Republic or in Northern Ireland to Irish citizenship. By then immigration was rising on both sides of the border. Interpretation of the right to Irish citizenship by the Irish courts (derived from the 1987 High Court ruling in *Fajujonu v. Minister of Justice*) also extended rights to the family members of Irish-born children of immigrants. The Department of Justice, preoccupied with preventing asylum seeker families with Irish-born children being granted residency status, successfully challenged this ruling, making it possible to deport families with a child who was entitled to become an Irish citizen. In 2004 the then Fianna Fáil/Progressive Democrat coalition government introduced a Citizenship Referendum proposing to remove the birthright to citizenship altogether from the Irish-born children of people who were not already Irish citizens. Removal of this birthright was supported by 79.8 per cent of those who voted in the 2004 Referendum. A new section was added to Article 9 of *Bunreacht na hÉireann*:

> Article 9.2.1: Notwithstanding any other provision of this Constitution, a person born in the island of Ireland, which includes its islands and its seas, who does not have, at the time of his or her birth, at least one parent who is an Irish citizen or entitled to be an Irish citizen is not entitled to Irish citizenship or nationality, unless otherwise provided for by law.

This constitutional amendment had implications for children whose parents were not Irish citizens or, if they lived in Northern Ireland, did not have parents who were born there. It undermined the principle of a citizenship birthright for all persons born on the island of Ireland which had been inserted into the Irish Constitution following the 1998 Belfast Agreement. The British and Irish governments issued an interpretive declaration, stating that the Belfast Agreement was not intended to extend birthright citizenship to the children of migrants. Assurances were given that the entitlement to Irish citizenship of children born 'on the island of Ireland' to British national parents would not be altered.[8] Under the Irish Nationality and Citizenship Act 2004 children born of foreign national parents on the island of Ireland on or after 1 January 2005 are not automatically entitled to Irish citizenship. However, those born since 1 January 2005 are entitled to Irish citizenship if one or both their parents is British or entitled to live in Northern

Ireland or the Irish state without restriction on their residency. It is relatively easy for many Irish-born children of immigrants to become Irish citizens. Parents must prove they have a 'genuine' link with Ireland evidenced by having lived three out of the previous four years of 'reckonable residence' in either the Republic of Ireland or Northern Ireland immediately before the birth of their child. 'Reckonable residence' does not however include periods of Irish residence for asylum seekers before being granted refugee status.[9]

Post-2004 regulation of migration

To a considerable extent Chinese, Lithuanian, Latvian, Polish and other migrants who settled on either side of the border have been similar people from similar places who migrated for similar reasons.[10] From the early 1960s some Hong Kong Chinese from the New Territories where Hakka and Cantonese are spoken settled in Northern Ireland and in the Republic. Mostly they established restaurants and takeaway food businesses. They moved to both parts of Ireland from Britain where Hong Kong Chinese migrants had run similar businesses. As British subjects they could move to the Republic without having to obtain work permits or visas. In Northern Ireland, Hong Kong Chinese settled mostly in Belfast though also in towns including Craigavon, Lisburn, Newtownabbey, North Down and Bally-mena.[11] In the Republic, they opened businesses in Dublin but also in several other cities and towns.

Prior to EU Enlargement, migrant workers from Eastern European countries arrived both north and south of the border to work as farm labourers. By 2004 some 3,000 migrants, mostly from Lithuania and Latvia, worked for about 120 mushroom growers in the Republic. Many appear to have been paid substantially less than the minimum wage and some were made to work up to sixteen hours per day in difficult conditions.[12] Research undertaken in Northern Ireland found that similar kinds of migrants from similar places were similarly exploited by similar agribusinesses.[13] Some mushroom pickers described being recruited by a Northern Ireland agency only to be shipped across the border to work on farms in the Republic.[14]

In 2004, following EU Enlargement, both the United Kingdom and the Republic of Ireland immediately removed visa requirements from the EU's new member states, prompting large-scale migration from these to both countries. The decision to do so at the same time (when all other pre-2004 member states except Sweden decided to phase in free movement) reflected the established common travel area between both jurisdictions. As a result, migrants from countries such as Poland, Lithuania and Latvia (who prior to 2004 required visas) could now freely travel to the Republic or Northern Ireland and move between both jurisdictions. Before 2004 both jurisdictions attracted migrants from such Eastern European countries, but the scale of such migration increased hugely once visa requirements were removed.

In the twelve months following EU Enlargement some 85,114 workers from the new EU member states became registered workers in the Republic of Ireland (being issued national insurance numbers). This represented more than a tenfold increase from the numbers admitted from the same countries during the final year preceding free movement. The 2006 Census identified 63,276 Poles living in the Republic of Ireland. By 2011 this number had risen to 122,585 and Polish had overtaken Irish as the second most commonly spoken language in the Republic.[15] By 2011 there were 81,318 migrants in Northern Ireland not from elsewhere in the UK or the Republic. Just under a quarter (19,658) of these were Polish. Lithuanians (7,241) comprised the next largest group.[16] Other than English, Polish became the most commonly spoken language (by 17,731) followed by Lithuanian (6,250).[17]

Many Lithuanians and Latvians settled in counties adjoining the border between both parts of Ireland. Migrants who settled on both sides of the border were joined by former neighbours and classmates as well as members of their extended family. For example, a study of Lithuanians in Northern Ireland found that a concentration of migrants from the same Silute region had settled in Dungannon.[18] By 2006 Lithuanians made up 3 per cent of the population of county Monaghan, with higher concentration in the county's rural towns: 9 per cent of the population of Monaghan Town, 7 per cent of Carrickmacross and 6 per cent of Clones. Although noticeably concentrated in Monaghan, almost every town in the Republic with a population of more than 1,500 had some Lithuanian residents by 2006.[19]

Like the Lithuanians, but on a far larger scale, Poles settled all around the island. Prior to the possibility of Brexit it was perhaps incidental whether such Poles settled north or south of the border. Most were young adults who initially envisaged themselves as temporary migrants. Most were young adults who initially envisaged themselves as temporary migrants when they arrived and most did not have children at the time. [20] Various studies of Poles in the Republic and Northern Ireland tell similar stories of how temporary stays became longer ones, how single migrants connected with family members or started new families of their own, set up community organisations, Polish scout troops and shops that sold Polish food. [21] In both Northern Ireland and in the Republic a system of Polish Saturday schools was quickly established. The impetus was partly to prepare children for re-entry into the Polish education system, suggesting that some parents expected to return eventually to Poland. These were usually funded by the Polish government, and followed Poland's school curriculum in Polish-language studies, history, geography and, in some cases, maths. [22] Of the 122,585 Poles identified in the 2011 Republic of Ireland Census, 25,291 (20.6 per cent) were children or teenagers.

Some implications of Brexit

How existing immigrants from EU countries will be treated in Great Britain and Northern Ireland is as of yet unclear but there are indications that many will have access to permanent residency status and to UK citizenship. Issues and questions that can be identified at this stage include: (1) How and to what extent will the experiences of EU migrants currently resident in Northern Ireland and Britain become different after Brexit, or be perceived as different after Brexit? (2)How might Brexit affect the behaviour of EU migrants? For example, will a higher proportion living in Northern Ireland seek to naturalise or will Brexit result in the relocation of some such migrants to the Republic of Ireland or lead to others returning to their countries of origin? (3) How will post-Brexit stratifications on the mobility, employment, welfare and settlement rights – the software of migrant control – likely impact on migrants from the EU?

Polish organisations in the United Kingdom have expressed concern that the political campaign to leave the EU and the results of the Brexit referendum have increased levels of racism, xenophobia and anti-immigrant nationalism. By 2016 the number of Polish nationals in the UK had reached one million and the overall EU27 population was estimated to be around 3.5 million.[23] Opposition to free movement from other EU countries played a significant part in political campaigns to leave the EU. British insistence on immigration controls became a red line issue in Brexit negotiations with the EU. A 17 March 2017 article in the *Irish News* noted that there was 'great fear and concern' among the 30,000 Polish nationals living in Northern Ireland. [24] Even if the residency rights and other entitlements of migrants who have settled in Northern Ireland are not undermined by Brexit some of these may come to feel more like outsiders. This emerged as a theme in interviews with Poles in Belfast conducted by Marta Kempny (see Chapter 7).

In the aftermath of the Brexit referendum some newspaper articles speculated that some Poles would relocate to the Republic of Ireland and that future prospective migrants from EU countries would choose Ireland over the United Kingdom as their destination. An October 2016 article published in *The Guardian* claimed that Poles working in Ireland were expecting 'an influx of their compatriots over the coming weeks and months as Britain becomes an increasingly uncertain and hostile destination after the Brexit vote'.[25] The article quoted Wojciech Bialek, who ran Together-Razam Centre, a Polish organisation in Cork, as saying that Poles in the UK believed that they would have greater security and safety in the Republic of Ireland. The article noted that Aer Lingus and Ryan Air operated 126 flights a week between Warsaw and Dublin and Shannon airports, and that these airlines also served emigration hotspots such as Rzeszów in south-east Poland. Another interviewee, Dublin-bound Marcin Raganowicz, returning from Warsaw to Dublin with his five-year-old Maya, who was born in Ireland, believed that in choosing to migrate to Ireland rather than the UK he made the right choice: 'Poles in Britain are afraid they will be thrown out. People in Ireland are really friendly. You do not hear anyone complain about the Poles.'

Such newspaper articles posit emerging distinctions between the experiences of and perceptions of Poles living in both Irish jurisdictions and perceptions among prospective immigrants that might affect future decisions about where to migrate. Various studies have found it difficult to predict the intentions of Poles to stay in the UK or return, not least because many Poles arrived in Britain with no firm plans. Their views changed over time.[26] As put in one analysis, one of the features of post-Enlargement Polish migration to the UK was the 'deliberate indeterminacy' or intentional unpredictability of many migrants – their tendency 'to keep their options deliberately open. Post-2004 arrivals enjoyed rights to free movement and automatically acquired permanent residency status after five years of exercising free movement rights.' [27] They may not have intended to remain permanently in the UK, yet found themselves becoming settled there without having proactively planned to do this.

Research undertaken in 2016 sought to gauge the likely responses to Brexit of Polish migrants living in the UK by asking 894 interviewees about their future plans (for the next five years).[28] Forty per cent of respondents stated that they intended to apply for a permanent residency certificate, suggesting an intention to remain in the UK as long-term residents, and 32 per cent intended to apply for citizenship. Another 22 per cent had no concrete plans to leave, bringing the total likely to stay to 94 per cent.[29] Poles and other EU citizen migrants in Ireland and in the UK have tended not to naturalise because there was no real necessity to do so. Brexit seems to have pushed more Poles into making concrete plans for the future, including aspirations to become British citizens or apply for permanent residency status, a prerequisite for applying for citizenship.[30]

When asked what they would do if Britain left the EU, just 6 per cent stated that they would move to a third country.[31] Ireland was not referred to in this study but it may well be the case that some Poles and some from other EU member states currently living in the UK may relocate to the Republic. The findings suggest that those with less education and older respondents are less likely to relocate. Those respondents considering relocation tended to be young and among the most highly qualified. Younger Poles (those under thirty years) and better-educated Poles thought of themselves as more mobile. The study found that compared with those under thirty, older migrants (those over forty) were more than twice as likely to apply for permanent residency or citizenship in the event of a Brexit. Higher-qualified individuals were four times more likely to apply for citizenship than those with secondary education, and 2.7 times more likely to do so than those with vocational qualifications.[32] Overall, the research suggested that post-referendum anxiety about Brexit, and feeling 'insecure' about the durability of currently enjoyed rights, had made Polish migrants twice as likely to seek naturalisation than previously.

By contrast, Poles in the Republic of Ireland are far less likely to seek to become Irish citizens and it is likely that, even if Britain does not leave the EU, or if in the event of a Brexit the residency rights of migrants are not significantly undermined, a far higher proportion of Poles will naturalise in the British case. According to the *Growing Up in Ireland Survey* data from 2011 only 5 per cent of the mothers from EU Accession states of children living in Ireland had Irish citizenship.[33] By comparison some 72 per cent of mothers with children in Ireland born in the United Kingdom (including those from Northern Ireland) had Irish citizenship.[34] Unlike their parents, many of the children of Polish immigrants have already become Irish citizens (those born to parents with sufficient 'reckonable residence' in Ireland). Around two-thirds of children born in Ireland to a parent from an EU Accession state had Irish citizenship. This is unlikely to translate into political influence until they become adults.

Although Poles in the UK and Northern Ireland may well in the future continue to feel more insecure than those in the Republic, they will in one crucial respect be more integrated and may constitute a significant electoral bloc. Rob Ford, a British academic expert on anti-immigrant politics, has observed that if many of the 3.5 million EU migrants had been entitled to vote, the Brexit referendum outcome would, most likely, have been different. EU citizenship in Ireland as in the UK does not come with full political rights. The kind of reciprocal arrangement that allows Irish citizens to vote in UK elections and vice versa does not extend to other EU countries.[35]

Much of the focus on Brexit in the Republic of Ireland and in Northern Ireland has been on concerns about border controls between the Republic and Northern Ireland. However, an April 2018 article in the *Irish Times* reported the views of (unnamed) senior Gardaí that Brexit would, by necessity, lead to new restrictions on migrants entering the Republic of Ireland with a view to subsequently travelling illegally to the United Kingdom. Between 1999 and 2015 some 16,000 deportation orders were signed in the Republic of Ireland. Some 40 per cent of intended deportees remain unaccounted for; it is presumed that most of these moved to the UK, finding it easy to do so because of the common travel area and the low level of border checks during this period.

It is likely that there will be greater pressure on the Irish state to prevent such migrants entering the UK after Brexit. Senior Gardaí anonymously briefed the media that 'Ireland could become a sort of Calais-style camp; people coming here and staying to just wait for their chance to get to Britain', and that it is 'all but certain' immigration checks would be introduced within the common travel area for the first time. These also claimed that because of the shortage of accommodation in the Republic, centres or camps would need to be built in Ireland if asylum seeker numbers began to climb. In effect, although a common travel area between Ireland and the United Kingdom would still operate, it is likely that a system of immigration checks would be introduced for the first time since the Second World War aimed at preventing non-Irish citizens from entering the UK.[36]

Immigration controls are not just regulatory systems involving policing of entry points such as passport checks at airports, but are also the workings of social security systems and labour market controls. A 2017 UK government position paper which addressed the possible impact of Brexit on migration upon the Irish–British common travel area described it thus:

> When considering the nature of the [common travel area] as a border-free zone, it is important to note that immigration controls are not, and never have been, solely about the ability to prevent and control entry at the UK's physical border. Along with many other Member States, controlling access to the labour market and social security have long formed an integral part of the UK's immigration system.[37]

When migrants arrive in Ireland or the UK from outside the EU this is only the beginning of what can be an arduous process of establishing a viable residency. As put in a 2017 report by the Centre for Cross Border Studies,

> Basic aspects of everyday life – such as being able to register at an address or with a GP, opening a back account, finding employment, enrolling your children in school and so on – all depend on the existence and enactment of rights which vary according to a person's citizenship, and are linked to reciprocal agreements between states. 'The border' comes into existence when a decision is taken by the relevant authorities at each of these points regarding whether or not a right exists that can be enacted. If no right exists then the person is not granted access to a network of resources, services and entitlements.[38]

Borders, as such, do not just regulate simple physical movement. As expressed internally, through the impact of differing levels of rights and entitlements, they treat some migrants as outsiders to a greater degree than others. In 2013, when she was Home Secretary, Theresa May sought to introduce what she called a 'really hostile' environment for people living in Britain illegally. People are now required to produce their passport or other documentary evidence of their residency status in order to open bank accounts, rent somewhere to live or access health care. The 'hostile environment' approach has arguably turned landlords, bank officials and healthcare professionals into a kind of border police. Such internal scrutiny has, in part, substituted for checks at hard borders. It has resulted in controversial deportations of elderly Commonwealth migrants, the 'Windrush generation' who legally came to Britain during the 1950s.[39]

Internal administrative borders operating within both Northern Ireland and the Republic have long categorised and stratified migrants based on their citizenship and residency status. As again put by the Institute of Cross Border Studies, some months before the Windrush deportations controversy:

> We need to be careful then, if we expect that the lack of visible physical infrastructure at the geographical UK–Ireland land border by itself suggests openness. While the invisibility of border controls and infrastructure at this border has undoubtedly had enormous positive practical and symbolic effects, particularly in Northern Ireland, there is a complicated relationship between the visibility and openness of borders. Each can affect the other but, again, in ways that vary across different groups of people, and depend on the spatial, material, and practical aspects of border enforcement.[40]

In thinking about the potential impact of Brexit on the lives of immigrants it is useful to consider the current experiences of those from non-EU countries and the pre-2004 experiences of those from countries that had not yet joined the EU. Research on the experiences of these migrants in both jurisdictions has identified similar patterns of marginalisation. For example, Filipinos working in the Northern Irish fishing industry and in other sectors have experienced very similar patterns of exploitation made possible in both cases by the lack of any meaningful access to rights.[41] Research has identified similar forms of exploitation of Filipinos in the Republic.[42] Such exploitation, like the kinds identified among Eastern European migrants prior to 2004, is at least partly due to having a precarious immigration status and, as a result, less meaningful access to employment rights.

It is likely that the experiences of future migrants from EU countries who move to Northern Ireland will diverge from those who settle in the Republic, and it may also be the case that such newcomers in the North may face more restrictions than compatriots who arrived before Brexit. Newcomers from EU countries are likely to be regulated in similar ways to non-EU migrants at present and may have lesser social citizenship rights and entitlements to social security and health services than their longer-settled compatriots. The Treaty of Maastricht (1992) which introduced the principle of free movement also contained provision for reciprocal rights to social protection benefits to EU citizens living in each other's countries. Following Brexit there would be no treaty impediment to removing such rights to newcomers.

Notes

1 E. Delaney, '"Almost a class of helots in an alien land": the British State and Irish immigration 1921–45', *Immigrants and Minorities*, 18:2–3 (1999), 240–265, pp. 242–243.
2 Ibid., p. 249.

3 C. Wills, *That Neutral Island: A Cultural History of Ireland During the Second World War* (London: Faber and Faber, 2007), p. 317.
4 Delaney, '"Almost a class of helots', p. 255.
5 Wills, *That Neutral Island*, p. 218.
6 I. Maher, 'Crossing the Irish land border after Brexit: the common travel area and the challenge of trade', *Irish Yearbook of International Law* (Oxford: Hart, 2018), p. 7.
7 Anthony Soares, 'Migration at the Northern Ireland (Brexit) border: identities, commodities and connections', Centre for Cross Border Studies, Keynote Lecture delivered at Discourses of Migration conference, University of Warwick, 7 September.
8 S. Mullaly,'Children, citizenship and constitutional change', in B. Fanning (ed.), *Immigration and Social Change in the Republic of Ireland* (Manchester: Manchester University Press, 2007), pp. 27–29.
9 www.citizensinformation.ie, accessed 30 January 2019.
10 B. Fanning, *Migration and the Making of Ireland* (Dublin: UCD Press, 2018), p. 200.
11 F. Meridith, 'The Chinese community of Northern Ireland', Culturenothernireland.org, www.culturenothernireland.org, accessed 31 January 2019.
12 Mushroom Workers Support Group, *Harvesting Justice: Mushroom Workers Call for Change* (Dublin: MRCI, 2006), pp. 5–6.
13 L. Allamby, J. Bell, J. Hamilton, U. Hansson, N. Jarman, M. Potter and S. Toma, *Forced Labour in Northern Ireland: Exploiting Vulnerability* (York: Joseph Rowntree Foundation, 2011), pp. 19–20.
14 Mushroom Workers Support Group, *Harvesting Justice*, p. 17.
15 Figures cited from the Central Statistics Office unless otherwise stated. www.cso.ie, accessed 30 January 2019.
16 K. Bell, N. Jarman and T. Lefebvre, *Migrant Workers in Northern Ireland* (Belfast: Institute for Conflict Research, 2004), pp. 27–28.
17 A. Krausova and C. Vargas-Silva, 'Northern Ireland Census profile' (2011), www.nisra.gov.uk, accessed 30 January 2019.
18 N. Liubinine, 'Lithuanians in Northern Ireland: new home, new homeland', *Irish Journal of Anthropology*, 11:1 (2008), 9–13, p. 12.
19 Mushroom Workers Support Group, *Harvesting Justice*, p. 17.
20 M. Kempny, *Polish Migrants in Belfast* (Cambridge: Cambridge Scholars Press, 2010).
21 M. Kempny-Mazur, 'Between transnationalism and assimilation: Polish parents' upbringing approaches in Belfast, Northern Ireland', *Social Identities*, 23:3 (2017), 255–270.
22 N. Nestor, 'The Polish complementary schools and Irish mainstream education', in J. Plackechi (ed.), *Irish Polish Society Yearbook, Vol. 1* (Dublin: Irish Polish Social Society, 2014), p. 31.
23 Office for National Statistics, 'Population of the UK by country of birth and nationality', www.ons.gov.uk, 2017, accessed 30 January 2019.
24 S. McGonagle, '"Great fear" amongst Polish community in north over Brexit', *Irish News*, 31 March 2017.
25 A. Duval Smith, '"The only problem is the weather": Poles eye up Ireland after Brexit vote', *The Guardian*, 20 October 2016.

26 K. Burrell, 'Staying, returning, working and living: key themes in current academic research undertaken in the UK on migration movements from Eastern Europe', *Social Identities*, 16:3 (2010), 297–308.

27 J. Eade, S. Drinkwater and M. Garapich, *Class and Ethnicity – Polish Migrants in London*', Research Report for the RES-00–1294 ESRC Project (Surrey: CRONEM, University of Surrey, 2007), p. 21.

28 D. McGhee, C. Moreh and A. Vlachantoni, 'An undeliberate determinancy? The changing migration strategies of Polish migrants in the UK in times of Brexit', *Journal of Ethnic and Migration Studies*, 43:13 (2017), 2019–2130.

29 Ibid., p. 2118.

30 Ibid., p. 2121.

31 Ibid., p. 2121.

32 Ibid., p. 2121.

33 The *Growing Up in Ireland* survey is a longitudinal study of more than one-quarter of those 41,185 infants born between 1 December 2007 and 30 June 2008 who are registered with the Department of Social Protection as in receipt of children's allowance payments. Having first stratified the population by marital status, county of residence, mother's nationality and number of children per household, a final sample of 11,134 participants was arrived at. Taken together, this means that *Growing Up in Ireland* collected information on 27 per cent of all children born in Ireland during the sampling period. See A. Röder, M. Ward, C. Frese and E. Sánchez, *New Irish Families: A Profile of Second Generation Children and their Families* (Dublin: Trinity College Dublin, 2014).

34 Ibid., p. 22.

35 R. Ford and M. Goodwin, 'Britain after Brexit: a nation divided', *Journal of Democracy*, 28:1 (2017), 17–30.

36 C. Lally, 'Brexit will put major pressure on immigration controls – gardaí', *Irish Times*, 3 April 2018.

37 H. M. Government, *Position Paper on Northern Ireland and Ireland* (London: HM Government, 2018), p. 11, para. 33.

38 Centre for Cross Border Studies, *Briefing Paper 1: A Roadmap*, Brexit and the UK–Ireland Border Briefing Paper Series (Armagh: Centre for Cross Border Studies, November 2017), p. 5.

39 'Editorial: May's "hostile environment" must be dismantled', *The Observer*, 22 April 2018.

40 Centre for Cross Border Studies, *Briefing Paper 1: A Roadmap*, p. 7.

41 Allamby et al., *Forced Labour in Northern Ireland*, p. 36.

42 T. Dundon, M. A. Gonsález-Pérez and T. McDonough, 'Bitten by the Celtic tiger: immigrant workers and industrial relations in the new "glocalized" Ireland', *Economic and Industrial Democracy*, 20:4 (2007), 501–522, pp. 509–510.

15 Bashir Otukoya*

Hyphenated citizens as outsiders

'Where you from?' is the usual question an Afro-Irish is greeted with when encountering an ethnic-Irish. 'Letterkenny, Donegal' is the answer I usually give the intrigued stranger. 'Letterkenny? Naw, where you really from?' is the usual response, signalling that my answer is incorrect. Hesitant to respond, knowing that the answer I provide could make or break this brief encounter, I take a deep breath and answer 'Nigeria'. 'I knew it!' one man exclaimed, before further probing, 'and how long have you been here young man?' 'Seventeen years', I answered quickly to change the conversation, knowing already where it was about to end. 'Ah sure you're practically one of us', the stranger said with a smile, and resumed fiddling with his mobile phone where he sat opposite me on the long bus journey home to Donegal.

Hyphenated citizens are positioned in a precarious situation. One longs to be accepted into both one's 'home' and host society, only to be met with questions of identity that conflict the mind. One's longing to belong can never be satisfied, because one is for example neither Irish, nor Nigerian, enough. One carefully threads along the blurred concept of 'home', unable to determine where 'home' is. Not at one's own will of course, but because one's self-assertion to a particular identity is met with enquiry from those who deem that identity theirs: 'are you one of us?' For fear of being branded as 'lost in Europe' by one's fellow ethnics, or worse, being perpetually branded a foreigner by one's ethnic-Irish neighbour, the hyphenated citizen must endeavour to remain inside the thin line of identity on both sides of his/her hyphenation. One must retain one's cultural identity while integrating into another. Failure to do so will determine that one is not 'one of us': one is an outsider.

This chapter examines, from a Nigerian-Irish perspective, three difficulties encountered by hyphenated citizens in their efforts to become accepted as belonging to the Irish nation. The first difficulty is legal in nature and lies within the host (Irish) society; there exist rules and processes pertaining to citizenship that remind immigrants who have become naturalised Irish citizens that they are still outsiders. The second difficulty is sociological and lies within the 'home' society. This concept of home is perplexing, because for some immigrants 'home' is their host society: but for the sake of convenience, I take 'home' to mean their ethnic (Nigerian) society. This chapter serves to explore the added difficulty a hyphenated citizen might have in ensuring his/her dual (or multiple) identity is recognised and accepted by his/her own ethnic fellows. In seeking this assurance, young migrant adults experience a level of acculturative dissonance when conflicted with principles of cultural identity from both their home and host societies. The third difficulty is therefore psychological and lies within the 'self'. The chapter reveals how years of tormenting questions of identity reshape one's perception of the world, to the extremities that almost every comment is perceived as discriminatory, except where otherwise disputed. This notion of the 'outside self' reveals why a discourse on 'defending against racism' is a more suitable alternative to 'fighting racism'. Indeed, the lines of political correctness have been blurred due to a loss or lack of understanding of what comments are deemed racist and what are not. In essence, the chapter aims to reveal the experience of a hyphenated citizen as an outsider, from a Nigerian-Irish perspective.

Hyphenated citizens as outsiders in their host society

In the first place, naturalised citizens are not considered 'true' citizens because their identity is hyphenated. They are perceived to be conflicted in their national loyalty and, as a result, they are treated as outsiders. Secondly, the discrimination they face is twofold, because whichever side of the identity they proclaim to be a part of, theyare not part of that identity to a satisfactory level. For example, not all British citizens are the same. There are the Scottish, the English, the Welsh and, controversially, the Northern Irish. They differ in their culture, heritage, accents, language; but their 'British values' are perceived to be the same.[1]

Then there are the new forms of British, who too are distinguished by the aforementioned categories, but who are also perceived to share 'British values'. Their citizenship or/and nationality are hyphenated; they are British-Irish, British-Indian, British-African, British-Arab or, controversially, 'non-citizens'.[2] These hyphenated citizens, though equal under the law, have been perceived as not nationalistic enough to deserve hyphenated titles like Irish-Welsh, or Nigerian-Scots. Rather, it is their shared British citizenship that endows them with their British hyphenation.[3]

In Ireland, the realities of hyphenated citizens, such as 'black-Irish' or 'mixed-race-Irish', are not yet as advanced as they are in the neighbouring countries.[4] Indeed, second-generation migrants grow up grappling questions of national identity that are unfamiliar to ethnic-Irish citizens. 'Half Irish, half Nigerian; why can't I be both?' is a popular mind-boggling question among second- and third-generation migrants in Ireland.[5] While these migrants challenge the self-reflexivity of their national identity, the current political atmosphere centred around the fallout of the United Kingdom's referendum to leave the European Union ('Brexit') based on an anti-immigration rhetoric creates a much larger public debate concerning identity, citizenship and nationality. It poses the age-old socio-political question: 'are they one of us?'[6]

We are not.

The question is divisive. Depending on the context or purpose of the question, the answer will always vary. But to the individual to whom the question is referred, the question internalises and becomes the answer: 'am I one of them?'

The harsh reality of this question lies not in its 'insider–outsider' dichotomy, but rather in that the question is framed in a sociological sense. Framed in a legal sense, the answer is apparent. Ethnic-Irish citizens and naturalised-Irish citizens are perceived as equals, regardless of their level of national attachment or lack thereof. But this perception remains merely a perception. The truth of the matter is that the equality that citizenship guarantees refers only to those citizens who are 'part of the nation', those who are aptly referred to as nationals.[7] They are nationals because their proximal affiliation to the nation is that of blood or descent. All other citizens, that is, those who attain their citizenship by way of naturalisation, are not nationals. They are not 'true' citizens. Their loyalty and/or attachment to the state is not whole. Their citizenship is hyphenated.

Internal exclusivity

Nationals are wholly citizens – their legal rights are fully protected. Citizens, particularly those who are naturalised, are not necessarily nationals – their legal rights are subject to discretionary intervention. Citizens who attain their citizenship by naturalisation are at risk of losing that citizenship by virtue of Section 19 of the Irish Nationality and Citizenship Act 1956, as amended, a threat from which all other citizens are immune. How can we proclaim an inclusive citizenship if a particular group of citizens can be denaturalised? Naturalised citizens are not truly citizens in the inclusive sense. They are citizens in the passport-wielding sense, but no more than that. This is citizenship as 'internal exclusivity'.

According to Brubaker, citizenship is characterised as both 'internally inclusive' and 'externally exclusive', echoing the accepted definition of citizenship as an instrument of political membership.[8] His characterisation exhibits citizenship as exclusionary closure[9] defining those who belong to the national polity, and consequently defining those who do not. Citizenship internally recognises a rule of law that protects and binds citizens while externally creating a formal state membership based mainly on birth. I suggest another characterisation: citizenship is 'internally exclusive'. Citizenship obtained through naturalisation is not citizenship in the traditional sense; citizenship is but a mere instrument of mobility. Citizenship obtained through naturalisation fails to satisfy the conditions of traditional citizenship, including civic participation or an ethnic affiliation with the host state. The naturalised citizen does not need to identify with the host state, though it is commonplace to find that they do. Moreover, citizenship by naturalisation is significantly different from citizenship by birth (*jus soli*) or by descent (*jus sanguinis*). The latter is truly internally included, the former is internally excluded.

While citizenship internally includes those with membership to its polity, it is not alien in internally excluding those with the same membership, but which was obtained subsequently to, or in tandem with, a previous membership to another polity. More clearly, persons who acquire citizenship by naturalisation are distinguished with lesser social, civil, political and legal protection than those who acquire citizenship by other means. The most noticeable example of the internally exclusive characteristic of citizenship legislation lies in its name; 'Irish Nationality *and* Citizenship Act' (emphasis added), making a clear distinction between nationality and citizenship. The distinction is important, not least because it reinforces the significance of the disciplinary definitions of nationality and citizenship, but also because the legislation itself seeks to demarcate society into two spheres of citizenry: those who are internally included and those who are internally excluded. The title of the legislation suggests that the acquisition of nationality is far and distinct from the acquisition of citizenship. While the administrative processes of Irish citizenship acquisition determine this to be true, the wording of Article 2 of the Constitution clearly affirms that no such distinction is to be made.[10] The entitlement to be 'part of the nation' is bestowed upon 'every person born in the island of Ireland' as well as those 'qualified in accordance with law'. Put like this, to be an Irish national, one must first be a citizen. The Constitution had no intention of differentiating nationals from citizens, yet legislation does. One can only question the intentions of the authors of the citizenship legislation for choosing a paradoxical title as opposed to a more aptly named 'Irish Nationality Act'.[11]

The citizenship acquisition process itself is exclusionary. The Irish process, strengthened by ministerial discretion, can be seen as restrictive, full of impediments and uncertainty that may not lead to citizenship at all. The conditions for attaining Irish citizenship by naturalisation are set out in Section 15 of the Irish Nationality and Citizenship Act 1956. This lays out the five naturalisation conditions that one must satisfy in order to be eligible for naturalisation. The applicant must be over eighteen; must have been resident in Ireland for five of the previous nine years; must be of good character; must have an intention to continue to reside in the state after naturalisation; and must swear an oath of loyalty and fidelity to the state.

Criticisms of these conditions are rare, considering that Ireland is renowned for its 'easy' and 'open' naturalisation system – naturalising more immigrants than any other European country.[12] Ireland's naturalisation system is seen as 'easy' and 'open' because, unlike most of its European counterparts, the applicant is not required to have any knowledge about the state's history or the customs of the state, the official languages of the state can be neglected, and the applicant's understanding of the civic structures of the state has no bearing on the granting of naturalisation. Yet its 'easiness' can be questioned when naturalised Irish citizens are required to depict 'super-citizen' attributes (see below) before and after they are granted citizenship.[13] Making sense of these conditions; some criteria are more obscure than others. While age, continuation of residence and declaration of fidelity to the nation are conditions which remain untested in the Irish courts, the last two remain the subject of theoretical legal complications for both the state and the naturalised/naturalising individual. They are complicated because they are incoherent, inconsistent and uncertain. For example, by what metric is an intention to continue residency measured? Does a mere declaration provide ample evidence of the citizen's fidelity to the state and loyalty to the nation?

Super-citizens

Naturalised citizens are required to go beyond exercising their civic duties, while the civic duties of 'Irish-born' citizens are, by comparison, limited and mostly non-mandatory. The naturalised citizen is required to be of 'good character' before being awarded citizenship, but the inconsistency and the lack of guidelines in explaining what actions are deemed to be of 'bad character' leave the applicant in perpetual fear of the law, rather than understanding, acknowledging and respecting the law. This fear acts as a mode of authority over naturalised citizens, who now feel they must be of 'good character' at all times – a requirement of all citizens, but with explicit added pressure placed particularly on naturalised citizens. Naturalised citizens are required to remain in the state, first for a minimum of five years before naturalisation, and indefinitely thereafter. Only naturalised citizens are explicitly required to make a declaration of 'fidelity to the nation and loyalty to the State', while all other citizens, though required to have such loyalty, are not expected to make a declaration to this effect. This political duty is imposed upon all citizens, both 'nation-born' and naturalised, but for the former it is a discretionary imposition: 'it is an option, personal to him and to be exercised at his discretion'.[14] The latter must attest their loyalty and fidelity by way of a declaration, which, arguably, can at times be impersonal to the assignee. These so-called 'conditions of citizenship' are ideals for what the 'perfect citizen' ought to be and detract from the empirical realities of the modern-day conception of citizenship, which remains rife with voter apathy,[15] a disregard for other civic duties like jury duty[16] and a distancing of physical presence from the nation of which that citizen is part.[17]

In another example, Section 19 of the 1956 Act lays out the circumstances in which a naturalised citizen may lose their Irish citizenship, one of which states that if the naturalised citizen leaves the country for a period of seven years without reason 'and without reasonable excuse has not during that period registered annually in the prescribed manner his name and a declaration of his intention to retain Irish citizenship with an Irish diplomatic mission or consular office or with the Minister', the naturalised citizen may lose his/her Irish citizenship.[18] In arguably a clear breach of EU free movement rights, naturalised citizens are required to remain in the state or risk losing their citizenship if they do not register annually with the local Irish embassy. In contrast, there are the thousands of Irish emigrants who have left the emerald isle for pastures new, and who are yet to return after decades of political non-activity within the state, while their citizenship remains intact.

Naturalised citizens as outsiders in their 'home' society

Acculturation is a deeply disturbing psychological task every immigrant must undertake to be whole in the perception of oneself in one's place in one's new society.[19] Fuelled by social and political pressures, the immigrant must adopt the culture and/or citizenship of their new home if theyare to be considered integrated. One must be careful however, for one risks being under-integrated, whereby one is perpetually perceived as a foreigner, and with that comes its own socio-political, and in the extremes, racial, xenophobic and discriminatory consequences.[20] Extreme caution is advised, for the immigrant also risks being over-integrated, whereby the owners of the adopted culture might perceive one as threatening to their society.[21] One's self-assertion in an adopted culture will face backlash, because no matter how 'Irish' the immigrant perceives oneself to be, one will never be truly Irish enough.[22] One is branded a 'plastic Paddy', for example.[23] Yet the naturalisation requirements of becoming an Irish citizen suggest that the immigrant must act in a 'super-citizen'-like manner, to act 'more Irish than the Irish themselves'. However, in the 'home' society of the hyphenated citizen, this poses a significant problem.

Over-integration encourages seclusion

The problem is twofold. The first is that the hyphenated citizen is perceived as having disposed of his/her cultural background and is consequently disowned by his/her ethnic peers. Over-integration, much like under-integration, is easily evidenced in modern Irish society. In a bid to satisfy the self-imagined integration process, the immigrant, with an aim of attaining Irish citizenship, or merely for integration purposes, attempts to meet the imagined standards of 'Irishness' s/he perceives. One, for example, attempts to learn the Irish language, only to find that the language is not widely used, nor is it encouraged.[24] Indeed, one Irish-speaking Dutch journalist based in Galway once wrote a dark and controversially speculative article discussing the potential for future fascists to use the language as a rallying point against immigrants.[25] Regardless, the Irish language is an integration tool undisposed to immigrants, which is why one who is successful in utilising the language as often as the Irish themselves is perceived as having fully integrated into Irish society.[26] This can be seen as positive; but more so a negative if that individual loses, in its place, the ability to speak his/her native language.

In another example, one attempts to play the national sport (Gaelic football, hurling or camogie) but fails, and is instead recognised for playing a *more* internationally recognised sport like rugby, or joins the local Olympic team. The failure can at times, perhaps subconsciously, be deliberate. On the one side, until recently, only a small minority of migrants participated in the national sport, mainly because there was no encouragement or engagement for ethnic minorities to participate. Even with the more internationally recognised sports, there appears to be a preference to attain 'white players' (for want of a better description) to play for the national teams. Rugby is a prime example, wherein the manager and members of the Irish rugby team were designated as '100 per cent Irish' in 2016 even though head coach Joe Schmidt is a Kiwi ('New Zealander'), Olly Hodges is Australian and hooker Richardt Strauss is South African.[27] Only in recent times have ethnic minority sportsmen, such as Niyi Adeolokun, a Nigerian-born Irish rugby player, and Shairoze Akram, a Pakistani-born Gaelic football player, come to be recognised as legitimate Irish players. It is important to note that the distinction between the ethnic minority players and the white players is that the former attained their 'Irishness' by naturalisation, whereas the latter were 'gifted' their citizenship. More still, their limited fame as recognised Irish players only comes to media attention by virtue of being 'the first' something (insert unusual Irish characteristic here, e.g. 'first black', 'first Pakistani' etc.), and not initially as a result of their skills.

Secondly, one fails to engage in the national sports for lack of support from one's home society. One of the main reasons why the national sports are seen as a cultural treasure in Irish society is because of the communal support that is provided to local teams, comprising players who grew up in that community. Players who are new to that community, or ethnic minority players in general, find it difficult to attain such support, not from the local community but from their home society. The reasons for the lack of support are somewhat justified; for example, ethnic minorities, Africans and Arabs in particular, tend to be religious in their upbringing. Attending church or mosque on a Friday night, or on a Sunday morning (both times when training or matches usually take place), takes precedence over playing a sport that the parent of the individual sees no real future in – except whereby that individual is perceived to be accomplished as being 'the first' something. Furthermore, since knowledge of the history of the state, of which a national sport plays a vital part, is not an integration requirement for citizenship (indeed there are none), the importance of home societies to encourage young minority groups to engage in the sport is unfounded. It is not difficult to imagine the discomfort a player might have, perhaps at a national stadium such as Croke Park, whereby an array of white faces wearing colourful jerseys is cheering on their local team but there are few black faces in the crowd cheering on that 'first something player'. Certainly, a lack of support from one's home society can be discouraging. On the other hand, it serves to favour the individual as having more opportunities within the host society, since s/he is perceived as having integrated, though s/he is favoured to the disdain of her/his home society.

One can become overly exertive of one's level of Irishness by, for example, braiding one's hair in the colours of the county Gaelic football club,[28] or making music dedicated to national sports and heroes in the hope of being recognised as having integrated.[29] In another example, one expressly makes clear how integrated one has become by publishing news articles exclaiming same.[30] Such exclamations come with a price of being categorised by the home society as having forfeited one's ethnic origins.

In the extremities, where skills and talents are not disposed to the individual, the hyphenated citizen integrates by way of becoming friends either with other migrant groups to the exclusion of his/her own ethnic group, or exclusively with white-Irish groups. While in the eyes of the host society, this is a positive display of integration and multiculturalism that showcases Ireland as a welcoming and receptive society, in the eyes of the home society the individual is condemned as being 'Westernised'. In extreme cases, some are bullied, neglected and told they are 'lost in Europe' or 'too white'. These individuals are disassociated from their ethnic groups and forced to accept the Irish identity as their only identity, albeit to the scrutiny of that ethnic group and the Irish society themselves. One longs to belong, but to no avail.

Becoming friends with only white-Irish people can also occur in situations where the population of ethnic minorities is relatively low, whereby the individual is not given the opportunity to associate with his/her own ethnic group. The opposite of this is also true, whereby the individual becomes friends solely with his/her own ethnic group, to the exclusion of white-Irish groups. This arises in situations where the population of ethnic minorities is relatively high. Both these circumstances arise out of the housing policies in Ireland.[31] Cheap housing, or council housing, allocates a large population of ethnic minorities to a particular area, usually within the major cities, leaving a minority of that population to reside in small towns and rural areas without a proximal engagement with their ethnic peers.

In any event, befriending only members of a particular ethnic group, for example a black individual having only white friends, or a black individual having only black friends, can be damaging to the social cohesion of the changing Irish population. In the former example, the individual suffers a psychological damage to his/her identity, and in the latter it is society which suffers the damage. In this circumstance, whereby no integration takes place because it is perceived as being non-essential, hostility among the different ethnicities can occur. Hostility breeds ignorance and ignorance breeds hatred.

Over-integration encourages racism

The second problem is more severe, because such over-integration, like under-integration, disrupts the understanding of what contents, either implicit or explicit, can be classed as discriminatory. The individual suffers psychological and, in the extreme, physical damage as a result of such confusion, but to the home society as a whole the damage is more significant. Fabu-D, a Nigerian-Irish comedian, provides a prominent example. In a bid to achieve an acceptance of his integration into Irish comedy, often calling himself the 'black paddy', he describes himself as 'the black Conor McGregor', and aspires to become 'the black Tommy Tiernan of Ireland'.[32] This is perhaps an admirable thing to say to a white journalist writing for a white-owned media outlet reporting to a predominantly white audience. However, to the black community Fabu-D and others like him (such as the African-Irish Dude) are seen as causing more harm than good, since they grow in popularity at the expense of the black community. Quite frankly, were they to be told by a white-Irish, his jokes would be considered racist. His YouTube videos grow in popularity worldwide, playing on black stereotypes, like the one entitled 'Black people don't like sun bathing', which, if presented by a white person, would be considered racist, but is instead considered acceptable because it is classed as comedy, and worse still, because it comes from a black man. Yet some (mainly white individuals) have commented that rather than offend, his videos educate his audience to help answer questions that might be perceived as too offensive to ask; such as whether black people get sunburnt. Indeed, his videos not only entertain but also help enlighten viewers on the cultural differences (and similarities) between the culture of the white-Irish and of the black-Irish.

However, this type of comedy, and indeed most of his videos, permits white-Irish viewers to engage in online comments that are outright discriminatory but are passed off instead as 'banter' and 'craic'. This online acceptance of racism further skews the relationship between black ethnics and white ethnics in Ireland. Since the joke is being told by a black man, white people accept it as comedy; but what it does is subconsciously feed the stereotypes to the minds of its white audience, to the extent that such online comment-ing transposes to real interactions, where clear racist jokes are being told in the midst of the so-called 'black friend', who is expected and psychologi-cally forced to accept it as a joke. The phrase 'It's OK, he's my friend' is not a suitable excuse to entertain an all-white guest with racial jokes at the 'black friend's' expense. Unfortunately, most 'black friends' will accept the joke and carry on, so as to avoid any awkwardness. More worrying still, some will entertain the joke and also engage in quite clearly discriminatory jokes that are accepted as normal because the black guy is laughing too. S/he is not. In her/his mind, it instils a confusion so terrifyingly great it disturbs, at a psychological level, the friendship. The black friend no longer sees the teller of the joke as a friend, but instead someone with whom caution should be taken, because in the mind of the black friend, if one is at such liberty to make jokes at his/her expense in his/her presence, one can only question that liberty when the black friend is not present. More than this, it blurs the line between political correctness and free speech. Suddenly, what once might have being acceptable becomes, at the very least, question-able. Which is why questions such as 'where you *originally* from?' can be perceived as implicitly racist, though they may not be intended to be. The experience dictates that caution should now be taken when encountering the white race.

More still, damage is caused to the white friend and society as a whole, for s/he now privileges having a black friend as justification for engaging in racist jokes. Nothing is more damaging than one who is ignorant in his/her discrimination, permitted and somewhat encouraged to discriminate by a black man who uses racial stereotypes as a utility of integration. The attempt to become one of *them* comes at the greater expense of losing what it means to be one of *us*.

Naturalised citizens as outsiders in their selves

Hyphenated citizens perceive themselves as outsiders on both sides of the societies they perceive themselves as belonging to. They do not identify themselves as belonging fully to the host (Irish) society because society has laws and policies pertaining in particular to citizenship acquisition which indicate that they are not full members of society. On the other hand, they also do not fully belong to their home (Nigerian) society, whereby they are rejected from their ethnic identity as a result of having acquired another. The individual is thereby in a psychological limbo where s/he cannot be placed in either society.

Young migrant adults experience acculturative dissonance as a result of this psychological limbo, especially when conflicted with principles of identity from both their home and host societies. Years of tormenting questions of identity reshape one's perception of the world. Questions of ethnic or national identity, and the answers to these, often determine the interactional relationship between the individual, the society and the state. One question which remains prevalent, though perhaps on a subconscious level, is the question of 'home', because from it derives other questions of identity, such as, Where is home? Am I home? If this is not home, why am I here? If I go somewhere else, will that be home? Will I belong there? Why don't I belong here? These questions are most commonly experienced by young migrant adults, and are often elevated when questions of ethnic or national identity arise – 'Where are you from? … No, where are you *really/originally* from?', a popular conversation starter in Ireland. One other way of these identity questions arising is through intentional racist comments like, 'why don't you go back home to your own country?'[33]

The harm caused by these types of question is often unintentional and unfamiliar to the Irish; 'regionalism' and 'placement' often mapping the routes of friendly conversations: 'O'Donoghue? A Galway man is it?'[34] Yet the harm exists. Minute as they may appear, or as is recorded, they lead to cognitive dissonance and acculturative dissonance, the extent of which slowly eradicates social integration while promoting segregation and ghettoisation. In the United States, reports have correlated acculturative dissonance with youth delinquency, youth violence and an increase in the population of juvenile detention centres.[35] These reports are not too distant from the realities of the so-called youth-driven 'race wars' that occur unrecorded here in Ireland.[36] The reasons for such delinquency appear logical; if a person is constantly asked where he is *really* from throughout his lifetime, despite that lifetime being spent on Irish soil, he is moulded into believing that he is not *really* from there. He removes himself from society and finds commonality with others like himself, those perceived as not belonging. Yet the 'where you *really* from?' question has been argued to have no harmful intentions.

In addition, the severe level of cognitive dissonance that orbits a young migrant's mind when questions of identity arise are further complicated by questions of state loyalty: If one had two passports, to which state does one's loyalty lie? In a hypothetical situation where Ireland proclaims war with Nigeria, am I Nigerian, or am I Irish?[37]

Am I Nigerian? Well, my passport says so, and my native language, Yoruba, is unequivocally Nigerian. I am dark in colour, like other Nigerians I know, I was born in Nigeria and my parents are Nigerian – to other

Nigerians it is quite obvious that I am Nigerian, although some have argued that I am not Nigerian enough; whatever that may mean.

Am I Irish? I certainly feel Irish, I can speak just about the same level of leaving cert Irish that my white-Irish friends can, I most certainly can ask if I may go to the toilet in Irish!: 'An bhfuil cead agam dul go dtí an leithreas?' I am a 'local' (a regular customer) at a nearby pub. When Donegal won the All-Ireland finals in 2012, I led the crowd into chants singing 'Jimmy's winning matches' in reference to Jim McGuiness, the Manager at that time. On St Patrick's Day, the dark pigmentation of my skin is concealed with green dye. I participate in the plane-landing ritual of the clapping of hands, bless myself when an ambulance drives by, go to Mickey D's (McDonald's) for breakfast on Friday mornings as a treat, and, when I can, I have the roast on Sundays for dinner – I must be Irish! – at least my Irish friends dictate me as such, though some have argued that I am not Irish enough; whatever that may mean.

Yet my skin colour, my perplexing accent, my perceived religion, my ancestry, my name, but most prevalently, society, tells me different. Even with my Irish passport, my Irishness is questioned; am I not Irish? In part if not whole? But what does this even mean; to be Irish?

Satirical articles suggest that 'there's nothing more Irish than an Irish Mammy', they suggest that 'being Irish means you're probably Catholic … but you never go to Mass'. Traditionally, being Irish meant that you were ethnically white and predominantly Catholic – at least until the rise in immigration after 1997 this has mainly been the case. But the question of Irishness in light of the changing ethnography of Ireland is far too complex to remain in the school of comedy, sociology or Irish studies; the phenomenon must travel far into the school of politics, and of law. The question of 'Irishness' must be viewed in its entirety; by examining Irishness under a politico-legal lens, in terms of citizenship and national identity.

So, I ask again; what does it mean to be Irish? Being Irish means that I can own land;[38] become an Officer in the defence forces;[39] own Irish-registered ships and aircraft, or shares in companies owning them[40] – all of which non-Irish members of the population are hindered from doing. Being Irish means, by default, being a European citizen. It means that I am able to leave and re-enter Ireland as I please, and I am able to do so freely within the EU. Being Irish means I am able to vote in both local and national elections, and that I am able to judge or be judged by a *true* member of my peers in a court of law – the two most democratic rights of all.[41] Yet when we are asked what it means to be Irish, we forget the privileges, rights and powers that are bestowed upon us by virtue of being Irish. Perhaps, then, it is fair to proclaim that only those who are naturalised will truly appreciate the significance of being Irish, having endured the hardships that come with the hyphenation.

Conclusion

What can be done to alleviate some of the concerns raised in this chapter? An easy first step is to continue engaging in the discussions contained within this book. A second step might be to reconsider some of our views and perceptions of our 'visibly different' counterparts. The steps that follow these are more complex, requiring, for example, changes (or rather introduction) to state policies on immigrant integration and law reform on the laws governing citizenship acquisition, in particular naturalisation. In addition, perceiving oneself as an outsider in society need not be a disadvantage. For example, I have already outlined how being 'the first' something can be beneficial in attaining recognition of one's skills and talents, even if that means being the first (or only) black person in one's workplace or neighbourhood. Being multilingual is another, coupled with the ability to manoeuvre social awkwardness and in educating the ignorant. Your difference need not be a negative; indeed there is a certain speciality in being different that disadvantages those in the majority.

The truth of the matter is that we are different. We are different in colour, our accents are confusing, our religions vary, we have little ancestry here, nor do our names sound Irish (though the argument can be made that pronouncing Caoimhe is just as difficult as pronouncing Olatunde). We are not at liberty to choose our physical appearance, our biological character, nor even our cultural background, and I suspect, if given the choice, we would not change a single strand of our DNA. However, we can change the society we live in and a case is being put forward here for a socio-legal change in the way we perceive those who are Irish in whole or in part, either by law or by heart.

Notes

* A note of thanks to those whom I interviewed in the process of writing this chapter, in particular Alex Hijman and Wuraola Majekodunmi who provided an insight into the experience of living as an immigrant who speaks Irish. To Doxa Moba who provided many examples for the content of this chapter and Eógan Hickey who reviewed the contents of same. Some of the content of this chapter has been published elsewhere and has been cited accordingly.

1 ETHNOS Research and Consultancy, *Citizenship and Belonging: What Is Britishness? A Research Study* (London: Commission for Racial Equality, 2005); U. Maylor, "I'd worry about how to teach it': British values in English classrooms', *Journal of Education for Teaching*, 42 (2016), 314–328.

2 C. Joppke, 'Multicultural citizenship', in E. Isin and B. Turner (eds), *Handbook of Citizenship Studies* (London: Sage, 2002), p. 245.

3 D. Miller, 'Will Kymlicka "Multicultural Citizenship within Multination States": a response' *Ethnicities*, 11 (2011), 303–307, p. 303.

4 These realities are not pleasant. See L. Michael, *Afrophobia in Ireland: Racism against People of African Descent* (Dublin: ENAR Ireland, 2015); F. Gartl, 'Mixed race Irish in state care subjected to colour specific abuse, Oireachtas told', *Irish Times*, 23 October 2014.

5 Z. Boladale, 'Irish or Nigerian? why can't I be both', *Irish Independent*, 19 June 2015; D. Van Nguyen, 'Half-White, Half-Asian, but no less Irish' *Irish Examiner*, 15 August 2015.

6 For a good example of an evaluation of this question, see P. Vohra, 'One of us? Negotiating multiple legal identities across the Viking diaspora', *Ethnic and Racial Studies*, 39 (2016), 204–222, p. 204.

7 The distinction between nationals and citizens is fundamental in the understanding of the concept. On a less significant note, the distinction can be language-based. The definition provided here is based solely in an Irish perspective. In other states, 'nationality' is seen as legal citizenship and 'citizenship' is referred to as social citizenship; see for example, K. Kovács, Z. Körtvélyesi and A. Nagy, 'Margins of nationality: external ethnic citizenship and non-discrimination', *Perspectives on Federalism*, 7 (2015), 85–116, p. 85. Some states however do not differentiate between the two definitions and use both 'citizens' and 'nationals' interchangeably. For individual European Union member state definitions see, 'Citizenship or nationality?', http://globalcit.eu/glossary_citizenship_nationality/, accessed 3 February 2019.

8 R. Brubaker, *Citizenship and Nationhood in France and Germany* (Cambridge, MA: Harvard University Press, 1992), p. 21.

9 Also termed 'social closure', C. Piola, 'The reform of Irish citizenship', *Nordic Irish Studies*, 5 (2006), 41–58.

10 'It is the entitlement and birthright of every person born in the island of Ireland, which includes its islands and seas, to be part of the Irish Nation. That is also the entitlement of all persons otherwise qualified in accordance with law to be citizens of Ireland. Furthermore, the Irish nation cherishes its special affinity with people of Irish ancestry living abroad who share its cultural identity and heritage' – Article 2 of the Constitution of Ireland, 1937 as inserted after the Good Friday Agreement 1998.

11 Most European states opt to use 'citizenship' or 'nationality' in their legislation, but not both. See for example, British Nationality Act 1981; Dutch Nationality Act 1892; Italian Citizenship Act 1992 (Statute 91/92).

12 M. M. Howard, 'Comparative citizenship: an agenda for cross-national research', *Perspectives on Politics*, 4:3 (2006), 443–445; M. M. Howard, 'The impact of the far right on citizenship policy in Europe: explaining continuity and change', *Journal of Ethnic and Migration Studies*, 36:5 (2010), 735–751; MIPEX, 'Access to nationality | MIPEX 2015', mipex.eu/access-nationality (MIPEX, 2015), accessed 3 February 2019.

13 See B. Otukoya, 'Super-citizens: equal powers come with greater responsibilities', *Cork Online Law Review*, www.corkonlinelawreview.com/single-post/2017/01/18/Super-Citizens-Equal-Powers-comes-with-Greater-Responsibilities (corkonlinelawreview.com, 18 Jan 2017), accessed 3 February 2019.

14 *Lobe and others v. Minister for Justice*, Equality & Law Reform [2003] IESC 1, 160.

15 I. Honohan, 'Civic republicanism and the multicultural city', in W. J. V. Neill and H. U. Schwedler (eds), *Migration and Cultural Inclusion in the European City* (Basingstoke: Palgrave, 2007), p. 63.

16 For example, Section 34.1 of the Juries Act 1976 obligates a person called for jury service to respond to their call for jury duty, otherwise a fine of €500 may be imposed, with the exception of those under Section 9.2 of the Act and those ineligible as of right. Despite this legal sanction upon failure to participate in what should be a voluntary civic duty, some 'are prepared to pay a jury tax rather than incur a multiple of this from lost earnings because of a potential commitment to a long drawn out jury trial'; E. Byrne, 'Problem with our attitude to jury service', *Irish Times*, 30 June 2009.

17 Measured in terms of net migration (immigration less emigration).

18 Irish Nationality and Citizenship Act 1956, Section 19(c).

19 E. K. Bailey, 'From cultural dissonance to diasporic affinity: the experience of Jamaican teachers in New York City schools', *Urban Review*, 45 (2013), 232–249, p. 232.

20 Michael, *Afrophobia in Ireland*.

21 Indeed more and more European member states, like Britain, are implementing citizenship tests as part of their naturalisation policies for fear of perceived loss or damage to their national identity. M. Paquet, 'Beyond appearances: citizenship tests in Canada and the UK', *Journal of International Migration and Integration*, 13 (2012), 243–260, p. 243; C. Joppke, 'The inevitable lightening of citizenship', *European Journal of Sociology*, 51 (2010), 9–32.

22 B. Otukoya, 'I'm Irish, but the Irish don't know that I'm Irish', 18 August 2015, www.thejournal.ie/readme/irish-by-heart-2277271-Aug2015, accessed 3 February 2019.

23 The term originally refers to second-generation Irish citizens who emigrated to London during the 1980s. Having grown up in an English society but self-identifying as Irish, they were referred to as 'plastic Paddy' – fake versions of a true Irishman. Modern definitions refer the 'plastic Paddy' to be a non-Irish national who knows little about 'actual Irish history and culture but claim to be "Irish"'. J. Nagle, *Multiculturalism's Double-Bind: Creating Inclusivity, Cosmopolitanism and Difference* (London: Routledge, 2016), pp. 162–163; R. Cullen, *The Little Green Book of Blarney: The Importance of Being Irish* (White Plains, NY: Peter Pauper Press), p. 37.

24 C. Healy, O. Parkinson and Immigrant Council of Ireland, *On Speaking Terms: Introductory and Language Programmes for Migrants in Ireland* (Dublin: Immigrant Council of Ireland, 2007).

25 A. Hijman, *Foinse* (2005), cited in A. Killick, 'Immigrants to Ireland and the Irish language – 2005 and onwards', www.independentstateofhappiness.com/index.php/ga/gradaim-buaicphointi/imeasc-cuntas-gearr (2014), accessed 3 February 2019.

26 Indeed the Immigrant Council of Ireland suggests that learning the Irish language would be a form of integration because it is essential to some employments and activities: Immigrant Council of Ireland, *Getting On: From Migration to Integration: Chinese, Indian, Lithuanian and Nigerian Migrants' Experiences in Ireland* (Dublin: Immigrant Council of Ireland, 2008), p. 149.

27 P. Duncan, 'Citizen Schmidt: Ireland rugby coach now one of our own', *Irish Times*, 2 September 2015.

28 M. Hilliard, 'Mayo v Dublin: "It's bringing two cultures into one place on my head"', *Irish Times*, 14 September 2017.

29 B. Hughes, 'Rap trio Phat KiiDZ score YouTube hit with "GAA Jersey"', *Irish News*, 30 July 2016. Following their success with 'GAA Jersey', the Donegal trio went on to release another song entitled 'Conor McGregor'.

30 Otukoya, 'I'm Irish, but the Irish don't know that I'm Irish'.

31 C. Paris, 'Housing and the migration turnaround in Ireland', *Urban Policy and Research*, 23:2 (2005), 287–304.

32 S. O'Connor, 'Blind Date star Fabu D's one year homeless hell', *Irish Mirror*, 28 October 2017; S. Pownall, 'Irish comedian Fabu_D says he looks "like a black Conor McGregor" on TV3's Blind Date', *Irish Mirror*, 21 October 2017.

33 Michael, *Afrophobia in Ireland*.

34 T. Inglis and S. Donnelly, 'Local and national belonging in a globalised world', *Irish Journal of Sociology*, 19 (2011), 127–143, p. 127.

35 M. Rabin, 'Cognitive dissonance and social change', *Journal of Economic Behavior & Organization*, 23 (1994), 177–194, p. 177; T. N. Le and G. Stockdale, 'Acculturative dissonance, ethnic identity, and youth violence', *Cultural Diversity and Ethnic Minority Psychology*, 14 (2008), 1–9; Bailey, 'From cultural dissonance to diasporic affinity'.

36 G. MacNamee, 'Irish teens wield lethal weapons as they clash in vicious "race related" pitch battle', *Irish Mirror*, 14 May 2015.

37 However hypothetical, Section. 19(d) of the Irish Nationality and Citizenship Act 1956 states that a naturalised citizen's citizenship may be revoked if 'the person to whom it is granted is also, under the law of a country at war with the State, a citizen of that country'.

38 Land Act 1965, Section 54.

39 Defence Act 1954, Section 41.

40 Mercantile Marine Acts 1955, 2006, Section 16; Irish Aviation Authority (Nationality and Registration of Aircraft) Order 2005, SI 634/2005, Section 7. Although there are no restrictions on non-citizens to establish a registered company in the state, they are however excluded from the enjoyment of the freedom of markets, as only nationals of an EU member state may enjoy the freedom of establishing companies within the EU. Companies are assimilated to nationals of the EU member states where they are formed and have their 'registered office, central administration or principal place of business'. See Treaty on the Functioning of the European Union 2010 OJ C 83/01, Article 54.

41 Stemming from the exclusion of non-citizens (with the exception of those under Section 8.2) to register as a Dail elector under the Electoral Act 1992, Section 8. In America, voting is seen as a fundamental right, which cannot be denied to citizens, save in accordance with the law. See National Voter Registration Act 1993; V. Francis, *Preserving a Fundamental Right: Reauthorization of the Voting Rights Act* (Washington: Lawyers' Committee for Civil Rights Under Law, June 2003). The right to a trial by a jury of your peers is seen to be fundamental in most common law states; however, whether there are fair representations on the jury, in a multicultural state, has led governments to rethink the design of the jury; see, J. Van Dyke, 'Jury service is a fundamental right', *Hastings Law Quarterly*, 2 (1974–5), p. 27; Law Reform Commissioner, Report on Jury Service (LRC 107–2013).

Bryan Fanning and Lucy Michael

Conclusion: shades of belonging and exclusion

Normatively, integration refers to the process by which immigrants become accepted into a society, both as individuals and as groups.[1] However it comes to be defined, the implicit assumption is that some degree of conformity represents 'successful' integration.[2] But conformity to what? Theories of segmented assimilation suggest that different groups of immigrants are confronted with the challenge of adapting to different parts of the social and class structure of the host society or have opportunities only to slot into particular spaces. The various kinds of adaptation documented throughout this book, as well as the range of barriers experienced by different groups, exemplify patterns of segmented assimilation in both Irelands. It can be seen in differentiated access to housing, employment and education. Some of this is influenced by stratifications in rights and entitlements experienced by migrants on arrival. Some of the differences between the experiences of some immigrants and others might be accounted for by racism. There is also significant evidence that pathways to assimilation or integration are shaped heavily by gender and class, so that patterns of employment, education and social interaction for any group or part of a group are affected not just by the characteristics of the migrant group, but by gender and class divisions in the host society.

Sociology is concerned (among other things) with understanding social reproduction, how society changes from one generation to the next in terms of values, culture and beliefs, and the relationships between this changing social structure and individual agency. Here, it is not just identity rules of belonging that matter but the capabilities that contribute to successful adaptation within a particular host society. Overlapping aspects are captured by concepts such as habitus, cultural capital, acculturation and capabilities. The characteristics, dispositions, skills and forms of knowledge understood to foster integration can change over time as well as differing from place to place. Some immigrants in both Irelands have considerably lesser rights or poorer options than many citizens. Some, because they do not speak English, do not have meaningful access to their rights and may not be able to make use of education and skills they acquired in their countries of origin.

Of course, there are many marginalised people in both Irelands other than immigrants. It may not simply be the case that these lack human capital. They may also be disempowered by a relative lack of capabilities that confer upon them skills that might help them get on better in life.[3] Amartya Sen has argued in his writings on capabilities that people make choices based on the information they have access to and can understand. He is critical of overtly simplistic accounts of human motivations proposed by economists that ignore 'all other motivations other than the pursuit of self-interest'.[4] He argues that 'so-called rational choice theory' actually takes the rationality out of choice; it ignores the conditions, contexts and individual capabilities which inform the actual choices open to people.[5] Education, from this perspective, is not just about conferring skills and qualifications. It potentially empowers people by enabling them to choose in a more informed way, to advocate on their own behalf and to be taken more seriously by others. Many parts of the world are generically modern, with comparable education, health and administrative systems, similar supermarkets, brands and mass-produced foods and goods, all sharing a globalised mass media. Well-equipped immigrants may even fare better from the outset than marginal groups within a given host society. Economic rules of belonging, where those with marketable skills find favour, do not just apply to migrants.

The basic capabilities needed by any immigrant (or indeed anyone else) seeking to avoid discrimination and find work that matches their skills, abilities and aspirations include various kinds of knowledge in addition to what economists call human capital. But not being able to speak the language of the host society places people at a huge disadvantage; they are utterly dependent on intermediaries in their own families and communities. There is a significant body of research which shows that dependency induced by language barriers leads to exploitation. Also, not having a secure legal status, being a so-called 'illegal immigrant' or an undocumented one, makes it very difficult for migrants to seek help and support.

There is, however, a need to understand language and rights as part of a broader sphere of capabilities. Immigrants and others who are failed by the education system are likely to become outsiders even if they have citizenship rights, even if they speak the language of the host community. Conversely, well-educated English-speaking immigrants may have considerable advantages over some members of the host community. Some may possess forms of cultural capital that are valued within the host society. Pierre Bourdieu defines cultural capital as skills and dispositions that confer advantage on a person in a given society.[6] Cultural capital may be understood as a form of intellectual capital that affects the life chances of individuals even as it reproduces a specific social order. It confers status-enhancing forms of knowledge, norms and habits. The unequal distribution of cultural capital is seen to result in cultural hierarchies (defined in terms of socio-economic status as well as in terms of ethnic or religious divides) alongside material ones.[7]

Various chapters have described how some immigrants experience initial periods of state-induced marginalisation, have become excluded from employment, are shunted towards disadvantaged schools or encounter racism. Others describe immigrant experiences that are in many respects positive ones. While there is an urgent need to address some institutional barriers, address discrimination and provide supports for vulnerable migrants, it is important to acknowledge that many immigrants are doing well, that their migration journeys have been successful ones, that many are making significant positive contributions to the societies in which they have settled, that many have experienced the communities into which they have settled as welcoming places, that the day-to-day problems many immigrants face are often the same as those experienced by anybody else.

Viable lives

The biggest challenge facing immigrants (or anyone else) is to build viable lives for themselves and their families. If they fail to do so (or are failed by institutional barriers or discrimination) this potentially sets up future inter-generational problems for the host society as well as those who come to be excluded. The term 'functional integration' denotes what migrants themselves might consider as viable lives in the host society, as distinct from the host society's expectation of integration.[8] Migrants might arrive in Ireland, or anywhere else, hoping to make a living or build better lives for their families at home. Some have clearly experienced dysfunctional and damaging levels of exploitation. Others might be part of a supportive community that is somewhat marginal within the host society, but within which day-to-day life is nonetheless socially and economically viable.

By such criteria, many immigrants on the island of Ireland are functionally integrated. Many are at least as well integrated as many Irish-born people. Ireland is a society where economic rules of belonging matter greatly and where cultural belonging has never stemmed emigration or other kinds of marginalisation. Irish Travellers, recognised as a marginalised community since the 1960s, are included in this book because the kinds of inequality that they have experienced in both the Republic of Ireland and in Northern Ireland exceed those of other marginal Irish communities that have experienced intergenerational class inequality and social exclusion, those being compounded by racialised discrimination. The struggles of Pavee Point and other Traveller organisations to redress institutional discrimination in education, healthcare and in other areas of social policy have had limited success and demonstrate the difficulties of challenging the structural barriers in these areas. The formal recognition of Traveller ethnicity by the Irish state in 2017 came after decades during which Irish politicians and political parties were complicit in anti-Traveller racism and during which Traveller cultural distinctiveness was denied by the Irish state. The situation of Travellers is in some ways analogous to those African Americans who continue to experience racism, disproportionate incarceration and a form of ghettoisation. Most are marginalised but there are a few Traveller music, film and sports stars as well as some public intellectuals and activists. Some Travellers have also done well in business but there is not much of a Traveller middle class.

The kinds of exclusion and marginalisation experienced intergenerationally by Travellers in education, employment, housing and health have proved exceedingly difficult to shift. The nature and extent of exclusion experienced by many Roma if anything exceeds that encountered by Travellers because of linguistic barriers and very low rates of literacy. A number of chapters in this book have highlighted anti-Roma racism, including attacks on Roma homes in Belfast and Waterford, and even the repatriation of Roma subject to organised racist harassment. We need always to be careful to avoid over-deterministic claims about the impact of racism on people's lives for all that there is an urgent need to take racism seriously in both Irelands. Otherwise what are we to make of the statement of one young Roma woman at a 2015 community event in Belfast that she loved living in Northern Ireland, which had been her home for the past fourteen years, and that she and her family felt safe and included there.[9] It may well be the case that many Roma see themselves as living viable lives and, although many experience relative deprivation, their migration journeys to Ireland reflect a measure of success, particularly in offering better prospects for the next generation.

For many Roma in Ireland, the likelihood of future intergenerational marginalisation is all too real, not just because of racism but because of language deficits and poor education. Of the immigrant-origin communities examined in this book, the Roma perhaps experience the greatest accumulation of barriers even if, as EU member state citizens, they have most of the same rights as Irish citizens. Other groups can also be described as particularly at risk of intergenerational exclusion because of combinations of low levels of capabilities and racism and due to their assimilation in deprived neighbourhoods where long-term Irish residents are also marginalised.

Several chapters focus on those whose experiences of lesser rights and entitlements contribute to their marginalisation. The experiences of migrants have come to depend very much on how they are classified by the host society. Since 2004 migrants from the Eastern European countries that joined the EU at that time have settled in the Republic of Ireland and in Northern Ireland without hindrance. Others requiring visas from countries such as the Philippines and India work in healthcare and other sectors and have become Irish citizens in large numbers. Tens of thousands from places like China and Brazil came as students and have been allowed to work during their stay.

By contrast – and unlike in most other EU countries including the United Kingdom – asylum seekers in the Republic of Ireland have been prevented from working. In 2017 the Republic of Ireland's Supreme Court ruled that this absolute ban was unconstitutional. The Burmese Rohingya man whose case led to the ruling had spent eight years in enforced unemployment before getting refugee status. At the time of writing, considerable institutional barriers remain which effectively prevent most asylum seekers from applying for a work permit. Various studies cited in Chapter 5 of the exceedingly high rates of unemployment among African-Irish have concluded that the long periods of compulsory joblessness experienced by asylum seekers, as well as 'severe racism', had much to do with this. Both Irelands are racist societies and institutional commitments to addressing racism in both jurisdictions have been weak.[10]

Many immigrant communities are internally stratified on the basis of social class. Alongside Indians, Pakistanis and Filipinos who have become citizens, homeowners and hold middle-class jobs, there are others who have migrated to both Irelands to do badly paid work. The Filipino care workers described in Chapter 6 worked for low pay but most had become Irish citizens. They were considerably better off than undocumented Filipinos interviewed in some other studies in Northern Ireland and in the Republic of Ireland.[11] They had not fared as well as better-paid qualified nurses, many of whom had purchased houses and settled with their families in Ireland.[12]

The sole chapter in this book on Ireland's Muslim community focuses on young people who are far from the most marginalised within the Republic of Ireland's education system (although there are evident stratifications between the experiences of children of asylum seekers and other Muslims with secure residency status or Irish citizenship). There is some evidence to suggest that Muslims in both Irelands are on the whole not as economically marginalised as in some other European countries.[13] Ireland's Muslim communities, both in the North and in the Republic, were founded and came to be led by medical students, some of whom became permanent residents or established the first mosques. The 2011 Northern Ireland Census identified some 3,832 Muslims.[14] At 2002 the Republic's Muslim population stood at 19,147.[15] Of these, around two thousand were medical doctors.[16] The 2016 Census identified 63,443 Muslims living in the Republic. For several decades this community was decidedly middle class, different in profile from the Muslim communities in a number of other European countries which attracted many poorly educated post-colonial settlers, like France, or guest workers, like Germany. But by the turn of the century this profile had begun to shift. Ireland continued to attract Muslim medical students, doctors, nurses and other middle-class professionals. However, others arrived to fill comparatively poorly paid jobs in service industries.[17]

The 2002 Census had identified 5,472 Muslims who were citizens of African countries. Most of these were asylum seekers. This number rose to 6,909 by 2006 and to 15,376 by 2011. A 2010 study of Somali Muslims who arrived as refugees found them living in deprived areas, experiencing high levels of unemployment because of language barriers and low levels of education, with their children finding the education system difficult.[18] The settlement of some of the most vulnerable immigrants in Ireland's most disadvantaged urban localities sets up scenarios potentially similar to and as difficult to fix as those that have played out in other Western cities with marginalised immigrant-origin populations.

Chapter 12 examines evidence that immigrant-origin children have been disproportionately shunted into schools in disadvantaged areas, partly as a result of residence patterns and partly because of schools' admissions systems. One-quarter of African children were found to attend a disadvantaged school (compared with 9 per cent for the overall population) and one-quarter were likely to have limited fluency in English. It seems likely that children from such families were the ones most likely to find themselves living in poverty in disadvantaged areas and attending disadvantaged schools whereas the children of well-educated Africans, fluent in English and better off, may be less likely to be living in marginal areas or attending marginal schools. Some Africans are as such far more at risk of growing up as outsiders than others. Stratification along class lines is greatly exacerbated by the compounding factors of what Chapter 13 refers to as non-employment and labour market disadvantage, by lesser language fluency and low opportunity for residential and economic mobility, as well as by the lower overall capacity to escape the effects of institutional and direct racist discrimination.

Invisible lives

Perhaps the most striking characteristic of many new immigrant communities has been their near-invisibility within Irish society. Compared with many other European countries immigration stayed off the political radar, and political emphasis upon the integration of immigrants, which tends to be driven by host community anxieties about immigration, has been half-hearted at best. Many immigrant inhabitants of twenty-first-century Ireland are largely invisible to and within the major institutions of both jurisdictions, including within the media, within universities and within the political system. They go about their lives like anybody else. They exist below the radar, except sometimes as the focus of hostility. Comparison with the Irish in Britain during the decades after the Second World War is useful here. There was some degree of acknowledgement that Irish-born immigrants encountered some hostility and discrimination but this is not recognised within legislation such as the Race Relations Act 1966. Irish-born people and their descendants who identified as Irish were statistically invisible; they were not counted (i.e. disaggregated) within administrative data that might identify the nature and extent of barriers or discrimination. This changed, thanks to activism by Irish groups in Britain along the lines of subsequent activism by Traveller organisations in Ireland. The Irish in Britain had to become politically visible before they could become visible to policymakers. Some community activists interpreted high levels of deprivation among the Irish as evidence of 'racial discrimination'. However, this discrimination fell outside the narrower definition of racism then prevalent in academic scholarship and the terms of reference of the Commission for Racial Equality.[19] Similar issues might attend to xenophobia or anti-refugee sentiment in Ireland today.

To address this, community activists and academic researchers collected a substantial body of empirical evidence of experiences of institutional and individual discrimination among the Irish in Britain in areas such as education, policing and the criminal justice system, health and employment.[20] During the 1990s Irish organisations in Britain sought recognition of Irish ethnicity, believing that formal recognition and being counted in Census data were crucial to address forms of marginalisation. In many respects what these groups sought was similar to what Traveller organisations have since sought in the Republic of Ireland.

Many immigrant communities have established some degree of infrastructure in the form of places of worship, shops and community organisations. There are now a significant number of immigrant-led organisations in both Irelands. Some serve specific immigrant-origin communities (such as the Chinese Welfare Association in Belfast or Forum Polonia in Dublin); there are pan-African organisations such as the Africa Centre and single-issue collectives such as AkiDwa, which campaigns against female genital mutilation. Most immigrant communities have not mobilised as ethnic blocs like the Travellers or the Irish in Britain.

Poles, who are the largest immigrant-origin community in both the Republic and Northern Ireland, very quickly established a network of Polish-language schools. Their community activism appears to be very much focused on the Polish diaspora and on cultural events such as the now-annual Polski Eire festival. The shared Catholicism of Poles in both Irelands is potentially a rallying point. It is also likely that shared feelings of Polish nationalism work to foster a cohesive sense of Polish identity. None of this has translated yet into political influence in either of the two Irelands. Several Polish candidates stood unsuccessfully in the 2009 and 2014 local government elections and Forum Polonia has run voter registration campaigns. Although Poles constitute some 3 per cent of the population of the Republic of Ireland, they punch politically far below their weight. Most have not become Irish citizens.

The second largest immigrant group as revealed by the 2016 Republic of Ireland Census were those born in the United Kingdom. Of a total of 124,267 some 53,183 of these were citizens of the United Kingdom. The third largest group, Lithuanians (36,552 in 2016), who also constitute a significant population in Northern Ireland (around 7,000), are strikingly invisible within both academic research and in policy debates. In compiling this book, we sought unsuccessfully to redress this. Most of the chapters in this book are built on specific doctoral studies, research projects by non-governmental organisations (NGOs) or upon research commissioned by the state. Census data tell us that about a third of the Lithuanian population in the Republic live in the vicinity of Dublin and that many others live in counties on both sides of the border between the Republic and Northern Ireland. A number of studies of migrant exploitation in agriculture on both sides of the border appeared just before and after the Enlargement of the EU in 2004. These interviewed Lithuanians as well as migrants from other countries. In effect, these studies provided snapshots of people's lives at that particular time. The experiences of those who went on to settle on both sides of the border have not been tracked. In the absence of proper research all there is to go on are a few newspaper stories here and there. Some of those who initially worked as agricultural labourers are likely, a decade later, to be part of well-established Lithuanian communities in towns like Clones in County Monaghan. If an Irish government minister or their Northern Irish equivalent were asked how well have these integrated, or (our question) how and to what extent (if at all) are these outsiders? she could do no more than shrug her shoulders. Insofar as Lithuanian migrants are effectively invisible to elected officials, public services, NGOs and even academic researchers, their lives in Ireland are invisible ones.

A high proportion of non-EU-origin immigrants have become Irish citizens. These have yet to wield any discernible political influence. The sole exception is the Dublin 15 area, where there is a relatively high concentration of African immigrants. Several Nigerian candidates stood unsuccessfully against one another in the 2009 local government election and Congolese-born Edmund Lukusa, a Sinn Fein candidate, was elected in 2015. In Northern Ireland, Anna Lo successfully moved from leading the Chinese Community Welfare Association to chairing the Northern Ireland Council for Ethnic Minorities, which she co-founded, before being elected as a member of the Northern Ireland Assembly. She did so as a member of the Alliance Party, which stood apart from the two main host community ethnic blocs that dominate Northern Irish politics.

The invisibility of migrants within this political landscape is compounded by the ways in which administrative data are disaggregated. The use of the 'other' category in Northern Irish equality legislation and in policy documents makes explicit outsiders of those who do not fit into the two main communities. Occasional panics about violent racism in Northern Ireland have, as Chapter 3 shows, resulted in the main work on anti-racism being located within policing and criminal justice, rather than in community development and social policy. Institutional responses to racism have been far poorer in the Republic of Ireland, where there has been little political or policy acknowledgement of either violent racism or other manifestations of racist discrimination.

One problem with thinking of immigrant communities as ethnic blocs is that it makes less visible those groups who have low numbers or are highly dispersed. Another is that it tends to emphasise the differences between groups, rather than the shared experiences along the lines of gender, age, class and within arrival contexts or subsequent systems of rules and rights. For example, LGBT Poles appear to have been marginalised within Polish civil society to some extent and may well identify primarily with lesbian and gay communities in Ireland that cross ethnic lines.[21] Victims of female genital mutilation living in Ireland did not mobilise as Nigerians or Somali but as part of AkiDwa, a collective which brings together women from many different ethnic backgrounds. Multiculturalist approaches which have tended to favour ethnic blocs through political recognition or funding have, in places, achieved greater political visibility for migrants and subsequently greater recognition for rights, but in the absence of large numbers are less useful in creating institutions and services (as well as systems and rights) which can be equally inclusive of the heterogeneity within migrant groups.

The lens of 'superdiversity' offers an alternative approach.[22] Places like London have been described as superdiverse, with immigrant populations from dozens of countries of origin. Ireland, with more than two hundred nationalities among its migrants and these highly dispersed across the country, may not look exactly like London but the concept of 'superdiversity' can still be applied. Some analysts have described a 'diversification of diversity' where national origin is not an adequate category to capture differences in religion, ethnicity and the main spoken languages.[23] Disaggregation of ethnic data has, in the UK, demonstrated the value of identifying subgroups which are extremely disadvantaged compared with others in the same ethnic or national group.

The Republic's 2016 Census identified migrant communities of more than 10,000 persons from 15 different countries, with communities from a further 25 countries of between 1,000 and 10,000 persons. To put this into historical perspective, the Republic now has perhaps two dozen immigrant communities that are already larger than its Jewish community, which dates back to the late nineteenth century. But the word 'community' may not capture the religious, linguistic and cultural diversity to be found among migrants from some countries of origin. For example, many Lithuanian nationals are in fact ethnic Russians and form part of a Russian Orthodox religious community alongside migrants from other Baltic states. It is useful to be able to recognise differences between Catholic Igbo, Pentecostal Christians and Muslims among the Nigerian-Irish population. In places like Dublin 15, Nigerians with different religious and cultural backgrounds live alongside other Africans as well as migrants from many other countries. All settled in Dublin 15 because of the availability of housing there at a particular time, a factor that also accounts for 'superdiverse' immigrant communities in some inner urban areas in Belfast as well as inner city Dublin. Chapters 4 and 7 respectively address how some migrants may choose superdiverse areas for safety and convenience while others seek to settle in more homogeneous areas, perhaps because these are more middle class.

Superdiversity is a useful concept in thinking about the needs of diverse immigrant populations that include groups that are, in effect, invisible to policymakers. It would not make sense for the Republic or Northern Ireland to design policies aimed at supporting immigrants by configuring these separately for all immigrant communities. However, lessons about barriers encountered by specific groups can be extended to address the needs of other groups. While Traveller-specific issues can be identified in areas such as healthcare, education and housing, it is also the case that similar institutional barriers apply to the Roma. Other kinds of barrier experienced by Roma might also apply to other immigrant groups, and so on. It is crucial that public services, schools and healthcare for diverse or superdiverse communities become fit for purpose. Yet various chapters have described the policy approach of 'mainstreaming' as failing the minority groups it is designed to serve.[24] In essence, lip service is paid to the idea and the work to design services and guarantee access to these on an equal footing for everyone has yet to be done. Examples of good mainstreaming practice that might be drawn on include FGM and HIV sexual health campaigns aimed at supporting people from many different ethnic and linguistic backgrounds.

Integrated lives

Media debates about integration tend to fixate on culture, that is, on the ability (or not) of immigrants to fit in with the culture of the dominant ethnic group. New immigrants may not be particularly interested in becoming Irish, either of the two main kinds of Northern Irish or British, initially at least. This, we have argued, is not necessarily a problem when it comes to achieving functional integration. However, racism and xenophobia can have much to do with how immigrant-origin minorities are perceived within the host society or, as examined in Chapter 10, how they are represented in the media.

There are two good reasons why immigrants should become citizens if possible in the places where they settle. The first, addressed in the previous section, is that people who vote are taken more seriously by politicians than people who don't. Those who are not entitled to vote in both the Republic of Ireland and Northern Ireland include the vast majority of immigrants from EU member states. Poles may constitute the largest immigrant-origin community in both jurisdictions, but they are politically irrelevant.

The second reason is that citizenship has a symbolic value. Insofar as more than 150,000 immigrants, most from non-EU countries, have taken out citizenship of the Republic of Ireland since 2011 they have empirically shifted what it is to be a member of the Irish nation. The Enlargement of the EU in 2004 coincided with a Referendum in the Republic on citizenship in which almost 80 per cent of those who voted endorsed a proposal to remove an existing constitutional right to Irish citizenship from the Irish-born children of immigrants. During the Referendum debate Irish citizens were generally referred to in the media as 'nationals' and immigrants as 'non-nationals'. Unlike in the United Kingdom there has been, to date, no significant political backlash against the removal of all controls on migration from the new EU member states Voters in the Referendum inevitably drew on their own strong preconceptions of what it was to be Irish.[25] They did not need to reach for actual blood and soil justifications for their beliefs in national distinctiveness in order to draw such conclusions. Almost 80 per cent of those who voted in the Referendum apparently declared to immigrants: 'we're Irish, you are not'.

However, national identities are malleable political and institutional inventions that can be reinvented. Nations, as Benedict Anderson put it, are imagined communities and they have come to be reimagined over time.[26] The challenge for the Republic is how best to foster future social cohesion through more inclusive conceptions of Irishness – by turning immigrants into Irish citizens (which has begun to happen), and perhaps, over time, by shifting the centre of gravity of Irish identity a bit – as well as through social policies that leave nobody behind.

This is, as examined in the previous chapter, no simple task but it is much easier to see how this might work in the Republic than in Northern Ireland, where sectarian divisions and profound political disagreements about national identity persist. Here and there in writings about immigrants in Northern Ireland there is a sense of hope that somehow their presence might dilute sectarian divisions, by mixing up what it means to be Northern Irish a bit. But then there is the old joke told in Neil Jordan's film *Angel*, where a Jewish policeman is asked whether he is a Protestant Jew or a Catholic Jew.

While racist attacks on immigrants have been predominantly associated by the media and researchers with loyalists it also seems that many immigrants have settled successfully in Protestant neighbourhoods. It seems more difficult for immigrants to settle in socio-economically deprived Protestant or Catholic localities than into middle-class ones. Those who settle in disadvantaged localities, whether in Northern Ireland or the Republic, do so because they cannot afford to do otherwise or because they lack the necessary social capital and cannot read the lay of the land.

The Republic of Ireland has so far managed to avoid the kinds of toxic anti-immigrant politics that now plays out in many other Western democracies. It has no history of successful anti-immigrant political parties akin to France's Front Nationale or influential ones like the United Kingdom Independence Party (UKIP). Britain's decision to leave the European Union was driven, to a considerable extent, by opposition to the free movement of migrants from the post-2004 enlarged European Union. A majority of those who voted in Northern Ireland in the 2016 referendum on whether to leave the EU voted not to do so. As noted in Chapter 3, British debates about racism have had some normative influence in Northern Ireland. However, policy and legislative debate have been to a considerable degree influenced by the need to address local legacies of sectarianism, and the legislative consequence of equality policies that corral significant diversity under the category of 'other'.

The politics of immigration in Northern Ireland cannot be detached from the wider UK context. Several chapters address the implications of sectarianism in Northern Ireland for immigrant communities. There is a sense, examined in Chapters 2 and 3, that institutional preoccupations with sectarianism within the host communities have undermined responses to racism. Migrants quoted in Chapter 4 (African refugees) and Chapter 7 (Polish women) were keenly aware of the spatial segregation of Belfast into Protestant and Catholic areas. The case studies considered in Chapter 7 suggest that some Catholic Poles were unwilling to live in, as they saw it, more deprived Catholic areas, or to live in areas where there were many non-white immigrants.

In the Republic, there has been little evidence of an equivalent anti-immigrant political populism, at least at the time of writing. Yet there is an increasing anxiety about integration and failure to address far-right posturing, such as the occasional appearance of British and European far-right groups and attempts to create racial tensions in places like Drogheda or Balbriggan with racist posters in town centres and videos online. Fear of violent racism among some migrants is growing, as Chapter 4 notes, with African taxi drivers afraid that the racist abuse they now experience on a regular basis will end in injury or loss of life.[27] In Northern Ireland also, failure to address racism in employment has left even many highly skilled migrants, now fluent in English, trapped in low-paid and insecure jobs since few can access the graduate-level positions for which they are qualified.[28]

Migrants can be highly adaptable and, as we see repeatedly in this book, can at times respond to their problems in ways that sometimes circumvent or work around mainstream institutions. First-generation migrants are often preoccupied with establishing a foothold and may have obligations to provide for family members in their countries of origin as well as where they settle. The international experience is that the children of newcomers (the second generation) tend to acculturate to a greater extent than their parents. However, the degree to which such children acculturate tells us little about their capacity to deal with economic barriers or discrimination they will face in the future. What is certain, however, is that deliberate and unwitting institutional barriers can foster intergenerational exclusions and turn some migrants and their descendants into 'outsiders'.

We do not see integration or assimilation as having an endpoint of complete acculturation, but rather envisage incremental processes that play out alongside changes in wider society. The aim of any integration project should be to reduce the extent to which the host society treats immigrants as outsiders as well as to reduce the extent to which immigrants think of themselves as outsiders. However, it is not enough to change perceptions. Concrete measures are needed in both Northern Ireland and the Republic to strengthen socio-economic and political inclusion. For example, it is important that immigrants be encouraged to become teachers, civil servants, members of trade unions, members of political parties and become elected representatives; in short, to achieve full and equal citizenship.

Notes

1 R. Penninx, 'Integration: the role of communities, institutions, and the state', (2003), www.migrationinformation.org, accessed 31 January 2019.

2 H. Entzinger and R. Biezeveld, *Benchmarking in Immigrant Integration: Report written for the European Commission, European Research Centre on Migration and Ethnic Relations* (Rotterdam: ERCOMER, 2003), p. 8.

3 A. Sen, 'Capability and well-being', in Martha Nussbaum and Amartya Sen (eds), *The Quality of Life* (Oxford: Clarendon Press, 1993), pp. 30–53.

4 A Sen, *The Idea of Justice* (London: Penguin, 2009), p. 188.

5 A. Sen, 'Editorial: human capital and human capability', *World Development*, 25:2 (1997), 1959–1961, p. 1960.

6 P. Bourdieu, 'The social space and the genesis of groups', *Theory and Society*, 14:6 (1985), 723–744.

7 P. Bourdieu et al., *The Weight of the World: Social Suffering in Contemporary Society* (Cambridge: Polity Press, 1999), p. 186.

8 B. Fanning, *Immigration and Social Cohesion in the Republic of Ireland* (Manchester: Manchester University Press, 2011), pp. 81–82.

9 A. Shallice, *Why Roma Provide Opportunity for N.I.* (Belfast: Affinity/Integrate NI, 2015).

10 L. Michael, *Afrophobia: Racism against People of African Descent in Ireland* (Dublin: ENAR Ireland, 2015).

11 L. Allamby, J. Bell, J. Hamilton, U. Hansson, N. Jarman, M. Potter and S. Toma, *Forced Labour in Northern Ireland: Exploiting Vulnerability* (York: Joseph Rowntree Foundation, 2011), p. 37.

12 N. Humphries, R. Brugha and H. McGee, '"I won't be staying here long": a qualitative study on the retention of migrant nurses in Ireland', *Human Resources for Health*, 7:68 (2009), 1–19.

13 B. Fanning, *Migration and the Making of Ireland* (Dublin: UCD Press, 2018), p. 238.

14 G. Marranci, '"We speak English": language and identity processes in Northern Ireland's Muslim community', *Ethnologies*, 25:2 (2003), 59–75, p. 61.

15 All statistics from the Central Statistics Office unless otherwise stated. www.cso.ie, accessed 31 January 2019.

16 K. Flynn, 'Understanding Islam in Ireland', *Islam and Christian–Muslim Relations*, 17:2 (2006), 223–238, p. 228.

17 O. Scharbrodt, 'Muslim immigration to Ireland after World War II', in O. Scharbrodt, T. Sakaranaho, A Hussain Kahn, Y. Shanneik and V. Ibrahim (eds), *Muslims in Ireland: Past and Present* (Edinburgh: Edinburgh Press, 2015), pp. 49–72.

18 E. Moreo and R. Lentin, *From Catastrophe to Marginalisation: The Experiences of Somali Refugees in Ireland* (Dublin: Trinity Immigration Initiative/Horn of Africa People's Aid (HAPA), 2010).

19 M. Mac an Ghaill, 'The Irish in Britain: the invisibility of ethnicity and anti-Irish racism', *Journal of Ethnic and Migration Studies*, 26:1 (2000), 137–147, p. 144.

20 M. J. Hickman and B. Walter, *Discrimination and the Irish Community in Britain* (London: Commission for Racial Equality, 1997).

21 Fanning, *Migration and the Making of Ireland*, p. 236.

22 S. Vertovec, 'Super-diversity and its implications', *Ethnic and Racial Studies*, 30:6 (2007), 1024–1054.

23 R. King, M. Thomson, N. Mai and Y. Keles, *Turks in London: Shades of Invisibility and the Shifting Relevance of Policy in the Migration Process* (Brighton: Sussex Centre for Migration Research, 2008), p. 2.

24 J. Phillimore, 'Migrant maternity in an era of superdiversity: new migrants' access to, and experience of, antenatal care in the West Midlands, UK', *Social Science & Medicine*, 148 (2016), 152–159.

25 A. Thompson, 'Nations, national identities and human agency: putting people back into nations', *Sociological Review*, 49:1 (2001), 18–32.

26 B. Anderson, *Imagined Communities: Reflections on the Origins and Spread of Nationalism* (London: Verso, [1983] 2006).

27 L. Michael, *Reports of Racism in Ireland: 15th–16th Report of iReport.ie: January–June 2017* (Dublin: ENAR Ireland, 2018).

28 L. Michael, *Race Equality Works for Northern Ireland* (Belfast: Ulster University and Business in the Community NI, 2016).

Select bibliography

Ager, A., and Strang, A., 'Understanding integration: a conceptual framework', *Journal of Refugee Studies*, 21:2 (2008), 166–191.

Alba, R. D., and Nee, V., *Remaking the American Mainstream: Assimilation and the New Immigration* (Cambridge, MA: Harvard University Press, 2003).

Allamby, L., Bell, J., Hamilton, J., Hansson, U., Jarman, N., Potter, M., and Toma, S. et al., *Forced Labour in Northern Ireland: Exploiting Vulnerability* (York: Joseph Rowntree Foundation, 2011).

Barrett, A., and Duffy, D., 'Are Ireland's immigrants integrating into its labour market?', *International Migration Review*, 42:3 (2008), 597–615.

Barrett, A., McGinnity, F. and Quinn, E. (eds) *Annual Monitoring Report on Integration 2016* (Dublin: ESRI, 2018).

Becker, H., Cosgrave, C. and Labor, M., *Family Reunification – A Barrier or Facilitator of Integration? Country Report Ireland* (Dublin: Immigrant Council of Ireland, 2013).

Bosswick, W., and Heckmann, F., *Integration of Migrants: Contribution of Local and Regional Authorities* (Dublin: European Foundation for the Improvement of Living and Working Conditions, 2006).

Boucher, G., 'Ireland's lack of a coherent integration policy', *Translocations*, 3:1 (2008), 5–28.

Bourdieu, P., 'The social space and the genesis of groups' *Theory and Society* 14:6 (1985), 723–744.

Carr, J., *Experiences of Islamophobia: Living with Racism in the Neoliberal Era* (New York: Routledge, 2016).

Corcoran, M., and Peillon, M. (eds), *Uncertain Ireland* (Dublin: IPA, 2006).

Crenshaw, K., 'Demarginalizing the intersection of race and sex: a Black feminist critique of antidiscrimination doctrine, feminist theory and antiracist politics', *University of Chicago Legal Forum*, 139 (1989), 139–167.

Crowley, N., *Empty Promises: Bringing the Equality Authority to Heel* (Dublin: A & A Farmer, 2010).

Darmody, M. (ed.), *The Changing Faces of Ireland: Exploring the Lives of Immigrant and Ethnic Minority Children* (Rotterdam: Sense, 2011).

Darmody, M., Byrne, D., and McGinnity, F., 'Cumulative disadvantage? Educational careers of migrant students in Irish secondary schools', *Race Ethnicity Education*, 17:1 (2012), 129–151.

Darmody, M., McGinnity, F., and Kingston, G., *The Experiences of Migrant Children in Ireland* (Dublin: ESRI, 2016).

Darmody, M., and Smyth, E., 'Out-of-school social activities among immigrant-origin children living in Ireland', *Economic and Social Review*, 48:4 (2017), 419–439.

Department of Justice and Equality, *Migrant Integration Strategy – A Blueprint for the Future* (Dublin: DJE, 2017).

Department of Justice and Equality, *National Traveller and Roma Inclusion Strategy 2017–2021* (Dublin: DJE, 2017).

Department of Justice, Equality and Law Reform, *Planning for Diversity: The National Action Plan against Racism 2005–2008* (Dublin: Stationery Office, 2005).

Devine, D., Kenny, M., and Macneela, E., 'Naming the "other": children's construction and experience of racisms in Irish primary schools', *Race, Ethnicity and Education*, 11:4 (2008), 369–385.

Dundon, T., Gonsález-Pérez, M. A., and McDonough, T., 'Bitten by the Celtic Tiger: immigrant workers and industrial relations in the new "glocalized" Ireland', *Economic and Industrial Democracy*, 20:4 (2007), 501–522.

Entzinger, H., and Biezeveld, R., *Benchmarking in Immigrant Integration: Report written for the European Commission, European Research Centre on Migration and Ethnic Relations* (Rotterdam: ERCOMER, 2003).

Faas, D., Sokolowska, B., and Darmody, M., '"Everybody is available to them": support measures for migrant students in Irish secondary schools', *British Journal of Educational Studies*, 63:4 (2015), 447–466.

Fanning, B. (ed.), *Immigration and Social Change in the Republic of Ireland* (Manchester: Manchester University Press, 2007).

Fanning, B., *Racism and Social Change in the Republic of Ireland* (Manchester: Manchester University Press, 2012).

Fanning, B., *Migration and the Making of Ireland* (Dublin: UCD Press, 2018).

Fanning, B., and Michael, L., 'Racism and anti-racism in the two Irelands', *Ethnic and Racial Studies*, 41:15 (2018), 2656–2672.

Fanning, B., and O'Boyle, N., 'Immigrants in Irish politics: African and East European candidates in the 2009 local government elections', *Irish Political Studies*, 25:3 (2010), 417–435.

Fanning, B., and Veale, A., 'Child poverty as public policy: direct provision and asylum seeker children in the Republic of Ireland', *Child Care in Practice*, 10:3 (2004), 241–251.

Feldman, A., Gilmartin, M., Loyal, S., and Migge, B., *Getting On: From Migration to Integration: Chinese, Lithuanian and Nigerian Migrants' Experiences in Ireland* (Dublin: Immigrant Council of Ireland, 2008).

Garner, S., 'Ireland and immigration: explaining the absence of the far right', *Patterns of Prejudice*, 41:2 (2007), 109–130.

Garner, S., *Racisms: An Introduction* (London: Sage, 2010).

Geoghegan, P., 'Multiculturalism and sectarianism in post-agreement Northern Ireland', *Scottish Geographical Journal*, 124:2–3 (2008), 185–191.

Gilligan, C., *Northern Ireland and the Crisis of Anti-Racism – Rethinking Racism and Sectarianism* (Manchester: Manchester University Press, 2017).

Gilligan, R., Curry, P., McGrath, J., Murphy, D., Ní Raghallaigh, M., Rogers, M., Scholtz, J. and Quinn, A., *In the Front Line of Integration: Young People Managing Migration to Ireland* (Dublin: Children's Research Centre, Trinity College in association with the Trinity Immigration Initiative Children, Youth and Community Relations Project [Online], 2010).

Hainsworth, P., Gilligan, C., and McGarry, A., *Elected Representatives/Political Parties and Minority Ethnic Communities in Northern Ireland* (Belfast: Community Relations Council, 2008).

Harvey, B., *Travelling With Austerity* (Dublin: Pavee Point, 2013).

Haughey, F., *Racism in Northern Ireland: The Racial Equality Strategy from Policy to Practice. Summary Report of Main Findings* (Belfast: NICEM, 2014).

Haynes, A., Power, M., Devereux, E., Dillane, A., and Carr, J. (eds), *Public and Political Discourses of Migration: International Perspectives* (London: Rowman and Littlefield International, 2016).

Heisler, B. S., 'The sociology of immigration: from assimilation to segmented integration, from the American experience to the global arena', in C. B. Brettell and J. F. Hollifield (eds), *Migration Theory: Talking across Disciplines* (New York: Routledge, 2000), pp. 77–96.

Honohan, I., and Rougier, N. (eds), *Tolerance in Ireland, North and South* (Manchester: Manchester University Press, 2015).

Howard, M. M., 'The impact of the far right on citizenship policy in Europe: explaining continuity and change', *Journal of Ethnic and Migration Studies*, 36:5 (2010), 735–751.

Huddleston, T., Bilgili, O., Joki, A. L., and Vankova, Z., *Migrant Integration Policy Index 2015* (Barcelona and Brussels: CIDOB and MPG, 2015).

Hughes, J., Campbell, A., Lolliot, S., Hewstone, M., and Gallagher, T., 'Inter group contact at school and social attitudes: evidence from Northern Ireland', *Oxford Review of Education*, 39:6 (2013), 761–779.

Humphries, N., Brugha, R., and McGee, H., '"I won't be staying here long": a qualitative study on the retention of migrant nurses in Ireland', *Human Resources for Health*, 7:68 (2009), 1–19.

Irwin, J., McAreavey, R., and Murphy, N., *The Economic and Social Mobility of Ethnic Minority Communities in Northern Ireland* (York: Joseph Rowntree Foundation, 2014).

Joppke, C., 'Multicultural citizenship', in E. Isin and B. Turner (eds), *Handbook of Citizenship Studies* (London: Sage, 2002), pp. 245–259.

Joseph, E. 'Whiteness and racism: examining the racial order in Ireland', *Irish Journal of Sociology*, 26:1 (2018), 46–70.

Joyce, S., Kennedy, M., and Haynes, A., 'Travellers and Roma in Ireland: understanding hate crime data through the lens of structural inequality', in A. Haynes, J. Schweppe and S. Taylor (eds), *Critical Perspectives on Hate Crime Contributions from the Island of Ireland* (London: Palgrave, 2017), pp. 325–354.

Kempny, M., 'Between transnationalism and assimilation: Polish parents' upbringing strategies in Belfast, Northern Ireland', *Social Identities*, 23:3 (2017), 255–270.

Kempny, M., 'Tales from the Borderlands: Polish migrants' representations of the Northern Irish conflict in Belfast', *Space and Culture*, 16:4 (2013), 1–12.

Kenny, C., 'Finding a voice or fitting in? Migrants and media in the new Ireland', *Media, Culture & Society*, 3:2 (2010), 311–322.

Kingston, G., McGinnity, F., and O'Connell, P., 'Discrimination in the labour market: nationality, ethnicity and the recession', *Work, Employment and Society*, 29:2 (2015), 213–232.

Kingston, G., O'Connell, P. and Kelly, E., *Ethnicity and Nationality in the Irish Labour Market: Evidence from the QNHS Equality Module 2010* (Dublin: Equality Authority and ESRI, 2013).

Landy, D., "Challengers in the migrant field: pro-migrant Irish NGO responses to the Immigration, Residence and Protection Bill', *Ethnic and Racial Studies*, 38:6 (2015), 927–942.

Ledwith, V., and Reilly, K., 'Two tiers emerging? School choice and educational achievement disparities among young migrants and non-migrants in Galway City and urban fringe', *Population, Space and Place*, 19:1 (2013), 46–59.

Lee, A., 'Are you a Catholic Chinese or a Protestant Chinese? Belfast's ethnic minorities and the sectarian divide', *City*, 18:4–5 (2014), 476–487.

Lentin, A., and Titley, G., *The Crises of Multiculturalism: Racism in a Neoliberal Age* (London: Zed Books, 2011).

Lentin, R., and McVeigh, R. (eds), *Racism and Anti-Racism in Ireland* (Belfast: Beyond the Pale Publications Ltd., 2002).

Liubinine, N., 'Lithuanians in Northern Ireland: new home, new homeland', *Irish Journal of Anthropology*, 11:1 (2008), 9–13.

Loyal, S., *Understanding Immigration in Ireland: State Capital and Labour in a Global Age* (Manchester: Manchester University Press, 2011).

Maguire, M., and Murphy, F., *Integration in Ireland: The Everyday Lives of African Migrants* (Manchester: Manchester University Press, 2012).

Maguire, M., and Murphy, F., 'Neo-liberalism, securitization and racialization in the Irish taxi industry', *European Journal of Cultural Studies*, 17:3 (2014), 282–297.

Maguire, M., and Murphy, F., 'Ontological (in)security and African Pentecostalism in Ireland', *Ethnos: Journal of Anthropology*, 4 (2015), 1–23.

Malischewski, A., *Integration in A Divided Society? Refugees and Asylum Seekers in Northern Ireland* (Oxford: Refugee Studies Centre, 2012).

Marranci, G., '"We speak English": language and identity processes in Northern Ireland's Muslim community', *Ethnologies*, 25:2 (2003), 59–75.

Massey, D., *Space, Place and Gender* (Oxford: Polity Press, 1994).

McGarry, O., 'Knowing "how to go on": structuration theory as an analytical prism in studies of intercultural engagement', *Journal of Ethnic and Migration Studies*, 42:12 (2016), 2078–2083.

McGinnity, F., Grotti, R., Kenny, O., and Russell, H., *Who Experiences Discrimination in Ireland? Evidence from the QNHS Equality Modules* (Dublin: ERSI, 2017).

McGrath, B., and McGarry, O., 'The religio-cultural dimensions of life for young Muslim women in a small Irish town', *Journal of Youth Studies*, 17:7 (2014), 948–964.

McKee, R., 'Love thy neighbour? Exploring prejudice against ethnic minority groups in a divided society: the case of Northern Ireland', *Journal of Ethnic and Migration Studies*, 42:5 (2015), 777–796.

McVeigh, R., and Rolston, B., 'From Good Friday to good relations: Sectarianism, racism and the Northern Ireland state', *Race and Class*, 48:4 (2007), 1–23.

Michael, L., *Reports of Racism in Ireland: Quarterly Reports of iReport.ie* (Dublin: ENAR Ireland, 2013–2017).

Michael, L., *Afrophobia in Ireland: Racism against People of African Descent* (Dublin: ENAR Ireland, 2015).

Michael, L., *Race Equality Works for Northern Ireland* (Belfast: Ulster University and Business in the Community NI, 2016).

Michael, L., 'Anti-Black racism: Afrophobia, exclusion and global racisms', in A. Haynes, J. Schweppe and S. Taylor (eds), *Critical Perspectives on Hate Crime: An Irish Perspective* (London: Palgrave Macmillan, 2017), pp. 275–300.

Migrants Rights Centre Ireland, *Ireland is Home: Survey and Policy Paper on the Lives of Undocumented Migrants in Ireland* (Dublin: MRCI, 2015).

Moreo, E., and Lentin, R., *From Catastrophe to Marginalisation: The Experiences of Somali Refugees in Ireland* (Dublin: Trinity Immigration Initiative/Horn of Africa People's Aid (HAPA), 2010).

Murphy, F., and Vieten, U., *Asylum Seekers and Refugees' Experiences of Life in Northern Ireland* (Belfast: Stormont and Queen's University Belfast, 2017)

Mushroom Workers Support Group, *Harvesting Justice: Mushroom Workers Call for Change* (Dublin: MRCI, 2006).

National Consultative Committee on Racism and Interculturalism, *Building Integrated Neighbourhoods: Towards an Intercultural Approach to Housing Policy and Practice in Ireland* (Dublin: NCCRI, 2008).

Nestor, N., 'The Polish complementary schools and Irish mainstream education', in J. Plackechi (ed.), *Irish Polish Society Yearbook*, Vol. 1 (Dublin: Irish Polish Social Society, 2014).

Ní Chonaill, B., and Buczkowska, T., *Taking Racism Seriously: Experiences of Racism and Racially Motivated Anti-Social Behaviour in Social Housing* (Dublin: Immigrant Council of Ireland, 2016).

Ní Raghallaigh, M., *Foster Care and Supported Lodging for Separated Asylum-Seeking Young People in Ireland: The Views of Young People, Carers and Stakeholders* (Dublin: Barnardos and HSE, 2013).

O'Boyle, N., Rogers, J., Preston, P., and Fehr, F., '"New Irish" in the news', *Irish Communication Review*, 14:1 (2014), 3–16.

O'Connell, P., and McGinnity, F., *Immigrants at Work: Ethnicity and Nationality in the Irish Labour Market* (Dublin: Equality Authority and ESRI, 2008).

Papademetriou, D. G., Sumption, M., and Terrazas (eds), A. with Burkert, C., Loyal, S., and Ferrero-Turrion, R., *Migration and Immigrants Two Years after the Financial Collapse: Where Do We Stand?* (Washington, DC: Migration Policy Institute, 2010).

Pavee Point, *Policy and Practice in Ethnic Data Collection and Monitoring: Counting Us In – Human Rights Count!* (Dublin: Pavee Point, 2016).

Pavee Point Traveller and Roma Centre & Department of Justice and Equality, *Roma in Ireland – A National Needs Assessment* (Dublin: Pavee Point Traveller and Roma Centre & Department of Justice and Equality, 2018).

Pemberton, S., and Phillimore, J., 'Migrant place-making in super-diverse neighbourhoods: moving beyond ethno-national approaches', *Urban Studies*, 55:4 (2018), 733–750.

Penninx, R., *Integration: The Role of Communities, Institutions, and the State* (Brussels: Migration Policy Institute, 2003).

Phillimore, J., 'Migrant maternity in an era of superdiversity: new migrants' access to, and experience of, antenatal care in the West Midlands, UK', *Social Science & Medicine*, 148 (2016), 152–159.

Portes, A., and Rumbaut, R., *Immigrant America: A Portrait* (Berkeley, CA: University of California Press, 4th edn, 2014).

Portes, A., and Zhou, M., 'The new second generation: segmented assimilation and its variants among post-1965 immigrant youth', *Annals of the American Academy of Political and Social Science*, 530 (1993), 74–98.

Quinn, E., Joyce, C., and Gusciute, E., *Policies and Practices on Unaccompanied Minors in Ireland* (Dublin: ESRI, 2014).

Radford, K., Betts, J., and Ostermeyer, M., *Policing, Accountability and the Black and Minority Ethnic Communities in Northern Ireland* (Belfast: Institute for Conflict Research, 2006).

Ramsey, P., and Waterhouse-Bradley, B., 'Cultural policy in Northern Ireland: making cultural policy for a divided society', in V. Durrer, T. Miller and D. O'Brien (eds), *The Routledge Handbook of Global Cultural Policy* (Abingdon: Routledge, 2018), pp. 195–211.

Rumbaut, R., 'Ages, life stages, and generational cohorts: decomposing the immigrant first and second generations in the United States', in A. Portes and J. DeWind (eds), *Rethinking Migration: New Theoretical and Empirical Perspectives* (New York: Berghahn Books, 2008), pp. 342–387.

Sabenacio Nititham, D., *Making Home in Diasporic Communities: Transnational Belonging amongst Filipina Migrants* (London: Routledge, 2017).

Sen, A., 'Capability and well-being', in Martha Nussbaum and Amartya Sen (eds), *The Quality of Life* (Oxford: Clarendon Press, 1993), pp. 30–53.

Sen, A., *The Idea of Justice* (London: Penguin, 2009).

Soysal, Y. N., *Limits of Citizenship* (Chicago, IL: University of Chicago Press, 2007).

Stanley, M., *Immigration and Citizenship Law* (Dublin: Round Hall, 2017).

Svašek, M., 'Shared history? Polish migrant experiences and the politics of display in Northern Ireland', in K. Burrell (ed.), *Polish Migration to the UK in the 'New' European Union* (Farnham: Ashgate, 2009), pp. 129–149.

Taylor, S., *Responding to Racist Incidents and Racist Crimes in Ireland: An Issue Paper for the Equality Authority* (Dublin: Equality Authority, 2011).

Thompson, A., 'Nations, national identities and human agency: putting people back into nations', *Sociological Review*, 49:1 (2001), 18–32.

Threadgold, T., and Court, G., *Refugee Inclusion: A Literature Review* (Cardiff: Cardiff School of Journalism, Media and Cultural Studies, 2005).

Titley, G., 'Backlash! Just in case: "political correctness", immigration and the rise of preactionary discourse in Irish public debate', *Irish Review*, 38 (Spring 2008), 94–110.

Todd, J., Ruane, J., and Dunne, M., *From 'A Shared Future' to 'Cohesion, Sharing and Integration': An Analysis of Northern Ireland's Policy Framework Documents* (York: Joseph Rowntree Foundation, 2010).

UCD Study Team, *Our Geels: All Ireland Traveller Health Study* (Dublin: Department of Health, 2010).

Vertovec, S., 'Super-diversity and its implications', *Ethnic and Racial Studies*, 30:6 (2007), 1024–1054.

Wallace, A., McAreavey, R., and Atkin, K., *Poverty and Ethnicity in Northern Ireland* (York: Joseph Rowntree Foundation, 2013).

Zhou, M., 'Coming of age: the current situation of Asian American children', *Amerasia Journal*, 25:1 (1999), 1–27.

Index

EU authorised representative for GPSR:
Easy Access System Europe, Mustamäe tee 50,
10621 Tallinn, Estonia
gpsr.requests@easproject.com